Radically Gay

Radically Gay

Gay Liberation
in the Words of Its Founder

Harry Hay

Edited by Will Roscoe

Beacon Press // Boston

Beacon Press
25 Beacon Street
Boston, Massachusetts 02108-2892
www.beacon.org

Beacon Press books
are published under the auspices of
the Unitarian Universalist Association of Congregations.

First digital-print edition 2001

Library of Congress Cataloging-in-Publication Data
Hay, Harry.
Radically gay : gay liberation in the words of its founder / by Harry Hay ; edited by Will Roscoe
p.   cm.
Includes bibliographical references (p.   ) and index.
ISBN 0-8070-7080-7 (cloth)
ISBN 0-8070-7081-5 (paper)
1. Hay, Harry. 2. Gay men—United States—Biography. 3. Mattachine Society—History. 4. Gay libera-
tion movement—United States—History. I. Roscoe, Will. II. Title.
HQ75.8.H39A3   1996
305.38´9664´092—dc20   95-39290

Contents

Homophile, 1953–1969

Through the Gay Window, 1970–1980

Radical Faerie, 1980–1995

Reflections

Afterword

Chronology

About the Editor

Introduction

by Will Roscoe

Gay Liberation:
The Birth of an Idea

**With the full realization that, in order to earn for
ourselves any place in the sun, we must with
perseverance and self-discipline work collectively
. . . for the full first-class citizenship participation
of Minorities everywhere, including ourselves.**
Harry Hay, 1950

ACTIVIST, AUTHOR, TEACHER, AND VISIONARY, Harry Hay
is an American original. Through eight decades of living he
has witnessed—and left his mark on—some of the most significant social and cultural movements of the twentieth century, from
avant-garde theater and filmmaking to trade unionism and Marxism, Native American revivalism, and New Age spirituality. But
of all the movements he has witnessed and participated in, it is his
role in launching Gay liberation that has earned him a permanent
place in history.

By now the story of the early Mattachine movement should
be well known—how in 1948 in Los Angeles Harry Hay began
pursuing a "vision-quest more important than life," as he once
described it—the formation of an organization *of* homosexuals
for homosexuals. It had begun as a wild idea spun out at a Gay
party on a summer night. Hay had just come from signing a petition on behalf of the third-party candidacy of Henry Wallace. It
was the eve of the Cold War and Wallace represented for progres-

sives a bright spot on the political horizon. As the party-goers discussed the election, Hay suddenly had the idea that homosexuals
might organize themselves and lobby for a plank in Wallace's platform calling for reform of sex laws. Others brought up objections,
but Hay found answers for them all. That night he wrote up a
prospectus for an organization devoted to the welfare of Gay
people—"Bachelors Anonymous." The next morning, however,
a few phone calls quickly revealed that he was the only one of the
party-goers serious about actually undertaking such a project.

Two more years would pass before he found another Gay man
who would join him, Rudi Gernreich, and several months more
before these two, now lovers, found three more and launched the
Mattachine movement. They named the organization after a traditional European folk dance called *les Mattachines*, performed
in Renaissance France by fraternities of clerics (i.e., unmarried
men), called *sociétés joyeuses*, whose public performances
satirized the rich, powerful, high, and holy. The Mattachine
movement, launched in the midst of the anti-Communist, anti-
homosexual hysteria of the post-war era, would involve, in three
short years, an estimated five thousand homosexuals in California, while its name, carrying the promise of freedom, spread
throughout the United States and the world.[1] When a Mattachine
discussion group decided to start *ONE* magazine in 1953, the
organization was able to provide an initial mailing list of some
three thousand names. By that time, Mattachine had successfully
challenged in court the vice squad entrapment of one of its members—in those days an ever-present danger in the lives of Gay
men.

Then, as if jolted from a dream, the members realized their vulnerability to McCarthyism. Manipulating those fears, a small
band of conservatives attacked the original leaders, including

Hay, on the basis of their backgrounds as progressives and Leftists. Following their resignation in May 1953, the broad, grassroots base of Mattachine vanished, never to reach its pre-1953 levels again.[2]

Still, Mattachine chapters in various American cities and spin-off organizations, like ONE, Inc., pursued courageous publishing efforts and fought landmark civil rights cases, laying the groundwork for the explosion of Lesbian/Gay activism that followed the Stonewall riots in 1969. Today millions of Americans proudly claim Lesbian and Gay identity, but, as Hay likes to point out, in 1948 there was no such thing as a "Gay person" and no one lived a "Gay lifestyle." Gays were merely "sick heteros" leading schizophrenic lives of secret desperation.

When Hay wrote as the subheading of his prospectus, "a service and welfare organization devoted to the protection and improvement of Society's Androgynous Minority," he used a word that sparks sharp controversy to this day when applied to Lesbians and Gay men. This is not the term "androgyne," which Hay abandoned soon after writing this text. It is the word "minority," appearing no less than fourteen times in his prospectus, that remains hotly contested. Yet Hay's use of this term was instrumental in the history of Mattachine and the subsequent Lesbian/Gay movement. A central contention of this book is that *without the idea of Gays as a cultural minority there would be no Gay identity and no Lesbian/Gay movement today.*

The cultural minority thesis has been Hay's most profound and lasting contribution to Lesbian/Gay political theory. Hay argues that Lesbians and Gay men differ from heterosexuals much as African Americans, Latinos, Japanese-Americans, and other ethnic groups differ from Euro-Americans—in terms of shared values, modes of communication, historical heritage, psychological

orientations, and behavioral patterns. As he explained in 1983,
"We are a Separate People with, in several measurable respects,
a rather different window on the world, a different consciousness
which may be triggered into being by our lovely sexuality."

Since Stonewall, the Lesbian/Gay movement has modeled itself
after the agendas and tactics of other American minorities that
have simultaneously asserted a social identity and sought political
equality—not knowing that this was the original strategy that
started the Gay movement in 1950. Today's urban Gay communities increasingly function on a par with other ethnic, minority,
and neighborhood groups that make up the multicultural coalitions by which most large American cities are governed. In fact,
the history of the cultural minority model will show its intimate
relationship with those exciting, if sometimes chaotic, moments
of Lesbian/Gay history characterized by broad grassroots
participation.

As the founder of a major American social movement, Hay's
name should be commonplace. And yet, few Lesbians and Gay
men today recognize his name, let alone appreciate the ideas he
stands for and how those ideas made Lesbian/Gay liberation possible. They will be surprised to discover in this collection that the
issues that most bedevil the Lesbian/Gay movement today —
whether to foster Gay identity or minimize our differences,
whether to pursue coalition or single-issue politics—were
debated thoroughly forty years ago. In the decades since then,
all these positions have acquired a track record. We don't have
to guess what the consequences of any one of them will be.

Today's activists, however, show a marked disinclination for
making these kind of historical evaluations. The general attitude
seems to be that the Lesbian/Gay movement began whenever
one's own involvement with it began. If anything noteworthy hap-

pened before that time, it is part of the Gay Dark Ages and irrelevant to the present, so there's no need to know about it. Why is this so?

This lack of historical consciousness is due in part to the continued exclusion of factual information about homosexuality and homosexuals not only from popular media and school textbooks, but from scholarly histories as well. The typical Gay man or Lesbian, upon coming out of the closet today, might have heard of Harvey Milk and Martina Navratilova, of Rock Hudson and the radical religious Right, of Gays in the military—but very little else. There is no mechanism, except by the initiative of the individual, for Lesbians and Gay men to learn their own history. And this is a *very* serious problem when one realizes the role that the construction of the past plays in any social movement, not only in building identities but also in reproducing the movement for future generations. An extreme pragmatism, originally a makeshift imposed by the assaults of the Radical Right and, above all, the disaster of the AIDS pandemic, is now touted as a virtue by most Queer activists. What passes for "theory" today—clever essays in arcane terminology with the word "Queer" in the title—rarely offers points of articulation with daily life struggles. Even when the agenda is not set by us, our response to the assaults of the Right ought to be based on some reflection as to the nature of the people we would mobilize, the nature of the institutional forces and prejudices arrayed against us, and the strategies that will best achieve our goals.

This lack of historical awareness is also due to some serious oversights on the part of Gay historians and theorists. Lesbian/ Gay movement history has been made to conform to a neat closet-to-liberation, accommodationist-to-activist, homophile-to-Gay model that ignores the radical roots of early Mattachine. In fact, no new research on Mattachine has been done since John D'Emilio's 1983 *Sexual Politics, Sexual Communities*. An important goal of this collection is to acquaint Lesbians and Gay men with the true origins of their community and their movement by making available key documents from this period.

Before there could be a social movement of homosexuals, regardless of the presence of the necessary social conditions, someone had to think about homosexuals and homosexuality in a new way. Harry Hay was one of the first to do so. How he made that breakthrough is a story that will unfold in the course of this collection. For now, it is important to stress that this breakthrough was *and had to be* visionary in nature, not merely political. Considering the stigma of homosexuality in those years, only the passion of "a vision-quest more important than life" could make it possible for one man with a new idea to inspire others to adopt it. That's what Hay did in 1950 and what he continues to do to this day—inspiring us with his enthusiasm for being Gay, with his golden visions of the goodness, rightness, and beauty of that way of being. These visions are the heart and core of what the Gay movement is about.

Queer activists are not the only ones who can learn from the story of Harry Hay. Having traversed so many movements and communities in his lifetime, Hay offers a unique viewpoint on contemporary America—a "Gay window," as he would say. Moreover, if we consider Hay's life and work as an evolution, unexpected relationships between cultural and political movements are revealed. Most histories of twentieth-century America don't connect Native American revivalism with Marxism or Gay liberation or the history of folk music or New Age spirituality. Through Hay's life and writings we discover links between all these social and political currents. Further, we see how they *might*

be and *could be* connected in future coalitions that might yet put
the cause of social and economic justice back onto the American
political agenda.

As this collection reveals, Hay has remained relevant decade
after decade without repudiating any of his past. Rather, he has
managed to absorb each new wave of cultural and political
change, wrestling with it mightily to synthesize the new and the
old, and then announcing the results to the world. Hay's thinking
has grown by accretion. What might seem a series of agonizing
ruptures—between politics and art, or Marxism and spirituality—Hay has experienced as organic growth, albeit slow and
sometimes painful. And, too, part of Hay's personal dynamism
comes from the way he embodies contradictions. He is an opera
queen who has mastered Marxist dialectics; a farmhand who
could rein in a team of horses with one hand and today never fails
to appear in public without a string of fake pearls; a radical Gay
separatist who has never stopped working in coalitions with non-
Gays; a well-mannered scion of middle-class Edwardians and an
in-your-face activist; an indefatigable organizer who relishes the
solitude of the night, reading, writing, thinking, and surfing channels on TV.

Harry Hay is the Lesbian/Gay movement's living Malcolm X—
the unassimilable radical who returns in every generation to
inspire those young-at-heart unwilling to accept indignities that
their elders have learned to accommodate. He was there at the
beginning, in 1948, talking about homosexuals as a cultural
minority; he was there in the sixties urging stodgy homophiles to
make room for Gay liberation; he was there in the seventies challenging a new wave of Gay assimilationists with radical faerie
vision; he was there in the eighties, speaking to the Gay masses in
New York's Central Park on the twentieth anniversary of Stone-

wall, wearing a camouflage skirt over a pair of blue jeans. Hay always raises the stakes one more notch, challenging us to demand more, chiding us for seeking the approval of heterosexuals at the expense of our integrity. He is the Gay movement's antidote to complacency.

And he is not going to go away! It's been nearly fifty years since Hay founded Mattachine and he is still tugging at our sleeves. Lesbian and Gay communities and networks in every state and city, our own lives, testify to the accuracy of his view. Isn't it time we paid more attention to what this visionary has to say?

When I met Harry Hay in 1979, I knew I wanted to find a Gay "teacher." Not someone who would give me ideas—I had plenty of my own already—but someone with experience, political integrity, and above all a positive attitude toward being Gay with whom I could test my ideas. By that time in my life I had met many leaders of the Lesbian/Gay movement as well as Gay men prominent in New Age circles—but the former rarely seemed to view Gayness as anything but a sexual preference, while the latter were closeted and had no reflections on Gay living to offer.

In the summer of 1976 I was doing an internship in New York at the National Gay Task Force ("Lesbian" was added to the title later), and in the storage closet where the organization cranked out its mimeos, I found a small stash of old homophile publications. One of them was a book covered in black cloth with bold yellow letters that read *Homosexuals Today 1956*.[3] In it I read Hay's own account of early Mattachine and came to appreciate what that organization achieved. I wanted to learn more about him and his ideas, but I wasn't even sure he was still alive! A year later, I read in Jonathan N. Katz's *Gay American History* that Hay was, indeed, alive and well in New Mexico. We corresponded

briefly, then finally met at the 1979 Spiritual Conference for
Radical Faeries.

As our relationship developed in the years that followed—
really, a friendship of four that included John Burnside and my
lover Bradley Rose—I discovered that I had taken on much more
than a seasoned Gay political thinker and spiritual adept. I had
linked my destiny to a trickster, someone who would lead me on
wild adventures (and occasional wild goose chases) in search of
Gay spirit experiences. Brad and I found ourselves trekking on
foot into wilderness areas looking for sites for vision quests,
careening through the deserts of California and New Mexico
crammed into the cab of Hay's pickup, crawling over prehistoric
ruins once home to Gay ancestors, floating lazily through the California delta in a houseboat while we argued about the Spanish
Civil War. There have been quiet hours, too, sipping instant coffee
at two in the morning when the only sounds to interrupt our talk
were occasional avocados falling off the tree outside and banging
on the hood of Harry's pickup.

Just as I've learned not to predict what will happen on any given
visit with Harry and John, I've also learned to expect the sudden
challenges to my ideas, that great head shaking "no, no, no" when
he didn't like my answers. Hay's influence on my life and work has
been profound, as anyone who peruses my published writings will
see. It began in 1982, when Brad Rose and I lived with him for six
months. One evening we were discussing some point about Gay
people in the past and Harry made a sweeping gesture toward a
dark corner of the room where several file boxes were haphaz-
ardly stacked. "Of course, if you want to know more you'll have
to look at *that*," he said. *That* turned out to be the accumulated
notes and writings of twenty years of research.

As I came to appreciate the scope of Hay's research and his

11

thinking (this collection represents only a small fraction of his work), I determined to find a way to make his insights accessible to others. Appreciating the importance of the Native American Two-Spirit tradition for Hay, I decided to begin there. The best way to help others see what Hay saw in this tradition was to focus on the Two-Spirit role of a specific tribe and tell as full a story about that role and the people in it as I could. That was the beginning of the project culminating in *The Zuni Man-Woman*. Since completing that book in 1990, I have been following yet another of Hay's leads by looking into the evidence concerning what Hay termed "Berdache priesthoods" in the ancient world.[4] In all of these projects, I have always found core elements of Hay's speculations and instincts to be on target.

Today, Lesbian and Gay scholars are breaking new ground in every discipline, locating new evidence and compiling, analyzing, and theorizing it. But we can hardly expect the same approach to tell us which pattern of homosexuality is the most ethical, the most socially productive, the way of life most likely to lead to happiness and inner fulfillment. These are the questions Hay addresses. He is best read, I think, as an astute political thinker of unquestionable integrity, with mythopoetic powers of communication. One often wishes Hay wrote more clearly; constrained his claims; adopted more pragmatic stands; made less demanding calls for commitment. He makes himself easy to dismiss. But from Hay's point of view, if you're quibbling about the details of his interpretation of history, or about whether it is polite to use terms like "heteros," you are missing the point, you are not hearing the call. In the end Hay does not come to you—you must go to him, because you want to learn about Gay liberation from the source.

I may not be able to win any converts from those who already judge Hay too essentialist, utopian, radical, or separatist. Still an

actor at heart, his larger-than-life persona repels some as it
charms many. Hay's excesses are to me the marks of a human
being and a true queen; they endear him to me. I have edited this
collection in the hope of showing that his ideas, although often
condensed by Hay himself into axiomatic slogans and catch-
phrases, are not pipe dreams. They reflect years of research and
contemplation—and practical political experience.

Many of Hay's assertions—of the Berdache role as a uniquely
"contributive" social institution, of the relevance of Two-Spirits
and Fools (among others) to contemporary homosexuals—are
not ones that scholarship can settle, because they are not matters
of fact and evidence. They are interpretive questions to be judged
in terms of the ethics of the world we live in now. Hay is really saying this: if you are a Gay man who wants to explore and understand yourself, to find the meaning and purpose of being Gay,
who, at the same time, wants to contribute to society (whether
through politics, laughter, or art), then the tradition of the Two-
Spirit is the tradition you should study and appreciate—it is the
right model, the *right* connection to make.

Gay Brothers and Sisters, *listen* to our great old Pied Piper.
Not only to his enchanting tunes and images, but to the ideas he
brings, as well. He invites you to let go of your attachment to the
heterosexual world—just for a while, to see what it is like—let go
of your fear of judgment by your family, neighbors, boss and co-
workers, even your Gay friends, whoever is holding you back
from expressing your deepest values. Hay is saying: separate yourself from your oppressor. Leap from the nest. Come explore "this
new planet of Fairy-vision," who you might be in a world without
homophobia. Brothers, he says, listen to the question that your
sexuality is asking, that you are seeking to answer each time you
reach out to another brother in sexual feeling. Sisters, he says, find

your Lesbian consciousness, your dyke spirit, your other-
gendered, not-woman way in the world. Brothers and Sisters,
he says, listen to your inner voice, the one that sustained you when
you thought you were the only Queer in the world—that voice
and no other knows the way to the liberation of your spirit.

14

Notes

1. Marvin Cutler, ed., *Homosexuals Today: A Handbook of Organizations and Publications, 1956* (Los Angeles: ONE, Inc., 1956), p. 31.

2. According to Hal Call, one of those who, in his own words, "took the organization out of the founders' hands," the later Mattachine Society "never had as many as four hundred on our mailing lists" (Eric Marcus, *Making History: The Struggle for Gay and Lesbian Equal Rights, 1945–1990: An Oral History* [New York: HarperCollins, 1992], p. 65). For the history of Mattachine, see Stuart Timmons, *The Trouble with Harry Hay: Founder of the Modern Gay Movement* (Boston: Alyson, 1990), and John D'Emilio, *Sexual Politics, Sexual Communities: The Making of a Homosexual Minority in the United States, 1940–1970* (Chicago: University of Chicago Press, 1983).

3. See note 1 above.

4. See Will Roscoe, "Priests of the Goddess: Gender Transgression in Ancient Religion," *History of Religions* 35(3) (1996): 295–330.

Prologue

"How did he know?"

IT WAS MY FIRST SUMMER working in the Smith Valley and the year is 1925.

My father's brother has a ranch up there. He's my Uncle Tom, and his son, my cousin George, has a dairy right next door to their ranch. This is Smith Valley, Nevada, and I'm thirteen years old and my father has said, "Well now that you're thirteen years old you should be doing man's work and it's high time you went to work in the hayfields—just as other men do and as I did at your age." So I was sent up there to work.

Just getting there in the first place was a strange experience. I came through an area that didn't have any transportation. But I myself didn't know that and neither did my father know that when I started out. He assumed there was transportation all the way up and it turned out there wasn't any after I got to Mono Lake. So I had to go another 150 miles by getting rides with people and making arrangements to travel from this place to that place on hay wagons that were going in that direction, because there was no public transportation.

The first week there, I think I'm going to die because I've never done this kind of work before. I'm thirteen years old and I'm tall. But I don't have the musculature to go with that tallness and nobody realizes that. They forget about the fact that when a kid grows up he doesn't necessarily have the strength to go with it. I'm not accustomed to doing any of these things, so I'm having a terrible time the first week.

I'm hitching on the left-hand side of the wagon. On the right-hand side of the wagon is a man of about fifty and he's a Washo

Indian and a native of the area. He lives in that valley, on a ran-
cheria at the top end of the valley—you might say the land that nobody else wants at the head of the valley. Nobody knows a great
deal about it, except that the Washo people have always lived there
and they were natives of the area. He's a very good worker. He has
an impassive but a kind face. He has gray hair and white hair. His
name is Tom.

I'm working along, pitching hay from great hay shocks onto a
wagon and I'm having a very hard time. I don't really know how to
handle these shocks. I try to pull them apart, as my cousin shows
me how. But I can't do it and I make an awful mess of it and I take a
lot of time. So Tom picks up the shocks from his side of the wagon
and then he comes over on my side and picks up a couple and puts
them over, so that the wagon can move forward in a regular fashion and I'm not, apparently, holding things up.

This is a kindness on his part. But of course I'm thirteen and I
don't quite see it that way. So as soon as I get better, I get to the
place where I can not only handle the shocks on my side of the
wagon but the ones on his side, too. Then one day he explains to
me that that's not how you do it—but very kindly. He makes it
quite plain he'll take care of his side very nicely and all I have to do
is take care of mine. This is all going on in July. By about the middle
of August we make good teammates and we work well together.

One Saturday afternoon he says to my aunt, "Tomorrow we
have fandango." That would be the next day, Sunday. "You bring
boy. We dance. You bring him two o'clock."

So my aunt said to me, "Oh, that's wonderful, nobody in our
family has ever been invited before. They have these things called a
fandango every year. It's some kind of a ritual or ceremony. You
hear all kinds of interesting things go on, and the anthropologists

talk about them and it's always a story in the papers. But nobody that I've known has ever been invited before. Maybe it's because you work so well with Tom in the fields. But anyway, you go and then you tell us what happens."

So I thought, well, that's nice. I didn't know anything about this. I knew that they did things and had rituals. But I don't know very much about these local Indians.

By this time I've been involved in the Western Rangers for a couple years and I know about the Hopi and I know about the Shoshone and I know about the Cherokee.[1] But the Indians in Nevada and Utah were known as the "diggers" and the digger Indians were considered lowly savages—they were not considered particularly civilized. So I already knew about the "class system" among the Indians. The Pueblos were the elegant civilized people of a long time ago. But *these* Indians were considered the stragglers in the desert. So I wasn't at all sure what I was getting into. But since Aunt Laura had said, "We've always wanted to know what goes on there and you go there and find out," I thought, well, okay, this will be an adventure and I'll go.

The next day Aunt Laura drives me over in her brand-new 1924 Buick touring car—later on the ones that had the wind-up windows were called sedans, but this is called a touring car. It's open and has an open top. We drive along the road and all of a sudden she turns off to the left and we start moving up toward the north end of Smith Valley and we are going along a dirt track.

Pretty soon I realize that the mesquite and willow is up over the top of the car. We're in a sort of wilderness, like a willow jungle. We go along this track for quite a ways. I think we're lost but Laura says, "Well, pretty soon we're going to come to an encampment. So just don't worry." So we go on driving and driving.

All of a sudden there are two Indian women standing in the roadway. Aunt Laura stops and they say to her, "You don't go any farther now. You turn around and go back. We take boy. You come back eight o'clock."

So Aunt Laura says, "Well, I'll see you at eight o'clock. I'll be back for you at eight o'clock." I say thank you and then the women say, "You come now."

This is all strange, but nevertheless I know that there is one person I do know and it's Tom and he said to come. In fact, this is all *very* strange, but this whole summer has been strange for me. By this time I had met a number of odd situations and so I wasn't unprepared for odd situations this summer. I was just sort of being kicked around from one place to another and getting along, so it was okay.

In about, I would say, five minutes from when we left the car, we came to what looked like a large brush fence. It was an outlined wall made of layers and layers and layers of willow that had been crushed together along with some mesquite and sagebrush and chamiso. So it became largely impenetrable. It was caught in between wooden stakes and cactus pole stakes that had been driven into the ground in a variety of ways. You could see that it had been tied into the ground and this stuff was all lashed into place. It made a formidable barrier and no wild animal was going to get through that with any great ease. Probably it would be stopped from going through it at all.

I came to an opening and went sideways to go in. You went in between two layers that had been pulled apart. That was the entrance, and as soon as you'd gone through they brought it together again. So it became an impenetrable area all the way around.

The enclosure is maybe fifty to a hundred feet in diameter in all

directions. Inside this are a number of shelters that are shelters
against the sky, with heavy thatched material on top and what also
looks like thick weeds interwoven so that it was almost impervious
to rain. They were up on poles, standing high between eight and
ten feet from the ground. They formed a number of shelters and
there were things going on inside these shelters.

At one of these shelters at the far end there were a number of men
playing what was obviously a gambling stick game. There are several of these shelters where the men do this. Then there are other
shelters out and around which are probably used for sleeping or
maybe for eating, I don't know. Nevertheless they're all there and
I don't know what they all are, but I don't see them being used
necessarily.

To the right there is a sort of a dance circle. You can see that there
have been people dancing around and around, so you have a sense
of roundness. In the center there's a small fir tree and I know that
fir trees don't belong in this area. So it's been brought from somewhere else and it's sort of held in the ground by ropes. It's been
brought into place and put up and propped up. But anyway, it acts
as the center of the dance pit and people dance around it.

At the time that I come in there are some people who are dancing around it. They are both men and women and they are forming
a circle and doing a sort of shuffling dance, which goes around
it. Someone's beating a small drum about so big [indicates about
twelve-inch diameter—WR], quite fast, so that it has a high tone.
There is some singing going on in a language that I don't recognize.

To the left of me is a semicircle of fire pits [indicates small hole—
WR]. There are a number of jars that are pointed and they stand between hot stones and they reach down into this pit. I think that
some of these jars are made of leather or hides that are hardened

over a frame. The others are probably clay or basketwork that have been made waterproof or water-resistant with pitch and then maybe lined with leather or something. There was one thing they heated by putting hot stones in it. The others I think were pointed or rounded or had a point at the bottom and they reached into a heating center in the middle of hot rocks, which was another way of getting liquids and stews and things like that warm, because they served several dishes which were stewlike in character.

There are cooking pits here [to his left—WR] and then way over around behind that is where the boys and children are playing, which is their own area. It's sort of a round area and there are game areas and there is also a shelter. The boys are playing the same stick game that the men are, except that this is in the afternoon and they're out in the open—they don't care about going under the shelter. It's there that the old lady takes me, to these kids that are doing this.

A couple boys start to explain to me in elementary-type English how to play this game. But it's typically boys explaining how to play a game—you know, beginning in the middle and forgetting how much you don't know about the game. Little by little you stumble through a few things. So I was kind of monkeying around and trying to understand what was happening.

I became, however, aware of one other fixture in the area that I haven't mentioned to you before. That is almost directly in front of me as I come in the gate—I've come in looking in that direction [ahead], the dance ground is over here [left], the gamblers are here [right]. But right in front of me as I've come into it is another shelter with a sort of platform built up. The best way I can explain it is that it was put together with a lot of willow withes and it looked as though they were interwoven a little bit so there was a certain amount of spring in them. I guess to sit on them to make them more

22

or less comfortable. On top of that are a lot of skins which I think are rabbit skins that are woven—strips of rabbit woven together to make up sort of a blanket. There are about five or six of these.

23

On top of all of this is sitting one of the oldest men I have ever seen. I have seen, since this time, many very old men, but this is a very old man indeed.

I don't remember his body very well, in other words I don't remember the clothes he has on. I remember his face and I remember he had a sort of a hat, a cap that came over a portion of his head and his hair came out below. It was almost like it was made of something covered with feathers. There were strips of that. Then there were strips of what might have been a deer skin, or a very fine skin of some sort. So that it's like a ceremonial cap. Then there is a patterned scarf or bandanna that's tied around here [indicates forehead] as well—either to keep the hair down or it's the lower part of the cap or it's to keep the cap on.[2] Just what that is for at this point I don't think I can remember.

I'm aware of the fact that obviously he is blind.[3] He still has eyes but the eyes don't see any longer, because he doesn't move his face as though he did. His face itself is so parched, it's like parchment. The wrinkles are stiff. And I'm aware of the fact that he's very, very, very old and very frail.

The woman who had spoken to us down on the road, who seems to be the one assigned to take care of me, says to me, "Our sacred man, our old man, our beloved old man is here today. He's sitting over here. He knows you are here. He would like to speak with you. Is it in your heart to speak with him?"

"Is it in your heart to speak with him" is something I remembered all my life. Almost forty years later I was at Tonawonda, which is the home of the Seneca of the Iroquois Confederation in western New York, for the first North American Indian Unity

Conference in August 1967. And while I was there, I was taken to
meet some of the Indian medicine people. I was invited to come in
and then I was invited to speak—*if it was in my heart to speak to
them.* They used the same phrase. Here I am running into it in western New York and then later on as the regular ceremonial way of
greeting in New Mexico. But I first hear it in the Washo encampment in Smith Valley in 1925.

"Is it in your heart to speak with him?"

And I thought, "Well, yes of course, that's what I came for, to
find all the experiences, and of course I would like to speak to him."

So she takes me over to the little platform. It wasn't terribly high
but nevertheless it was sort of raised from the ground. She said to
me, "He is blind. And so when you speak with him and he speaks
with you he will feel what you say and will have to understand you
from your face. He will want to touch your face and when you answer he will want to touch your face. Is that all right?"

And I said, "Well, yes, I guess that's all right."

"Then kneel down and let him touch your face."

She brings me in and she says something to him. Then he says
something to her and then she asks me to give him my name and
where I have come from. Then he doesn't ask me direct questions
any longer. He runs his hands over my face and over my head
and across my forehead and back to my temples again and down
the side of my face. Then he feels my mouth, he feels my nose.
He's talking to the woman on the side and I say, "Is he asking
questions?"

"No, he is telling me what he hears and what he feels in you."

This goes on for quite a while. Apparently he is learning something from just touching me. I'm sort of amazed at this but then,
at this moment, I ask no questions because these were a different
people, they would approach this in a different way.

24

Finally, she says to me, "He is tired. You must go now."

But then, as she says that, he stops and feels back over here. He runs his hands up and down the side of my temples. Then he runs his hands across my forehead and he comes back to the side of my temples again. And every time he does this he says something. And it's the same thing he says; whatever it is he says, he says the same thing over and over and he says it to the woman who is behind me.

So when I get up to go away, I say to her, "But he kept coming back to the sides of my temples and then to the front and then he'd come to the sides again and each time he would say something and it would be the same thing and he said it to you, because you were behind me."

She said, "Yes, this is true."

"Well, could you tell me what he said?"

"Yes. He says we are to treat you well. We are to feed you well. We are to make you happy. Because someday you will be a friend. And then he wished you well. He touched you on the forehead."

Later on, Tom said to me, "The old man thinks you are a good man. He blessed you." So this is how I know about the blessing. This is why I mentioned it as the blessing.[4]

This is all very interesting, very strange. He does this. He says simply, "You will be a friend." And I simply take that as I take everything else that's coming that day. I don't know what any of this means. I've never been through any of this before and I was sort of absorbing it all. I only know that I assume that I'm going to put it all together when I'm finished. It's just that I'm going through these experiences and I'm receiving them all.

I'm served a clay bowl of food. There are a lot of things that I've never had before. There are things that smell interesting, but different, and some of them are not different enough that I like them. But I'm here and I'm these people's guest and so I do the best I can.

There are a lot of strange smells and things I don't necessarily like but I think I must eat a little of them to be polite. Because they're being polite and I must be polite, too.

I realize now that there was much food that was cooked without salt and, of course, at that time I'm not accustomed to saltless food. On the other hand, there were certain things, I think there were meats—and it might have been rabbit and it might have been rattlesnake and it might have been rat, I don't know what it was, but anyway it was meat. You know how you would have rabbit in your fricassee or in a rabbit stew?—there would be pieces of meat that came apart easily and chewed nicely. They were flavored, I guess, with herbs—herbs different than I know about. There were some things more than others I liked. There was a kind of a corn meal mush and that was nice when I would put that in the gravy. So I made for myself a good supper. And eight o'clock came much too soon, in a way. It wasn't even dark yet because this is summertime in Smith Valley and the sun doesn't go down until about nine o'clock. So eight o'clock it's still twilight, but it's still light.

We go back to the place along the trail that we came in on to start with. Pretty soon here's my aunt waiting in the car. So we go home. And on the way home I tell her all the different things that have happened to me. I tell her about the old man. And she said, "Oh, oh, that must be Jack Smith . . . uh, no, Jack Wilson. He's a very, very old man. He's one of their medicine men, I think, and they seem to think a great deal of him. Every year when he goes around there's always a story about him in the Yerington paper."

Mason Valley was the next valley to the east of us and Yerington was the largest town in the area, where the railroads and the highway and everything all came together. To the east of Yerington were some of the big cattle ranches and the great runs where the wild horses run in the springtime. Then the railroad comes up from

Wadsworth to Hawthorne. There's Walker Lake to the south of us and Hawthorne was an army depot [now a naval ammunition depot]. They also had a lot of copper mining and coal mining in that area. It all comes from Hawthorne and it comes up to the main highway at Yerington and joins the railroad and goes on over to Reno and then is distributed to San Francisco and other places. But Yerington was the main town and we're next to it in Smith Valley. We have just a little, tiny town [Wellington] and a post office and we are a branch of Yerington.

Outside of Yerington to the west and in the hills that go up toward the boundary between Smith Valley and Mason Valley was the old Wilson ranch. It had been there a long, long time. They had a number of people who had worked for them all their lives and apparently Jack Wilson had lived there. I think that his father, also, had been a worker on that ranch but I don't know what he was called. Anyway, Indians, because of the fact that they didn't have Christian names, were often named for the employer for whom they worked. Wilson was the name of this place and Jack Wilson, at least, was the name of this old man.

So Aunt Laura says, "Well, when Tom comes home tomorrow, I'll ask him if that was Jack Wilson. That could be. And maybe you met an important person. After all he's been in the papers many times."

Then I told her about the rest of the thing and she says, "Well, that's all very interesting. I have to talk to Tom about this and find out what this all means."

Apparently Aunt Laura talked to Tom quite a lot. He never talked very much to me or Uncle Tom but I guess he had talked to the women quite a bit. Phyllis used to talk to him and I guess Aunt Laura talked to him, too. So when Tom came home Monday morning to go to work she asked him if that was Jack Wilson and he said, "Yes, that is our old man, our sacred man. His name is Jack Wilson."

As I said, I simply thought, "Well, I went to this and Jack Wilson was a nice old man. It was an interesting experience and he gave me a blessing." And that was that.

Now the scene shifts to 1968 and here John and I are involved with the Committee for Traditional Indian Land and Life. It's a group of non-Indians who get very much interested in the traditional Indian way of life, and make it possible for several colloquiums to occur whereby traditional Indians, each coming from certain tribes and thinking they stood alone for their tradition, could all of a sudden come together and discover that there are other loners in each one of these other tribes standing for the same tradition. And to a large extent they can talk to each other because there are similarities in their stories.

This is the beginning of an indigenous Native American renaissance, a rekindling by the traditionals of tribes across the country of their traditional cultures. Here was this committee of about five hundred non-Indians from all different branches of the service industries, the movies, TV and radio, the music industry, and so on, who become very interested in the plight of the traditional Indians and want to help them restore and rediscover themselves, much as the counterculture people were rediscovering themselves in the '60s. They became tremendously interested in the Hopi Indian prophecies and the Four-Square Law of the Cherokee Nation and the fact that the Iroquois and particularly the Seneca had given Thomas Jefferson the ideas out of which the Declaration of Independence and the Constitution were eventually formed.[5] A lot of this information begins to come out. This had been happening two hundred years in the past but the kids are only finding this out in 1968, '69, and '70.

The committee that's doing this calls itself the Committee for Traditional Indian Land and Life. It met at the kaleidoscope factory in Los Angeles, and the kaleidoscope factory was owned by John and me.[6] As I said, it was made up of non-Indians under the guidance of traditional Indians. We were under the guidance of the traditional Hopi from Third Mesa in Arizona; Rolling Thunder was the medicine person from the Shoshone in Nevada; Calvin Rube was the medicine person for the Yurok and Hupa Indians in Northern California; and Semu Huaute (in 1966) presumably was a medicine person for the Pai-pai Indians along the Mexican-California border to the south. By 1968, he himself claimed to be Chumash. These were our guides from the four points. This particular committee was able to do things for traditional Indians in ways that the traditional Indians said no other white person had ever served them before. So we had a certain position there with them.

In the spring of 1969, somebody sent us a book on the great Ghost Dance religion, which had sprung up in the Plains in the latter part of the Indian Wars. It was a religion, a dance, and a way of believing where the Indians thought that if they no longer struggled, but believed in their own visions and danced their visions and sang their vision songs, the white man would go away and the buffalo would once more return. It was actually an attempt to do something peacefully and not in fighting and war. They would wear these Ghost Dance shirts and they would believe in the visions and the white man would disappear. It's a beautiful example of the kind of religion of the oppressed that a people who are about ready to go under may use as their last resort.

The man who brought this vision of a peaceful way of moving and a peaceful way of changing their lives was a Paiute visionary by the name of Wovoka. Wovoka's religion spread like wildfire through the whole of the western prairie and the western plains and had gotten as far as the Sioux in North and South Dakota.[7]

30   In 1890 there was what was known as the battle of Wounded Knee. All of the braves were away hunting and the United States Cavalry, the Third and the Seventh Cavalry in concert (this is what was left of Custer's cavalry, although this is twenty years after his death), swept through the encampment at Wounded Knee and killed off old men, women, and children. It was a miserable slaughter, where old Indians simply stood in the bitter cold of winter and were slaughtered by the cavalry. This was considered the last battle. This was considered what broke the back of the Indian movement. After that the Indians never fought again. And presumably they had used the Ghost Dance dancing and the shirts and the songs which made them invincible—which left them wide open and they were slaughtered to a person.

This story and the whole Ghost Dance religion and the Ghost Dance movement was investigated by James Mooney for the Bureau of Ethnography. The battle was in 1890. He went out in 1893 and he was there for three years. He interviewed all the people who were involved. He went to all the various campgrounds and all the battlefields. He interviewed all the survivors. He learned all he possibly could about it and he put this down in a magnificent book which was published by the Bureau of Ethnology in 1896. Then about 1910 or 1915, I guess, it went out of print. And it stayed out of print until Dover brought it back in the spring of 1969.

Somebody sent the Committee a copy of James Mooney's book and this arrived in the spring of 1969. I'm reading it because by this time everybody knows about Wovoka and everybody knows about the Ghost Dance. We've seen Ghost Dance shirts; we've heard a lot about the Ghost Dance and what it could have meant and how this was the true pacific nature of the Indian people; that this was how they really felt about things. They talked about various aspects of the Ghost Dance. The whole traditional movement has a lot of the same type of prophecy and visionism in common with what was going on in that time—sort of re-invoking it, making it possible to apply it in the twentieth century.

So I got interested and I'm reading about the thing. I look it over and it's talking about Wovoka and his father, who also seems to have been a visionary prophet of some sort. It mentions Wovoka and I turn the page and it says, "Of course, to most white people he was known by his English name, which was Jack Wilson."

And suddenly I check on the dates and discover that he died in 1932, at about 94. I saw him in 1925 when he would have been about 85, I guess.[8]

That's who I was blessed by. But I had no way of knowing that. All those years, I didn't know that. And then I remembered. I had forgotten all about it, that he had said, "Someday you'll be a friend."

You sort of wonder. You think of a story like that and then it's happening to you. You hear about it and you think it's odd. But you think about it. And I think, you know, as a matter of fact I was a friend all my life—how did he know? . . . How did he know?

Recorded January 15, 1985. Published as *A Blessing from Wovoka*, with Will Roscoe (San Francisco: Vortex Media, 1988).

Notes

1. Hay joined the Western Rangers, a Los Angeles boys' organization, in 1922. The leader of Hay's group, a young Canadian named Harry James (1896–1978), had friends at the Hopi villages, and on two occasions, in 1925 and 1927, Hay observed delegations of Hopis perform religious observances at the Pacific Ocean.

2. Caps made of animal skin were traditional garb for Paiute men.

3. As early as 1920 it was reported that Wovoka "was getting blind and deaf and has cataracts" (Michael Hittman, *Wovoka and the Ghost Dance* [Yerington, Nev.: Yerington Paiute Tribe, 1990], p. 167).

4. I introduced Hay to Randy Burns, co-founder of Gay American Indians and a member of the Northern Paiute tribe, in the summer of 1985. Burns was familiar with the dances held inside circles of brush, which he knew as "fandangos," and he confirmed several details in Hay's account. According to Burns, elders of his tribe touched the face and head in the manner described by Hay as both a blessing and a means of transferring power.

5. See Bruce E. Johansen, *Forgotten Founders: Benjamin Franklin, the Iroquois, and the Rationale for the American Revolution* (Ipswich, Mass.: Gambit, 1982).

6. The California Kaleidoscope factory.

7. According to James Mooney, Wovoka had become seriously ill in late December 1888. On January 1, 1889, while he lay in a fever, there was a total eclipse of the sun: "He fell asleep in the daytime and was taken up to the other world. Here he saw God, with all the people who had died long ago engaged in their oldtime sports and occupations, all happy and forever young. . . . He was then given the dance which he was commanded to bring back to his people. . . . Finally, God gave him control over the elements" (*The Ghost-Dance Religion and Wounded Knee* [1896; New York: Dover, 1973], pp. 771–72, 774). Wovoka proclaimed that all the earth would soon die and then come alive again. White people would disappear, and Indians—both dead and living—would be restored to their traditional life, free of death, disease, and oppression. In the dance he introduced, men and women stood hand in hand in a circle and shuffled back and forth, singing to the slow beat of a muffled drum. Sometimes dancers fell into trance states and had visions in which deceased relatives instructed them to revive traditional ways.

Word of Wovoka and his powers spread quickly, and tribes began to send delegations to Nevada to receive instructions directly from the Paiute prophet. All across the West, Indians adopted versions of the dance. The Sioux began wearing shirts decorated with symbols that they believed made them invulnerable to bullets. Whites responded to these developments with hysteria and demanded military protection. The army was de-

32

ployed to round up ghost-dancing Sioux and the result was the Wounded
Knee Massacre in December 1890, when trigger-happy soldiers mowed
down two hundred unarmed men, women, and children.

33

Wovoka preached nonviolence. "You must not hurt anybody or do
harm to anyone. You must not fight. Do right always. It will give you satisfaction in life" (ibid., p. 781). This philosophy made the Ghost Dance a
forward-looking social movement. The dancing itself helped unite and inspire dispirited Native American communities, and the visions dancers received fostered a revival of traditional culture, which amounted to a form
of resistance against overwhelming white pressure to assimilate. Most significantly, the Ghost Dance cut across tribal lines, pointing the way toward twentieth-century pan-tribalism.

8. Wovoka's year of birth has been variously recorded as 1856, 1857,
and 1858. He would have been 67 to 69 years old in 1925—old to a
thirteen-year-old but not quite as ancient as Hay recalls (Mooney, *The
Ghost-Dance Religion*, p. 771; Grace M. Dangberg, "Letters to Jack Wilson, the Paiute Prophet, Written between 1908 and 1911," *Bureau of
American Ethnology Bulletin* 164 (1957): 283; Paul Bailey, *Wovoka: The
Indian Messiah* [Los Angeles: Westernlore Press, 1957], p. 211).

Mattachine

1948–1953

I N 1948, WHEN HARRY HAY wrote his original prospectus for a Gay organization, homosexuality in America was illegal, homosexuals were dangerous perverts, and every move a homosexual made was fraught with the danger of self-disclosure and subsequent persecution. How, in such an environment, was Hay able to both articulate and act upon the idea of homosexuals as cultural minority?

Any answer to this question has to begin with Hay's seventeen-year involvement in the Communist Party of the United States of America (CPUSA). Hay was not just a committed member of the Party. At the time he resigned in 1951 he was a respected Marxist teacher. Like thousands of others of his generation, he had been drawn to the Party's uncompromising stands for justice and social change during the desperate years of the Depression. As Chuck Rowland, another former Communist active in Mattachine, recalled, "To most Americans, Communists were wicked, horrid people. Even to liberals. But the so-called liberals sat around and talked about socialized medicine, integration, and the rights of women. The Communists, on the other hand, were out there on the barricades or picketing or closing down something—doing something about it instead of just talking."[1]

Two defining moments in 1934 precipitated Hay's commitment to social change. That spring, he participated in his first demonstration and witnessed the brutality of the local police. Swept up in the excitement, he lobbed a brick at one of them and ended up fleeing into the mazelike tenements of downtown Los Angeles's Bunker Hill, where a famous drag queen named Clarabelle safely

38

hid him away.[2] Then, in July, Hay traveled with his lover, actor Will Geer (who ended his career playing TV's Grandpa Walton), to San Francisco to participate in the maritime strike that had paralyzed ports up and down the West Coast. When the National Guard fired on the striking workers, killing two and wounding scores of others, Hay heard the bullets whizzing past his ears. The massive public funeral march that followed left a permanent impression on him. "You couldn't have been a part of that and not have your life completely changed," he told one historian.

When Hay joined the Party in 1934, it was just beginning to implement the so-called Popular Front policy in response to directives from Moscow to form broad coalitions with all organizations and groups that opposed fascism, whether they advocated socialism or not. These policies were responsible for rapid growth in the Party's membership, which eventually peaked at around 100,000 in the early 1940s.[3] An important feature of Popular Front politics was the encouragement of cultural programs. The Party called on artists to foster social consciousness and mobilize the masses through their art. In Los Angeles, many of the writers, actors, and craftspeople in the burgeoning film industry joined Popular Front organizations. Hay himself was assigned to an artists' and writers' section of the Southern California branch of the Party, and spent much of his time in milieus where Leftists and artists intermingled. He signed up for nearly every progressive cause and organization that arose in the 1930s.

At first, Hay had little interest in the intricacies of Marxist theory, which seemed impenetrable to him. He blames this largely on local organizers, who were inept teachers and later proved to be FBI informers. In 1937, however, he began attending a series of Marxist discussion groups where dialectics, historical materialism, and the basic tenets of Marxist economic theory finally

"made sense." The rigor of Marxist thought, the insistence on
testing and revising theory through practice, the sense that the
seemingly scientific tenets of Marxism could clarify any and all
social problems appealed to him. "Everything began falling into
place," he recalls. During his years in New York City, between
1939 and 1942, when he had access to the Party's library, he read
the historical writings of Marx and Engels and took advanced
classes in Marxist theory with the intention of becoming a Party
educator.

Of course, Hay did not limit his reading to Marxist texts. His
interest in ancient history had been sparked at Stanford, when he
took a course in classical myths taught by a professor who had
studied under Jane Harrison. As early as 1933, he had read Robert Briffault's *The Mothers*, a classic statement of the so-called
"matriarchal" theory of human prehistory that Marxist historians had adopted.[4] By 1945, he had discovered the works of Gordon Childe, a Marxist archaeologist. He also read the Boasian
anthropologists, including Margaret Mead and Ruth Benedict.
The British classicists Jane Harrison and Gilbert Murray were
especially influential, and, in the 1950s, Robert Graves and
George Thomson, the latter a Marxist scholar whose *Studies in
Ancient Greek Society* was, for Hay, "an absolute eye-opener."[5]

Hay's Marxist background on its own, however, does not
explain how he came to see Lesbians and Gay men as a cultural
minority. To begin with, in Marxist doctrine, the working class
was the historically determined vehicle of social change. No other
group had the ability to alter the capitalist relations of production
that underpinned all forms of social inequality. Organizing labor
had to be the Party's primary mission; other causes were subordinate. If the possibility of a social movement of homosexuals ever
occurred to a Marxist before Hay, it would have been quickly dis-

missed as irrelevant if not detrimental to *class* struggle, much as nationalist movements and the cause of women's equality were viewed.[6] Why then, when Hay awoke that morning in August 1948, did he not dismiss the idea of forming an organization of homosexuals as the crazy talk of some tipsy queens? Wasn't he aware that such a program meant a drastic break with Marxist orthodoxy regarding class struggle? In fact, when Hay began writing his prospectus he was able to draw on an analysis, models, and specific policies that the Party had been promulgating for nearly two decades concerning one of America's largest and most exploited minorities—African Americans.[7]

In the 1920s, American Socialists and Communists alike considered African Americans simply one element of the oppressed population in the United States. Racial prejudice would be overcome once the contradictions of capitalism were surmounted by a working-class revolution. Any special program or effort on behalf of African Americans would be "reverse racism." This attitude changed dramatically in the late 1920s, when Moscow began issuing position statements concerning the rights of national minorities. While in practice, Stalin ruthlessly suppressed minorities, forcibly relocating some and slaughtering others, "Stalinism" was officially multicultural. This was the face that Moscow presented to the world and, as far as American Communists were concerned, this was the reality of Soviet socialism.

In 1928, the Sixth World Congress of the Communist International declared African Americans a "national minority"—a separate and distinct nation within the United States, centered in the "Black Belt," the region of the South where African Americans were a numerical majority. As a "nation," African Americans in this region had the right to secede and establish an independent "Negro Soviet Republic."[8] The rationale for these policies was based on a text by Stalin himself that Hay had often used in his classes. According to Stalin, "A nation is a historically-evolved, stable community of language, territory, economic life and psychological make-up manifested in a community of culture."[9] The first thing to note about this formulation is that it avoids relying on an essentialist notion of race or tribal descent to define a "nation." Rather, what binds the members of a nation is a history or collective memory into which individuals can project themselves and thereby derive an "identity." It also follows that a nation is "subject to the law of change, has its history, its beginning and end."[10]

By "community of language" is meant not only "the official government language" but "the colloquial language of the people." Interestingly, American Communists did not argue that African Americans spoke a dialect of English and therefore had a "colloquial language"—this aspect of African-American culture was not yet appreciated, even by sympathetic observers. (Similarly, the possibility of a "Gay English" has only recently been explored by linguistic experts.[11]) Rather, it was argued (somewhat lamely) that African Americans met the criterion of language because they all spoke English.[12]

Language alone is not sufficient to define a nation, however. Separate territory makes the English and the Americans distinct nations despite a common language. At the same time, economic integration within territorial boundaries can forge culturally different people into a single nation. However, it sometimes happens that a population within a territory is *not* integrated into the larger economic system and has the other elements of a distinct cultural identity. In this case, the minority constitutes a "nation" and has the right of self-determination.

The final criterion of a "nation"—a community of psychological make-up—is the least materialist. "Nations differ not only in their conditions of life, but also in *spiritual complexion*, which manifests itself in peculiarities of national culture" [my emphasis—WR]. Thus, even though England, America, and Ireland all speak one language, they are distinct nations "in no small measure due to the peculiar psychological make-up which they developed from generation to generation as a result of dissimilar conditions of existence." The discussion concludes by emphasizing that there is no *single* determining characteristic of a nation. "There is only a sum total of characteristics, of which, when nations are compared, one characteristic (national character), or another (language), or a third (territory, economic conditions), stands out in sharper relief."[13]

Stalin had insisted on the presence of all four criteria, intending to contain nationalist sentiment within the Soviet empire. The CPUSA had the opposite goal. By appealing to nationalist sentiment among American Blacks, it hoped to threaten the ruling class with the specter of a "peasant war" in the rural South allied with a proletarian revolution in the industrial North. Since African Americans lacked one criterion of a nation, an autonomous economy, they were deemed a "national minority," an emergent nation. Influential Blacks in the Party argued that the "Negro question" was the Achilles heel of American capitalism. By the late 1940s, with the rise of national liberation movements in China and Africa, some even suggested that the struggle of Blacks was replacing the struggle of the working class as the true revolutionary force in America.[14]

The other, more lasting consequence of the Party's outreach to Black Americans was to foster interest among Blacks and whites alike in African-American history, culture, and music. Marxist historians like Herb Aptheker and Philip Foner, along with pro-

gressive African Americans like W. E. B. Du Bois, challenged traditional portrayals of African Americans in United States history,
emphasizing their long-standing resistance to slavery. Leftist per-   43
formers and folklorists began to collect and record Black spirituals, folk songs, and jazz music. Because this culture had emerged
from the chrysalis of a struggle against oppression, progressives
argued that it was a valuable resource for present-day movements
as well.

   These policies and theoretical discussions, ongoing in the Party
throughout the 1930s and 1940s, were what enabled Hay to project American homosexuals as a cultural minority amenable to
political organization. He simply extended the Party's cultural
minority model to Gay Americans, arguing that they had two of
the four criteria—a language and a shared psychological make-
up—and that this was sufficient to consider them a cultural
minority. The rest could be "historically constituted." (And,
indeed, since 1950, the Lesbian/Gay minority has acquired the
dimension of a recognizable territory in several urban areas and
with it a degree of internal economic integration as well.)

   That Hay could make this extension of Party doctrine without
feeling any sense of contradiction or departure from Marxist principles speaks to the spirit of the Party as Hay knew it. His Communism was not the rigid orthodoxy of the Party in its declining
years in the 1950s, after his resignation, but the broad-based,
coalition politics and visionary outlook of the Popular Front,
in which the struggles of groups like African Americans were seen
as supplementing, inspiring, and sometimes leading the broader
movement for social and economic justice. These were politics
grounded in the activist's axioms that those with the greatest revolutionary potential were those with the least to lose—often,
but not always, this was the working class—and that those who

would be free, as Frederick Douglass once said, had to strike the first blow themselves. Any group that took this step had the potential to lead broader social change. If this had been the outlook of the New Left, it very well might have avoided the splintering of the late 1960s and early 1970s.

The Lesbian/Gay movement has often been portrayed by historians as arriving on the coattails of the Black civil rights and women's movements. That is, these movements developed the goals, principles, and strategies of identity-based politics, and Lesbians and Gay men borrowed them in the 1970s. But the origins of Mattachine as described here require a correction to this view. In the 1940s, the concept of "ethnicity" as a cultural-political identity not subject to assimilation was no less controversial when applied to Black Americans than to homosexuals. There is nothing "natural" about viewing Black Americans, Chicanos, women, and other groups as having a culture, history, or art, although we take such views for granted today. That we do so reflects in no small measure the enduring legacy of the 1930s Popular Front.

If the Party's position on African-American cultural and political self-determination provided a precedent for theorizing minorities, what actually convinced Hay that these theories could be applied to homosexuals? What enabled him to see in homosexuals *cultural* traits and *cultural* patterns—when society, homosexuals included, saw only pathology and degeneracy? Here Hay's research in music history proved instrumental.

Left-wing interest in folk music had grown steadily since the late 1930s. Roosevelt's New Deal programs and the Popular Front both encouraged artists to draw from traditional American themes and popular culture to create art and music accessible to the people. Hay dates his own interest in folk music to the summer

of 1937, when he worked on his grandfather's ranch in central
California and helped organize a dance for local people where he
heard a variety of traditional music. In 1940, while living in New
York, he met Pete Seeger and followed his efforts to revive folk
music. Five years later, after he had returned to Los Angeles, he
attended an early "hootenanny" organized by Earl Robinson, Ray
Glazer, and Bill Wolfe. In early 1946, Hay joined them in founding Los Angeles People's Songs, which later affiliated with People's
Songs, Inc., founded by Pete Seeger in New York, with the goal of
making folk music accessible to progressive campaigns and
causes.[15] Later that year, when the People's Educational Center
(PEC), which had been established by unions and progressives to
offer adult education programs, invited People's Songs to develop
a course on music history, Hay eagerly took on the assignment.
"Music, Barometer of the Class Struggle," the course he eventually offered in 1947 through PEC's successor, the Southern
California Labor School, was based on nothing less than a comprehensive Marxist theory of music history. Originally a series of
ten lectures, it soon grew to twenty sessions delivered over the
course of several months. Each session included detailed historical background and examples of recorded music. Hay often had
participants do exercises, such as composing and singing their
own rounds or developing variations on a ballad to demonstrate
how cultural and political resistance could be communicated
beyond the spoken word.

This research provided Hay with historical data and theoretical
tools he drew on in organizing Mattachine. First, he refined a
model of cultural survival based on the history of European folk
resistance to Church ideology and feudalism. Although both
Marx and Engels had been interested in pre-capitalist societies
and both envisioned socialism as a return to the values of these

46

societies, Hay's skill in reconstructing folk culture enabled him to make a unique contribution to Marxist historiography.[16] Marx and Engels had understood tribal modes of social organization as "barbarism," a stage on the ladder of social evolution leading to the present class society. In Hay's course, European folk culture emerges as a coherent non-patriarchal belief system in which women had high status and Gays enjoyed honored social-religious roles. Customs that Marx and Engels were likely to dismiss as "superstitions" Hay showed to be part of a mother-centered religion intrinsic to the agrarian mode of production and indispensable to its success. As he wrote in his lecture notes, "Ritual and magic are usable only on a group level, and serve to promote unity, to maintain identity, and even to offer the collective security needed to continue the struggle for survival so long as the group maintains a daily drive to maintain integration between all of its components." In the context of feudalism and Christianization, these cultural forms took on an added dimension, becoming modes of political resistance and cultural survival as well.

By arguing that the beliefs and practices of "ritual agriculture" (the predecessor to contemporary "scientific agriculture") survived until the nineteenth century and the break-up of traditional agrarian modes of production following the freeing of the serfs, Hay, in effect, brings the "matriarchate" and its institutions that much closer to us in time and relevance. Indeed, by 1950 Hay's Marxism had become decidedly feminist, incorporating a powerful analysis of gender inequality and its historical origins.[17] His discussions of women's roles in prehistoric society and the survival of matricentric cultural forms in Europe—what the Church considered witchcraft—anticipate the writings of Starhawk, Riane Eisler, Marija Gimbutas, Mary Daly, Arthur Evans, and others three decades later.

A second resource that Hay gained through his research were
specific examples of roles in which homosexuals were socially
productive members of their communities. Foremost of these were
the American Indian Berdache or Two-Spirit role and the Fool traditions of Europe. "Berdache," originally a Persian word, was the
term that European explorers used to refer to men living as
women, and, occasionally, women living as men, among North
American tribes. Native people today use the pantribal term
"Two-Spirit" to refer to these individuals, who were in fact members of a distinct third gender that combined male and female economic and social roles with traits unique to Two-Spirit identity.[18]
Hay had first read about Two-Spirits around 1945, in the Modern
Library collection edited by V. F. Calverton, *The Making of Man*,
which included contributions by Edward Carpenter and Edward
Westermarck. He was particularly impressed by (and often cited)
Ruth Benedict's account of Two-Spirits in *Patterns of Culture*.
As Benedict relates, Two-Spirits enjoyed a reputation not only for
excellence in crafts and domestic work, but in many tribes they
were religious specialists as well.[19]

Hay's statement in "The Homosexual and History" that "in the
Berdache we see arise the great social division of labor which
becomes the groundwork of industry as we know it today" is one
of his most provocative theses. In the ethnographic literature, the
role of Two-Spirits as specialists in arts and crafts is constantly
stressed. But in fact no other historian or anthropologist made
this connection between gender variance and economic specialization until the 1980s.[20]

The second exemplar Hay uncovered in his research were the
societies or guilds of fools, known as *sociétés joyeuses* in Renaissance France. As Enid Welsford describes them, "The *Sociétés
Joyeuses* were associations of young men who adapted the tradi-

tional Fool's dress of motley, eared hoods, bells and bauble and organized themselves into kingdoms under the rule of an annual elected monarch known as *Prince des Sots* [Prince of Fools], *Mère-Folle* [Mother Folly, a man dressed as a woman], *Abbé de Malgouverne* [Abbey of Misrule], etc. with the object of celebrating certain traditional customs, especially customs such as the *Charivari* which enabled them to keep up a running commentary on the affairs of their neighbours and to indulge a taste for satire and social criticism."[21] The most famous of all was the *Enfants-sans-souci* in Paris, organized under a Prince des Sots and a Mère-Sotte, with the motto *numerus stultorum est infinitus* (the number of fools is infinite). Always masked in public, the members of the society, through their plays, or *sotties*, gave voice to the people's complaints against both Church and king. The Basoche du Palais, an association of legal clerks organized in the early fifteenth century (whose members were required to be unmarried), "were able to take revenge with impunity in unlicensed speech upon the tyranny of their masters. . . . Not even the highest dignitaries in the country escape their satire." Their public performances were banned in 1547.[22]

Fool societies are believed to be a continuation of the medieval Feast of Fools celebrated by the inferior clergy in cathedral towns throughout Europe and England, usually on the day of the Circumcision. Following the singing of the Magnificat, the higher clergy turned over their staffs of office to an elected representative of the lower orders who, as "bishop or Pope or King of Fools," presided over the subsequent revelries. All sanctity toward religion and authority was suspended. The mass was burlesqued, asses were led into the church, and priests and clerks wore masks, danced in the choir, and dressed as women.

Another Fool tradition, perhaps even older, was represented by

the folk dance known in France as Les Bouffons or Les Mattachines. According to Enid Welsford, "The dance is a dance of
fools who perform a kind of combat in which swords are leapt
over, clashed together and woven into various patterns, culminating in a figure in which the swords are entwined over the heads of
one or more of the performers."[23] Some form of this dance
appears to have been known throughout Europe—as the
Matachin in Spain, the Mattacino in Italy, and the Moresca elsewhere.[24] It was often performed by the Fool societies. It was
closely related to the English sword and Morris dances, which
were typically accompanied by a Fool figure, sometimes cross-
dressed or dressed in both male and female clothes (and referred
to as the "man-woman"), who functioned as the dance leader.[25]

Most folklorists interpret these festivities and dances as surviv-
ing elements of pre-Christian "fertility rituals."[26] Hay, however,
argues that they are survivals of tribal initiation rites, originally
held at the beginning of spring, in which young people were given
impossible tasks or "fools' errands" (hence the origin of April
Fool's Day), and to the extent that they succeeded they were celebrated by the village.[27] Equally provocative is Hay's argument that
the figure of the Fool was the tribal religious functionary who presided over these rites, in a role similar to that of the Native American Two-Spirit. The Fool was able to serve in this capacity, as the
arbiter of transitions, transformations, and reversals, because he
performed all these operations in his own person. Cross-dressing,
or combining male and female dress, is, in fact, one of the most
common symbols throughout the world of the power to bridge
opposites. The literature on European folk traditions provides
many examples of the Fool dressed as a woman or in both male
and female clothes, of cross-dressing by men and women during
the Feast of Fools, and even cross-dressed Mattachine/Sword

dancers.[28] In this capacity, the Fool served as a deputy of pre-Christian goddess figures, a practice Hay traces back to the Berdache priesthoods of the ancient societies of the Near East (see "Christianity's First Closet Case," on pp. 218–37). Following Christianization, heretical movements like Arianism linked the tribal Berdache-Fool figure with Jesus, the son and deputy of the matron Mary.

Hay was especially drawn to the *sociétés joyeuses*, recognizing in their public and political satire the Renaissance counterpart of agit-prop theater, with overtly Queer elements. In fact, Hay had originally proposed "Society of Fools" as the name for the organization founded in 1950. Bob Hull, who had attended Hay's music classes, suggested the more ambiguous term "Mattachine." The need to explain the name to others would give members of the organization the chance to define themselves in their own terms.

It is important to note that, as a Marxist, Hay's focus was not on individual sexuality or even on roles or identities as such but on social *institutions*—the combination of roles and their associated practices, meanings, symbols, and historical heritage within the context of specific economic formations. Thus, the "Berdache institution" is not merely a social role for Native American men and women who were "different," but a combination of an identity and a role plus cultural practices, comprehensive knowledge, and symbols sustained by the larger community because of their contributions to a tribal level of production. How the individuals participating in this institution achieved sexual gratification was almost the last and least important element of it. That those who could best fulfill the requirements of the institution were often homosexually inclined was coincidental from the community's point of view. Conversely, the occurrence of occasional heterosexuals or heterosexual behavior in the "Berdache institution," from

Hay's perspective, does not negate his general characterization of it. Hay explains his use of the term Berdache in notes written in 1959:

> The writer has selected it because fundamentally it denotes a folk-evolved social institution. . . . The obdurate position that since heterogeneous Homophile patterns are historically recorded in widely separated areas of culture, *ergo* primitive ethics had a far greater latitude of permissibility toward deviant sexuality than have those traditional to more recent Western Cultures must be apprehended for the wishful thinking metaphysic that it is. . . . When we stumble upon recorded or secondary evidences of permissiveness towards Homophilia in a given archaic culture we must simultaneously search *for the institution that permitted it because it used it.*

The roles of the Two-Spirit and village Fool were examples of the "Berdache institution" because: the men who filled them were rarely married; their roles involved gender reversal or transformation in a religious context; they were community-sanctioned on the basis of the social contributions they made; some of them certainly had sex with men; and most of all because of their origins in the economic formation that Hay terms ritual agriculture, in which the mode of production is represented in terms of female fertility resulting in a flexible gender system.

With the examples of the Two-Spirit and the Fool and a model of emergent culture and cultural revival, Hay's view of Gay people and their subculture began to change. In the 1930s he had been introduced to vibrant, subterranean Gay networks in San Francisco and Los Angeles. He himself had mastered the refined camp mannerisms of the English actors he had worked with in the International Group Players, earning the sobriquet by which he is known among friends to this day—"the Duchess." Camp became the leading example of contemporary Gay culture for Hay. It was not only a language but also a powerful vehicle for social satire, which linked it to the traditions of the Feast of Fools and the *sociétés joyeuses.* Hay was also able to recognize the figure of the Native American Two-Spirit in some of the legendary queens he had known, like Clarabelle, the "mother" of Los Angeles's Bunker Hill. A man who lived in drag, Clarabelle had, by sheer force of personality, made himself the center of a network of friends and dependents.

One other element of Gay life had always fascinated Hay and figured in his growing sense of Gay culture—the ability of Gay men to find each other, in even the most faraway and unlikely places. In the 1930s, he had witnessed this every time he went cruising on Hollywood Boulevard, in Valentino and Lafayette Parks, and at the "magical Santa Monica Palisades." There's simply no mistaking another Gay man when he returns your gaze without a blink. This "eye-lock," as Hay calls it, points to the whole area of body language, where Hay believes a variety of distinct Gay patterns can be identified.

Hay's notion of Gay people as a minority was still mostly a hunch when the original group of Mattachine founders began meeting. It was their discussions that led him to develop this idea into a formal thesis. As Chuck Rowland recalled, "I kept saying, 'What is our theory?' Having been a Communist, you've got to work with a theory. 'What is our basic principle that we are building on?' And Harry said, 'We are an oppressed cultural minority.' And I said, 'That's exactly it!' That was the first time I know of that Gays were referred to as an oppressed cultural minority."[29]

As Hay and the others thrashed out the implications of this idea, they drew on two sources of evidence. First, there was the evidence provided in the discussion groups themselves, where participants were beginning to uncover unexpected commonalities in their lives. Nothing is more powerful than the experience of discovering you're not alone, that others share not only your sexual desires, but also your emotions, dreams, and basic values. A second source of evidence supporting the minority thesis were the historical examples of the Native American Two-Spirits and European Fool traditions that Hay had discovered in his research and frequently talked about in conversations and formal presentations. (More than seventy-five people attended two sessions of the Laguna discussion group at which Hay presented a version of "The Homosexual and History," included here on pp. 94–119.)

The extent to which Hay's thinking influenced others is apparent in Chuck Rowland's speech to the April 1953 Mattachine convention. "We must disenthrall ourselves of the idea that we differ only in our sexual directions and that all we want or need in life is to be free to seek the expression of our sexual desires as we see fit," he argued. "The heterosexual mores of the dominant culture have excluded us," and "as a result of this exclusion, we have developed differently than have other cultural groups." Homosexuals, he concluded, must develop "a new pride—a pride in belonging, a pride in participating in the cultural growth and social achievements of the homosexual minority."[30]

Hay continued to elaborate the cultural minority thesis in the years that followed. In notes written in 1960, he argues that, of the criteria for defining a national minority, the really decisive ones are a common language and a common psychological make-up expressed in shared cultural forms.[31] Citing examples from the Navajo and Pueblo Indians to Mennonite and Shaker religious communities, he argues that all groups "whose motivating persuasions and/or fundamental inclinations evoke decisive patterns towards a socially specific way of life, are to be seen as Social

Minorities." To underscore the importance of psychological make-up as a defining trait of a minority, Hay uses the example of the Nisei, the Japanese-Americans who were interned during World War II and threatened with repatriation when the war ended. If this had happened, Hay argues, the Nisei would have been just as much a social minority in Japan as they were in the U.S. Indeed, such was the case of the former American slaves who established a colony in Liberia. In considering the case of homosexuals, Hay makes the following observation: "The Homophile common psychological make-up manifests itself in a community of culture so phenomenologically remarkable that it transcends the mechanical barriers of formal language by creating an international behavioral language of its own, in addition to sharing the pedestrian language of each parental community. To be sure, the communities of culture differ in detail from one national community to another. But they are enough alike that no one need be a helpless stranger whatever the port of call."

Hay's cultural minority thesis was a crucial ingredient in the creation of the Mattachine movement. It is today the implicit mode of self-understanding and community organization of Lesbian/Gay communities wherever they exist. Hay's formulation of this model remains one of the best argued cases for a cultural politics of Lesbian/Gay liberation.

Notes

1. Quoted in Eric Marcus, *Making History: The Struggle for Gay and Lesbian Equal Rights, 1945–1990: An Oral History* (New York: HarperCollins, 1992), p. 28.

2. Hay claims it was the only time he was able to hit a target in his life (Stuart Timmons, *The Trouble with Harry Hay: Founder of the Modern Gay Movement* [Boston: Alyson, 1990], pp. 66–67).

3. Joseph R. Starobin, *American Communism in Crisis, 1943–1957* (Cambridge, Mass.: Harvard University Press, 1972), pp. 23, 100.

4. Robert Briffault, *The Mothers: The Matriarchal Theory of Social Origins* (New York: Macmillan, 1931).

5. George Thomson, *Studies in Ancient Greek Society: The Prehistoric Ægean*, rev. ed. (London: Lawrence and Wishart, 1954).

6. In fact, the American Communist Party mirrored the prevailing moralistic view of homosexuality. Article 10, section 5 of its 1938 constitution reads: "Party members found to be strikebreakers, *degenerates*, habitual drunkards, betrayers of Party confidence, . . . shall be summarily dismissed from positions of responsibility, expelled from the Party and exposed before the general public" (*The Constitution and By-Laws of the Communist Party of the United States of America* [New York: Workers Library Publishers, 1938], p. 20; my emphasis—WR).

7. Wilson Record, *The Negro and the Communist Party* (Chapel Hill: University of North Carolina Press, 1951), is the source for most details that follow.

8. These policies are explained at length in James S. Allen, *The Negro Question in the United States* (New York: International Publishers, 1936). For a recent review of these debates, see Michael Omi and Howard Winant, *Racial Formation in the United States: From the 1960s to the 1990s*, 2d ed. (New York: Routledge, 1994), pp. 42–44.

9. Joseph Stalin, *Marxism and the National Question: Selected Writings and Speeches* (New York: International Publishers, 1942), p. 12. I am aware that the reaction to this authorship will range from surprise to distress to horror on the part of many. Some will find it impossible to disassociate the name of Stalin from the ideas in this text. Yet, in fact, none of the ideas here is unique. Social scientists in the same period were developing non-essentialist (i.e., non racial) definitions of minorities and ethnicity. Donald Webster Cory had independently written of the "homosexual minority" in *The Homosexual in America: A Subjective Approach* (New York: Greenberg, 1951). However, given Hay's Party membership, it was inevitable he would encounter this particular text, and, in the 1940s, one would be hard pressed to find an authority who advocated cultural auton-

55

omy rather than assimilation for Blacks and other minorities. American social scientists still assumed that minorities would lose their cultural uniqueness once absorbed into Anglo-American society—or that they should, since cultural difference was considered an obstacle to success in a capitalist economy. They focused their research on "acculturation" and "assimilation" (see Stephen O. Murray, *Social Theory, Homosexual Realities* [New York: Gay Academic Union, 1984], pp. 6 ff.; Russell A. Kazal, "Revisiting Assimilation: The Rise, Fall, and Reappraisal of a Concept in American Ethnic History," *American Historical Review* 100[2] [1995]: 437–71). An exception was the work of Melville J. Herskovits, whose 1941 *The Myth of the Negro Past* offered confirmation for the Communist view of African-American culture.

10. Stalin, *Marxism and the National Question*, p. 12.

11. See, for example, William L. Leap, "Gay Men's English: Cooperative Discourse in a Language of Risk," *New York Folklore* 19(1–2) (1993): 45–70; and Leap, "Learning Gay Culture in 'A Desert of Nothing': Language as a Resource in Gender Socialization," *The High School Journal* (Oct./Nov. 1993–Dec./Jan. 1994): 122–32.

12. Record, *The Negro and the Communist Party*, pp. 67, 110. Hay points out that in this period African-American dialect was rarely represented in writing or other media unless the intention was to denigrate Black people.

13. Stalin, *Marxism and the National Question*, p. 16. The four-point model of a minority is an excellent example of what Wittgenstein meant by "family resemblance," what Rodney Needham terms "polythetic" (vs. "monothetic") classification (*Against the Tranquility of Axioms* [Berkeley: University of California Press, 1983]), and what others have called a "fuzzy category" (Stephen O. Murray, "Fuzzy Sets and Abominations," *Man* 19 [1983]: 396–99).

14. Starobin, *American Communism in Crisis*, pp. 200–201.

15. See Robbie Leiberman, *"My Song Is My Weapon": People's Songs, American Communism, and the Politics of Culture, 1930–1950* (Urbana: University of Illinois Press, 1989); and R. Serge Denisoff, *Great Day Coming: Folk Music and the American Left* (Urbana: University of Illinois Press, 1971).

16. See Eric J. Hobsbawm in Karl Marx, *Pre-Capitalist Economic Formations* (New York: International Publishers, 1965), pp. 50–51.

17. Hay's approach might be compared to that of the Subaltern Studies group in India, which, since the 1970s, has sought to develop histories from the "bottom up," focusing on groups otherwise left out of standard histories because they are illiterate or leave no written documents.

18. Honoring these preferences, which emerged in the early 1990s, I use the term "Two-Spirit" here instead of Berdache. Hay's most recent writings follow the same practice. Those written before 1990 primarily use "Berdache," which Hay always capitalized.

19. I have documented Two-Spirit roles in over 150 North American tribes. See *Living the Spirit: A Gay American Indian Anthology* (New York: St. Martin's, 1988) and *The Zuni Man-Woman* (Albuquerque: University of New Mexico Press, 1991).

20. See Will Roscoe, "How to Become a Berdache: Toward a Unified Analysis of Multiple Genders," in *Third Sex, Third Gender: Beyond Sexual Dimorphism in Culture and History*, ed. Gilbert Herdt (New York: Zone Books, 1994), pp. 329–72.

21. Enid Welsford, *The Fool: His Social and Literary History* (London: Faber and Faber, 1935), p. 203. Other key sources on European Fool traditions include Jean Benigne Lucotte du Tilliot, *Mémoires pour servir à l'histoire de la Fête des Foux* (Lausanne and Geneva, 1751); Petit de Julleville, *Les comédiens en France au moyen-âge* (Paris, 1885); E. K. Chambers, *The Mediaeval Stage*, vol. 1 (Oxford: Clarendon Press, 1903), pp. 347 ff.; James G. Frazer, *The Scapegoat*, vol. 9 of *The Golden Bough* (New York: Macmillan, 1935), chaps. 6, 8; Barbara Swain, *Fools and Folly during the Middle Ages and the Renaissance* (New York: Columbia University Press, 1932); Anton C. Zijderveld, *Reality in a Looking-Glass: Rationality through an Analysis of Traditional Folly* (London: Routledge and Kegan Paul, 1982); John Howard Lawson, *The Hidden Heritage: A Rediscovery of the Ideas and Forces that Link the Thought of Our Time with the Culture of the Past* (New York: Citadel Press, 1968), pp. 106–13; Natalie Z. Davis, *Society and Culture in Early Modern France* (Stanford: Stanford University Press, 1975), chaps. 4–5; William Willeford, *The Fool and His Sceptre* (Evanston, Ill.: Northwestern University Press, 1969).

22. Pierre L. Duchartre, *The Italian Comedy* (1929; New York: Dover, 1966), pp. 305 f.

23. Welsford, *The Fool*, pp. 70–71.

24. See Paul Nettl, *The Story of Dance Music* (New York: Philosophical Library, 1947), pp. 82–88; Barbara Lowe, "Early Records of the Morris," *Journal of the English Folk Dance and Song Society* 8(2) (1957): 61–82. Renaissance authors considered the Mattachin/Moresca a survival of the pyrrhic dances of the Greeks and Romans (Thoinot Arbeau, *Orchesography* [1948; New York: Dover, 1967], pp. 151, 82–83). The Curetes, Corybantes, and the priests of the goddess Cybele known as *galli* did, indeed, perform dances with swords (Will Roscoe, "Priests of the Goddess: Gender Transgression in Ancient Religion," *History of Religions* 35[3] [1996]: 295–330).

25. Various evidence suggests that the comic Female figure, often called the Bessy Bride or Dirty Bet, who appears with the Morris and sword dances, was not merely a woman portrayed out of convention by a man but a representation of gender reversal. Photographs from the late nineteenth century often show "her" wearing men's boots and sometimes a mustache. In some locales, the Bessy Bride appears to have "merged" with the Fool, resulting in a figure who wears a woman's skirt *and* men's pants and shirt (Chambers, *The Mediaeval Stage*, p. 200; Alex Helm, *The English Mummers' Play* [Woodbridge, Eng., and Totowa, N.J.: D. S. Brewer and Rowman and Littlefield for the Folklore Society, 1981], pp. 50–51). At Cheshire, the Fool was called Owd Molly-Coddle and the dancers referred to as Molly Dancers (Chambers, *The Mediaeval Stage*, 197). "Molly-coddle" is a term for effeminate men, specifically a man who does women's work (s.v., *Oxford English Dictionary*), and "Mollie" was an eighteenth-century term for Gay men. Finally, there is a report from 1655 of female Morris dancers appearing *with* a man dressed as a woman (Lowe, "Early Records of the Morris," p. 76). Most of the Fool traditions described here involved men, but in England, women appear as Morris dancers in some of the oldest records (Lowe, "Early Records of the Morris," p. 76; Sandra Billington, *A Social History of the Fool* [Sussex and New York: Harvester and St. Martin's], p. 109).

26. See, for example, Frazer, n. 21 above, and Francis M. Cornford, *The Origin of Attic Comedy* (1934; Gloucester, Mass.: Peter Smith, 1968).

27. Hay has in mind such "Fool's Day" customs as "hunting the gowk" or cuckoo, and the St. Stephen's Day wren hunt. These springtime rites were displaced to the Christmas season when the observance of New

Year's was moved from March 25 to January 1 in England in 1752 (Lewis Spence, *Myth and Ritual in Dance, Game, and Rhyme* [London: Watts & Co., 1947], pp. 44–49; Chambers, *The Mediaeval Stage*, p. 226).

28. Lowe, "Early Records of the Morris," p. 78; Chambers, *The Mediaeval Stage*, p. 84; Elizabeth Swann, "Maid Marian and the Morris," *Journal of the English Folk Dance and Song Society* 7(1) (1952): 20–25, esp. 20; Willeford, *The Fool and His Sceptre*, chap. 10.

29. Marcus, *Making History*, p. 32.

30. Quoted in John D'Emilio, *Making Trouble: Essays on Gay History, Politics, and the University* (New York: Routledge, 1992), p. 41. See also David L. Freeman [Chuck Rowland], "The Homosexual Culture," *ONE* 1(5) (May 1953): 8–11. In an interview in the 1980s, Rowland explained that by "culture" he meant "a body of language, feelings, thinking, and experiences that we share in common. As we speak of a Mexican culture. As we speak of an American Indian culture." Gay culture, however, is "emergent." It resides in the use of "certain language, certain words," like the word "Gay" itself. "This does not constitute a language in the sense that English is a language and French is a language, but it's more comparable to Yiddish culture." By using Yiddish words, even while speaking English, one can identify oneself culturally (Marcus, *Making History*, p. 33).

31. Party theorists often singled out "common psychological make-up" as a key characteristic. As Max Weiss wrote, "The Negro nation is still in an early phase of development." Contrary to predictions of some (often made regarding Lesbians and Gays as well) that once racial discrimination was ended Blacks would assimilate into the larger society, Weiss argued that the "Negro nation . . . is destined to flourish and to make untold creative contributions to a unified, democratic, bi-national United States" (Max Weiss, "Toward Clarity on the Negro Question," *Political Affairs* [June 1946]: 457–78, esp. 461, 466–67).

"We, the Androgynes
of the world"

IN 1948, Hay had all the concepts that would enable him to formulate his understanding of Gay people as a minority. Two events would trigger their combination into a gestalt. The first was the publication of the Kinsey report, *Sexual Behavior in the Human Male*. Hay himself had been interviewed by Kinsey, so he eagerly sought a copy of the book. The Kinsey research suggested that fully 10 percent of American males were significantly or predominantly homosexual. Rather than a few isolated misfits lurking about the red-light districts of the largest cities, there were, in fact, millions of homosexuals—everywhere. For Hay, this meant the potential for a mass-based social movement.

The second event took the form of less welcome news that Hay heard from the friend of a Gay co-worker that summer: "The guy worked in the State Department in Washington, and told me that kids were already getting kicked out of the Department because they'd all slept with someone named Andrew." It was the precursor of purges that would be conducted throughout the 1940s and 1950s. Suddenly, the bright prospect of organizing a movement of millions of Gay people was offset for Hay by a chilling realization: "The post-war reaction, the shutting down of open communication, was already of concern to many of us progressives. I knew the government was going to look for a new enemy, a new scapegoat. It was predictable. But Blacks were beginning to organize and the horror of the Holocaust was too recent to put the Jews in this position. The natural scapegoat would be us, the Queers. They were the one group of disenfranchised people who did not even know they were a group because they had never formed as a group. They—we—had to get started."[1]

Meanwhile, the façade of normalcy that Hay had carefully crafted over ten years of heterosexual marriage was crumbling. As he told his biographer, this was his "period of terror." He was plagued by dreams of blacking out and actually hurting his wife and daughters. "I was confronted by the horror of my own existence. I didn't know what to do." Furtive sexual liaisons and secret affairs with men were no longer enough. The pretext of heterosexuality had become unbearable.

Since its release, Hay had carried around his copy of the Kinsey report as though it were a Bible. He discovered that a passing reference to the report was an excellent way to determine if someone else was "sympathetic," as being Gay was described in the language of the time. On August 10, 1948, after attending a political event on behalf of Henry Wallace's presidential candidacy, Hay had a chance to use this ice-breaker at what turned out to be an all-Gay party. With other party-goers alternately encouraging and challenging him, Hay began spinning out the idea of how a discrete organization of homosexuals might lobby for the reform of anti-Gay laws. That night he drew up the prospectus for what became Mattachine.

Unfortunately, no copy of this original version of the "Call," as Hay has always referred to it, has survived.[2] The following text is a second, expanded version, hurriedly typed (and misdated July 7 instead of the actual date of July 9, 1950) so that he could show it to Rudi Gernreich the following evening.

The degree of detail in Hay's ideas for a Gay organization, even

before he had found his first convert, is striking. Equally striking
are the signs of the low self-esteem that even an intelligent Gay
man like Hay labored under in those years. Homosexuality is
referred to as a "physiological and psychological handicap." Hay
still accepted the view of homosexuals as afflicted with a compulsive sexual drive, and one of the models he had in mind was Alcoholics Anonymous. "Bachelors' Anonymous," in addition to its
social service, educational, and quasi-political functions, would
help homosexuals gain control of their sexual behavior and
form stable partnerships. Still, in 1948, even to suggest that
the problem of the promiscuous homosexual was promiscuity
and not homosexuality was a significant step forward in self-
understanding, as was the proposal that Lesbians and Gay men
could come to understand themselves *on their own*, without psy-
chiatric or professional guidance. Although Hay clearly has Gay
men in mind throughout most of the prospectus, he makes a pro-
vision for a separate order for women. In fact, many Gay men at
that time had never met a Lesbian, let alone gained insight into
Lesbian issues; only a few women participated in early Mattachine. Still, the Mattachine organizers always conceived of the
movement they were creating as being co-sexual.[3]

The use of the term "Androgyne" reflects Hay's attempt to find
an alternative to the self-denigrating terms of the Gay subculture,
on the one hand, and the pathologizing terms of medicine and
psychiatry, on the other. "Androgyne" rarely appears in Hay's
writings after this text. Concluding that Gay people couldn't be
adequately understood in terms of either male or female, Hay and
the other Mattachine founders coined the term "homophile" as
an alternative.

Here, then, in its entirety is the prospectus that launched the
modern Gay liberation movement.

Preliminary Concepts: INTERNATIONAL BACHELORS' FRATERNAL ORDER FOR PEACE & SOCIAL DIGNITY, Sometimes Referred to as BACHELORS ANONYMOUS

A service and welfare organization devoted to the protection and improvement of Society's Androgynous Minority.

A. Statement of aims and purposes.

    1. With full realization that encroaching American Fascism, like unto previous impacts of International Fascism, seeks to bend unorganized and unpopular minorities into isolated fragments of social and emotional instability;

        With full realization that the socially censured Androgynous Minority was suborned, blackmailed, cozened, and stampeded into serving as hoodlums, stool pigeons, volunteer informers, concentration camp trustees, torturers, and hangmen, before it, as a minority, was ruthlessly exterminated;

        With full realization that the full significance of the government indictment against Androgynous Civil Servants, veiled under the sentiment that they "by the peculiar circumstances of their private lives lay themselves wide open to social blackmail by a Foreign Power," lies in the legal establishment of a second type of GUILT BY ASSOCIATION;

        With the full realization that a GUILT BY ASSOCIATION charge requires that the victim prove himself in-

64

nocent against undisclosed charges (and is, therefore, impossible), and that a GUILT BY ASSOCIATION charge can be leveled on the evidence of anonymous and malicious informers (and, therefore, cannot be fought), and that under the Government's announced plans for eventual 100% war production mobilization all commerce and production would be conducted under government contract—thus making it impossible for Androgynes to secure employment;

And with the full realization that Guilt of Androgynity BY ASSOCIATION, equally with Guilt of Communist sympathy BY ASSOCIATION, can be employed as a threat against any and every man and woman in our country as a whip to ensure thought control and political regimentation;

With the full realization that, in order to earn for ourselves any place in the sun, we must with perseverance and self-discipline work collectively on the side of peace, for the program of the four freedoms of the Atlantic Charter, and in the spirit and letter of the United Nations Charter, for the full first-class citizenship participation of Minorities everywhere, including ourselves;

We, the Androgynes of the world, have formed this responsible corporate body to demonstrate by our efforts that our physiological and psychological handicaps need be no deterrent in integrating 10% of the world's population towards the constructive social progress of mankind.

2. We declare our aims to be to effect socially, economi-

cally, politically, and morally, the integration of the best interests of the Androgynous minority with the common good of the community in which we live.

65

3. We declare our aims to present the concept of our Fraternal Orders, fully subscribed to by our membership, as being similar in both membership service and community service and social objectives as the well-known and respected "Alcoholics Anonymous."

4. We aim, by helping our members to adjust emotionally and intellectually to the enlightened mores and ethics of the standard community, to eradicate the vicious myths and taboos that physiological deviation (degeneracy in its true scientific sense) precludes psychological and social degeneracy. (Within the recognized minorities, people are bad not because they are Jews or Negroes but because of the external nature of their political and economic environments. We must endeavor to understand ourselves and then demonstrate this knowledge to the community.)

5. We aim to aid in the dispelling of this myth by attempting to regulate the social conduct of our minority in such matters as, for example, exhibitionism, indiscriminate profligacy, violations of public decency; we aim to explore and promote a socially healthy approach to the ethical values of a constructed pairing between Androgynes; we aim to tackle the question of profligacy and Satyriasis as emotional diseases to be treated clinically.

6. We aim to dispel the fears and antagonisms of the community by making available clinical personnel, specialists, and apparati to educators, churchmen, and pro-

66

fessional practitioners to the end of discovering and applying group or personal techniques of therapy and/or guidance, to give advice or recommendations or assistance to outside community bodies perplexed by manifestations of an Androgynous nature or character; we aim by the above equipment to help curb the malingering and the inducements professed to be common to cases of juvenile delinquents; we aim by the above equipment to help community organizations adjust and alleviate where possible the emotional and psychological development of Androgynous tendencies in minors.

7. We aim, by making available to biologists, physiochemists, psychologists, and educators, clinical experience and data on the objectives, frustrations, daily patterns, oppressions, insecurities, compromises, and fruitions of the great body of average Androgynes, to represent to the community a codified social analysis upon which constructive and progressive sexual legislation may be comprehended and enacted.

8. We aim to contribute to the general welfare of the community by making common cause with other minorities in contributing to the reform of judicial, police, and penal practices which undermine the honesty and morale of the community.

9. We aim to contribute to the general morale of the community by bringing ourselves to realize that only in a national community embodying the right to freedom of conscience, the right to the expression of personal opinion, and the objective of a peaceful and mutually cooperative world affording equal place to cultural produc-

tion as to industrial production can our minority realize
and contribute its full value.

10. We aim to integrate ourselves into the constructive so-
    cial progress of society, on the side of peace, for the pro-
    gram of the four freedoms of the Atlantic Charter,[4] and
    in the spirit and letter of the United Nations Charter, by
    providing a collective outlet for political, cultural, and
    social expression to some 10% of the world's popula-
    tion, in which the collective force of their vote and voice
    may have substance and value.

B. Activities.
  1. A Service Organization providing:
     a. Committee channels to work for positive, scientifi-
        cally predicated, and morale building legislation.
     b. Committee channels to fight against, and eliminate,
        police brutality, political and judicial shakedown,
        and civic blackmail.
     c. Committee channels to educate public opinion.
     d. Committee channels to supplement community
        campaigns for minority rights; for safeguarding and
        restoring Constitutional Democracy on every Level;
        for promoting and insuring International Peace and
        the self-determination of nations and national mi-
        norities.
     e. Committee channels to make available to the com-
        munity whatever apparatus we may develop which
        has valuable community application (see A-6, 7, 8;
        see also B-3 below).
  2. A Civil Insurance Organization providing:
     a. Through dues payments and standard computed
        fees, legal services for all civil infractions, shake-

68

downs, frame-ups, blackmail, slander, and unwarranted invasions of personal privacy, as applicable legally to Androgynous experience.

b. Through standard fees, bail in all cases, preliminary to review by the Orders' Grievance Committee to determine if the action involves any of the protectable categories outlined in B-1 above.

(1) If clause B-1 is invoked, the Orders' insurance is to cover all basic costs of the case.

(2) If clause B-1 is NOT invoked, the Orders' insurance does not apply. (But the Orders' Service and Welfare Committees will endeavor to work and press for judicial and community leniency, and will offer to take such cases under guardianship and apply therapy or guidance under the jurisdiction and supervision of the Court.)

(3) If clause B-1 is invoked, the Order will make every effort to safeguard the social and economic well-being of the member and will undertake rehabilitation if necessary.

3. A Welfare and Educational Organization providing:

a. Educational Study groups and membership Forums on the issues which concern the civic responsibilities, general welfare campaigns, and constitutional requirements of the community as a whole, IN WHICH THE MEMBERSHIP BY ITS AIMS REQUIRES THE RIGHT TO PARTICIPATE.

b. Educational study groups and membership Forums on the special issues which the Order is sworn to promote and promulgate.

c. Cultural, creative, and recreational activities towards the end of improving the social conditions of culture, under the organizing impact of craftsman-and-audience constant participation.

d. Welfare groups to promote a better social integration of the membership Minority into the
community-at-large:

   (1) This shall include series of group discussions on
   ethics, hygiene, ethnology, social anthropology,
   social custom, morality, genetics, etc.

   (2) This shall include therapeutic groups conducted
   in accordance with the most advanced available
   techniques.

   (3) This shall include scholastic and laboratory research into the most advanced physiological and
   psychological theories, techniques, and applications, for the benefit of membership needs and
   aims, and the needs of the community as a whole.

   (4) This shall include committees and flying squads
   of specialists and qualified personnel, available
   for individual membership needs and problems,
   available to community needs and problems,
   and available to judiciary and governmental con-
   sultations, paroles, suspensions, and guardian-
   ships.

e. First Aid squads and single volunteers on a 24-hour
basis to provide therapy, guidance, or counsel to
members in emotional and psychological distress.

f. Social Service Committee to help new members, and
members new to this community, to adjust themselves to the duties, the responsibilities, and the privileges of the local Orders Chapter.

g. Public Relations Committee composed of civic
advisors, churchmen, attorneys, doctors, qualified

members, and interested persons to suggest activities and services based on current community interests.

h. The above suggested activities may be carried on under close supervision on a cooperative or token fee basis as determined by the membership body of the Chapter.

C. Membership.

1. Membership shall be declared to be completely nondiscriminatory as to race, color, creed, or political affiliation and shall be limited only to those actively affirming the principles of majority democracy, practiced within the Order, as outlined in A-1 above.

2. Membership shall be anonymous to the community at large and to each other if they choose: membership shall be protected by the device of fictitious names until such times as the organization is in a position to incorporate and set into operation the Civil Insurance plan.

3. Membership and inter-Order activity shall be Masonic in character; shall be understood to be sworn to protective secrecy except inasmuch as certain aims, purposes, and committees shall be declared as parties to community action or campaign.

4. Membership shall be determined by member-recommendation only and shall be confirmed by election. Members shall enter an initiate period for one year before being confirmed and during this period the Civil Insurance Coverage shall apply only at the discretion of the Executive Board. (Mechanics to be further determined.)

5. Membership shall, at all times, require of members and

initiate an established minimum of active and unsolicited participation in at least one Educational-Welfare activity and one Service activity of the Orders' Chapter. 71

6. Membership shall be classified into five degrees of rank which shall be determined and bestowed by membership vote.

a. Initiate Degree	Insignia . . . pin showing IBFO
b. First Degree (requirement: recognized participation in Service & Welfare activity)	Insignia . . . pin showing IBFO bar showing Androgyne (in Greek)
c. Second Degree (requirement: achievement in community integration activity)	Insignia . . . pin showing IBFO bar showing Berdache (in Hopi)
d. Third Degree (requirement: continual leadership in Orders' Aims and Purposes)	Insignia . . . pin showing IBFO bar design designating Order of St. Medardus[5]
e. Fourth Degree (requirement: the highest honor bestowable)	Insignia . . . pin and bars as described before, plus escutcheon and chain showing the Egyptian Ankh ☥, the sign of the Order of Pharaoh, the historic personification of the Androgynous Ideal

7. Membership shall agree to at all times, whether able to be involved or not, to lend a willing ear and voice to programs and purposes considered basic to the described objectives of the Orders.

72

8. Membership shall agree that at all times leadership principles and activity principles shall be weighed and accepted in terms of their adherence to the objectives, in spirit and in letter, as described in section A-1 above. Membership shall agree that at any time it becomes apparent that membership activity and sentiment is not in accord with the objectives and principles described in A above, that the dissenting member is required to submit his resignation, that the dissenting chapter is considered suspended preliminary to dissolution by the Executive Board, or that the organization as a whole is required to dissolve its incorporation and any and all connections with or interest in the name and prestige of this organization.

9. Membership shall subscribe to a minimum program of mutual aid and assistance, particularly to members who are new to a group or to a community. Similarly to Shrine and Masonic practice, insignia worn at an unconventional angle may be used to designate distress or need—and must be acted upon by all other members as quickly as possible.

D. Details of Organization (tentative and as yet incomplete).

1. The Orders shall be incorporated under the laws, duties and proscriptions attached to such non-profit organizations. Its corporate charter and by-laws must incorporate very precisely the objective and limitations of Section A and be subject to the proscriptions indicated in Section C-8.

2. The Orders shall be conceived to sub-charter supplementary subsidiaries such as:

  a. International Spinsters Orders.
  b. International Friends and Well-Wishers Auxiliaries.
  c. etc.

3. The Orders shall seek the aid and support of Church and Professional and Civic Leaders. The Orders shall seek the aid, and in return shall subscribe to the support of governmental reform bodies in the community; the Orders shall seek the cooperation and respect of all minority groups, physical and moral welfare groups, and any other groups, whose general aims and purposes—both nationally and internationally—subscribe to the objectives described in A above.

4. The Orders declare that, at all times, they publicly subscribe (though anonymously except through the public face of the Orders) to the aims, tenets, and objectives described in Section A. If any individual, group, Chapter, or Division deny or betray by intent or action any and/or several of these tenets at any time, the Orders reserve the rights to dissolve and expel the offending Chapters or members, and shall do everything in its power to make social restitution for the offenses (see C-8; D-11).

5. For purposes of mutual protection and supervision, all inter-order activities and meetings shall be declared as "closed" to membership only, except as they may be singly designated for community assistance services or campaigns by the Majority decision of the Membership involved, at each instance and each occasion.

6. Meetings and committees shall be designed for compactness and mobility . . . and shall be closely super-

vised to insure optimal subscription to the basic requirements of community behavior. Membership recreational activities, in the name of the organization, shall be planned and designed with the amenabilities and censures of the community in mind. (For example, play-party and square dancing will probably be always acceptable where social dancing might not.)

7. Groups shall be mainly geographical except in regard to recreational and welfare groups as outlined in B-3 above.

8. Membership Lists shall be planned with the Optimal Anonymity in mind; after full and protective incorporation has been executed membership lists in coded fictions and all data shall be handled by a bonded officer appointed by a duly elective and supervising governing committee.

9. The Orders, for the time being, shall be self-supporting as to needed funds and fees, and shall seek the services of paid functionaries ONLY when the scope of Organizational activity requires it.

10. Insignia, referred to in C-6, must be EARNED by the member, and shall be bestowed by elective vote only in respect to degree of participatory service upon the part of the candidate.

   a. Any member who shall, in the course of a year, not advance the degree of his standing must agree to a review of his privileges and responsibilities and must agree to attempt to reach common decision with the committee as to his future commitments.

   b. This shall be construed as one of a number of safeguards of the protective mantle required by the Orders against the infiltration of elements inimicable to the aims and principles of the Orders and its individual members.

11. In relation to the public responsibility assured by the Orders as indicated in D-4, and cross-references above, it must be understood that should investigation reveal that the violation were a first deviation, or an irrational or compulsive slip from the self-discipline sought and subscribed to by the Orders that the organization reserves the right to treat the member, or members, as penitents and to invoke the protection of therapeutic guardianship under the leniency of the community.

All the above, with the exception of the general sense and social orientation indicated in section A, is declared to be purely exploratory and open to complete expansion or rejection.

Respectfully submitted to whom it may concern . . .

Eann MacDonald

Dated July 7, 1950, but actually typed July 9.

Notes

1. Stuart Timmons, *The Trouble with Harry Hay: Founder of the Modern Gay Movement* (Boston: Alyson, 1990), pp. 132, 135.

2. Hay believes that Chuck Rowland burned the last copy during an episode of depression following the break-up of the original movement.

3. When I asked Hay about the role of women in early Mattachine, he provided me with the following recollections: "Del Martin and Phyl Lyons, next to Helen Sanders (Helen Sandoz) and Sten Russell (Stella Rush), their counterparts and first Editors of *The Ladder*, who moved from SF to LA in about 1956, were typical of the Lesbians who came forward *at all* during the first decade. Ruth Bernhard, who became a world-renowned photographer in the late '50s and '60s, was a major exception:

a truly marvelous European-born and -educated Woman, who was totally sure of herself as an artist as well as a person. Ruth was introduced to us through Martin Block's friend, the actor Phil Jones, and his actor-director friend Paul Bennard in approximately September of 1951. Geraldean Jackson (whose neighborhood name was Betty Purdue) had become part of the Echo Park–Silverlake Guild after the trial, in the Fall of 1952, and she, in turn, brought Jim Kepner to his first Mattachine Discussion Group meeting in late December of 1952 or early 1953. After *ONE* mag started, Ann Carll Reid and her lover Dawn Fredrick (who became Eve Elloree and *ONE*'s Art Director) showed up, with Ann Carll taking over the editorship from Dale Jennings after *ONE*'s first year in 1954. With the exception of 'Boopsie,' who showed up with Hal Call from San Francisco during the gathering of the First Mattachine's rupturous upheaval in April–May of 1953, these are all the women I know about in *first* Mattachine" (pers. comm., April 27, 1995).

4. The Atlantic Charter was a program of peace aims and a statement on international human rights enunciated by Churchill and Roosevelt in August 1941, which became the basis for the formation of the United Nations.

5. In the 1930s, a friend of Hay who had traveled through the Balkans showed him a small carving of a saint honored in that region named Medardus (or Medardos in Greek), who was the patron of life-long male companions. There is a French St. Médard, but I have been unable to confirm if this is the same figure Hay identifies.

"The heroic objective
of liberating one of our
largest minorities"

THESE ARE HAY'S REMARKS for the first discussion group meeting held in November 1950. Although brief, they reveal his sense of the historic nature of the meeting. The organizers ran this and subsequent groups without presuming that the participants were homosexual—hence Hay's reference here to "some of us as parents, or as potential parents." Even as attendance grew, many Gay men continued to bring female friends with them to provide a heterosexual "cover." As Hay recalls, "Nobody in our group ever seemed to know Gay people in California, let alone L.A. . . . It was always somebody else, not present, who'd had this homosexual experience or who knew someone somewheres-else who had."[1]

As the number of discussion groups increased, the organizers set up the Mattachine *Foundation* to serve as their official sponsor, and they each took responsibility for facilitating one or more groups. When individuals who seemed Gay attended discussion groups regularly (and appeared trustworthy), the organizers invited them to join the secret Mattachine *Society*. If they agreed, they underwent a simple but dramatic initiation ceremony and took a membership oath. Eventually, during the period of excitement generated by the organization's successful efforts in 1952 to defend Dale Jennings, a steering committee member, from vice squad entrapment charges, discussion group participants began to identify themselves as Gay, but in the atmosphere of betrayal and intimidation created by McCarthyism most Gay men and Lesbians instinctively avoided speaking about homosexuality in the first person.

78

Slogan "Children and Fools Speak the Truth": Les Mattachines (The Society of Fools)

I'd like to say that though forums and group discussions on social problems, social behavior, the rehabilitation of social ethics, etc., have been increasing in quantity, in scope, and thus naturally in quality on a community basis in recent years—nevertheless, I feel that the undertaking commencing here tonight may be one of historic importance and magnitude.

For myself, I feel it a great privilege to have been asked to attend and within my own limitations to participate. The direction, the objectivity, anticipated in the discussions planned, embrace questions which some of us as parents, or as potential parents, are deeply concerned—and about which little or no satisfactory knowledge or procedure has yet been advanced or even indicated.

In the deliberations on the questions to be discussed, some of the group may be able to comment, or analyze, or essay hypotheses based directly upon their own experiences and observations. Others of us may have to confine our suggestions, comments, and recommendations to levels of experiences recounted from hearsay or from second-hand, or to deriving generalizations from the experiences and observations of others. Occasionally some of us may be asked to participate as specialists in assigned fields of inquiry.

I personally feel that these differences of source-level are imma-
terial providing that we, in such groups as this, agree to participate to the fullest; providing we agree to disagree, object, criticize, analyze, summarize, specify, test, weigh, simplify, and finally to *prove* our conclusions by self-applications, thus bringing to the community generally the greatest body of socially derived, socially coordinated, socially oriented, and socially proven theory as we can possibly fashion. Fighting, arguing, hollering, and swearing has yielded magnificent harvests of social re-orientation and progressive legislation in the shape of Neighborhood Cooperatives, Third Parties, and Parents' Councils,[2] to name only a few. Such results may also be ours providing that this group keep always in mind the heroic objective of liberating one of our largest minorities from the solitary confinement of social persecution and civil insecurity . . . and instead guaranteeing them the basic and protected right to enter the front ranks of self-respecting citizenship, recognized and honored as socially contributive individuals.

> Delivered at the first Mattachine discussion group, November 1950.

Notes

1. Pers. comm., June 26, 1995.
2. The "third party" is a reference to the 1948 Wallace campaign. "Neighborhood cooperatives" and "parents' councils" refers to the Silver Lake and Echo Park Nursery School cooperatives formed by progressive parents, including Hay and his wife, in the 1940s.

"Should we be considered individuals or be considered a group?"

T O FOSTER DIALOGUE at the discussion groups, the Mattachine organizers often prepared comments and questions. The following are two examples of brief remarks that Hay presented at discussion groups in the 1951–1952 period. They give a good idea of the level of dialogue at these meetings.

Here again Hay emphasizes the need for homosexuals to understand themselves if they expect to win the understanding of heterosexuals. At the same time, although the defensive tone of the 1948 prospectus is largely gone, the preoccupation with self-destructive Gay behavior is still apparent. One of Hay's arguments for the minority thesis in this period was that Gays *needed* a culture, a community, to provide them with social standards and mores that would lead them away from anti-social behaviors. At the same time, Hay's use of the term "heteros," a reversal of the derogatory use of "homos," reflects the extent to which his sense of belonging to a minority had sharpened. He also offers a critique of heterosexual chauvinism that anticipates the 1980s analysis of heterosexism.

"Should we be considered individuals or be considered a group?"

Social Directions of the Homosexual

The public sees any Homosexual as a member of a group— a group which is characterized, in their minds, by people who stand around at parties and discuss their physical attributes, exhibit exhibitionism and callousness, and are as a whole degenerate. Heterosexuals, as well, talk openly of sex—the major difference being the gender of the sex and the implicative end-products of that sex. But this difference does not necessarily enter into the heterosexual's consideration and evaluation of the Homosexuals.

This situation should be a challenge to Homosexuals who have the capability to better their social habits. It should also be remembered that there is no separation of groups (as bull-sessions and tea-parties in heterosexual culture) and therefore Homosexuals need be all the more concerned in developing ethical standards to curb licentious conversations.

A Homosexual need not choose any ethic or responsibility, which often he does not, though as a result he sinks into degeneration and frustration. He chooses no ethical responsibility, and therefore he simultaneously chooses, by implication, not to belong to society.

In heterosexuality it is to be expected that there should be a stress on sexual matters because this is connected with their primary concern—reproduction—and thus is directive. The Homosexual copies this pattern and because it is not applicable, and nondirective, he is considered loose and degenerate. When the sex urge is thus not meaningfully used for procreation, this energy should be channelized elsewhere where its end can be creativity. Some societies have put this into practice, such as those people who deny sex to those creative workmen building canoes until their job is finished. Sex drains power that could be constructively put to use in other areas. This is especially lamentable in the case of the Homosexual, where unproductive sex becomes overemphasized and a basis for frustration.

Homosexuals are "lone wolves" through fear. In society as it now stands, they congratulate themselves for not being caught, as have their less fortunate brothers, and understandably retreat more within themselves. Like any human, the Homosexual has many things he wants not to be forced to face. Thus he is often an escapist. A Homosexual has no one to whom he must account, and in the end as well he must decide everything for himself. Though, in some instances, this is equally true of the heterosexual . . . the process for the latter is infinitely easier because the heterosexual has a socially predetermined pattern to follow and the opportunity to solicit upon it adequate guidance.

Though ethics are arrived at by the group, they are meaningful only when applied by the individual himself. It is essential that Homosexuals begin to direct their thinking in this way. Ghetto walls can be knocked down, but cooperation is essential. There are, however, difficulties to be overcome. Those in greatest need are sometimes the most reluctant to help each other or themselves, tending rather to think of personal experiences as things apart from the mutual effort toward betterment. Still others are not to be trusted until they have been shown the best way to overcome their difficulties. Heterosexuals have the opportunity to have their differences out with each other and thus are enabled to get along in relative harmony, but Homosexuals find this impossible and carry grudges and find freedom of expression impossible.

Homosexuals do not understand themselves and thus it is not surprising that heterosexuals do not understand them either. Because of pent-up frustrations and resentments the Homosexual psychologically rebels and becomes catty and takes on other char-

acteristics of instability. Each person considers himself terribly
maladjusted and peculiar. There is now no positive body of information from well-adjusted people.[1] Rather we find case histories of psychopathic and extreme cases that are negative and
retrogressive.

83

Some glad day there should be a body of knowledge that would
mean aid and progression, in that it would show that Homosexuals, as a group, have much in common and that they are not unique
cases. Should we be considered individuals or be considered a
group? We are essentially a group of individuals that have been
forced together by society. Society attacks the Homosexuals for
their non-conformity in sexual desire and objects completely on
the basis of this one characteristic. This attitude would change if
society could see the positive side and realize the potential ability
to offer a worthwhile contribution.

Homosexuals as a group are composed of a cross-section of society, and thus all types of individuals may be found within the
group. There are those few individualists who find it possible to
cope with the status-quo and make for themselves a stable niche.
The fact remains, however, that the majority of Homosexuals are
inept at adjusting without an acceptable atmosphere and an adequate pattern.

Dated October 4, 1951. Delivered at a Mattachine discussion
group.

Homosexual Values versus Community Prejudices

84

. . . To return to an examination of the basic American language and culture, we must realize that in the average consciousness humanity is divided into just two classifications—and that's all. Male and Female. Countries are fatherlands or motherlands. Ships are feminine. All living forms unless actually designated as feminine are spoken of in the singular as masculine. For example, "every person in the audience wore *his* overcoat." Not only has this primitive over-simplification persecuted and defeated the Homosexual in every attempt to bridge the gap between his minority and the mainstream of social contribution, *but this oversimplification has become the root of the hetero community's stupid hysteria concerning our threat to themselves.*

1. The stereotype is a stark and vicious example of the hetero's attempt to explain our social conduct and appearance in terms of black or white—that is, MALE or FEMALE.

2. The Homosexual, in these terms, as a lover of the male sex, must therefore be a feminine-man. If he loves his own sex—he therefore loves men. Thus, in the public mind, he is in competition with women and with the social objective of holy wedlock and with the eternal objective of the reproducing family.

The hetero's primitive over-simplification has an equally disastrous effect on us, too. Through the pressures of daily conditioning in language and culture we, too, accept the social stereotype that humanity is either male or female. And because it is our compulsion to love males—we perforce allow ourselves to be caricatured as feminine.

1. The latter is too much of an over-simplification. I should say we either allow ourselves to be caricatured as feminine, or we waste our days running around trying to persuade the world that we are 100% he-men studs with real balls. What's so important about this? Who are we trying to kid? Does this help society to accept homosexuality with any better grace?

2. How do we explain, not in person, but to that vast audience whom we will never see—known as the general public—that in the main we, like all Minorities, prefer the company and the intimacy of our own? That the men to whom we are attracted are Homosexual Men?

To tell them is a beginning—but to explain means to make them understand it in their terms—to justify it so that they can add it up in their values. HOW DO WE DO IT? I would like to throw out some general questions which might begin to find answers for all this:

1. Obviously, in order to learn to write these things in terms we know are understandable, we must have spoken them first—and gotten comprehension from heterosexuals. THUS how do we explain ourselves to our parents? How do we explain ourselves to our friends?

2. How do we explain our opposite attractions, the types we go for, in terms of male and female? Try it.

3. What are we doing when we try to convey the impression that we're 100% men with real balls?

4. How can we each of us begin to fight anti-homosexuality? —in terms of vicious stereotype jokes (particularly tie this in with anti-Semitism)

    – in terms of refusing to evade the word Homosexual in
    order to begin to restore to it some measure of dignity
    – in terms of our use of chauvinist words—supplanting
    "normal" with "heterosexual."

Delivered at a Mattachine discussion group, August 1952.

Note

1. This was the premise of Evelyn Hooker's research, which effectively countered the claim that Gay men were psychologically maladjusted.

"Perhaps I can begin to learn
a little humility"

HAVING LEARNED HOW to hold his own in the often fierce debates within the Communist Party and with critics outside the Party, Hay's political and organizational style has been described by some as heavy-handed, controlling, and even domineering. As Stuart Timmons relates, the phrase "Harry stormed out" came up again and again in interviews with his friends and colleagues as a description of how arguments with Hay often ended. Undoubtedly, Hay's complex and powerful personality contributed to both the rise and fall of early Mattachine, and to the ups and downs of the Radical Faerie network in the 1980s. For this reason, the following document is especially valuable.

In the summer of 1952, as attendance at discussion groups was beginning to swell in response to organizing efforts for the Dale Jennings entrapment case, Hay decided to engage in an exercise he had learned in the Communist Party known as "criticism/self-criticism." He had become concerned with the overall group process among the "fifth-order" organizers and his personal role in this process. He was also disturbed by the increasing belligerence of Dale Jennings, whose prominence within Mattachine was growing because of his trial. So while seeking to defuse tensions surrounding himself, Hay also hoped his self-criticism would inspire the others to engage in a similar exercise. Instead, as Hay recalls, they were appalled by his example and the whole matter ended there.

Nonetheless, the following document reveals Hay's awareness of his own limitations and his ability to reflect critically on them.

It confirms the assessment of Konrad Stevens, who recalled, "Harry would be domineering whenever he could get away with it, but he wasn't out of control, and the rest of us weren't so passive."[1]

[Untitled]

Since the time of my taking the first-order pledge I have been guilty of a repetition of infringements on sections 1 and 5 of the membership pledge.[2]

But the underlying cause of this infringement is so much more serious than the occasions of the infringements themselves that I should like to examine and analyze the cause in this first self-evaluation. The cause concerns serious underestimations on my part of section II of the Missions and Purposes. And it follows, because of the close interpenetrations of all the purposes upon each other, that I am guilty of infringements against the aims and objectives of Sections I and III also [see pp. 131–32].

Specifically, in regard to the Mission and Purpose TO EDUCATE, I find that I have, until recently, given thoroughly inadequate and insufficient thought to the insuperable cultural tasks that we face, namely the creation of vehicles of language that can articulate and communicate and evaluate the values, the patterns, the assets, the needs, and thus the codes that are special and peculiar to our minority.

Based on this insufficient thought, until comparatively recently, I have relied on the competitive—that is to say the undemocratic characteristics of my own personality—to impose by overbearing blasts of rhetoric and by emotional dynamics those tenets which I felt to be important but whose scope and sense were so clouded and inarticulate that their acceptance was obviously not to be won by logic and persuasion.

These tendencies and characteristics you have all rightly criticized: my predilection to domineer, to steam-roll by autocratic action, to patronize, to bluster on the basis of a dubious seniority, to disguise personal opinions as authoritative statements, and—topping all—upon being impinged by your criticism and resentments—being unwilling or incapable of admitting my mistakes.

I have been deeply disturbed by the several layers of conflict within myself, such as the stubborn reiteration of conviction on my part even in the face of most logical objections by you, and at a deeper level . . . the conflict between my unswerving conviction concerning many elements of our social responsibilities and my tendency to justify any means to gain their adherence, on the one hand . . . and the shattering evidence displayed in the floundering morale and lack of simple progress in this guild of councilors, which was directly attributable to the destructive results of principles and tenets intruded by pressure rather than welcomed by persuasion and comprehension.

In the course of this self-examination I have finally remembered a maxim, evolved through the long development of democratic fundamentals in mass movements. This maxim establishes that even if a member of a group has a conviction that may be absolutely right on a given subject, unless he can articulate that point and explain it to the satisfaction of all his fellow members then he is wrong—not the rest of the group who votes him down.[3] The remembrance of this truth, and the consequent recalling of the many times I have seen it proven in action, led me to the sudden illumination that the thing defeating me, defeating you, defeating our discussion groups, and all of our brothers, the thing which successfully impedes us from qualitatively changing our social direction from defensiveness to the attack . . . is our collective inability to

90

communicate the full sense of our impressions, our visual patterns, and therefore our constructive thinking to each other—let alone to our minority and further yet to the community.

This inability, not only conditioned for us but condoned by us, lies in the stalemate that our only vehicles of articulation, up to this minute, are the heterosexual languages of definition and measure, which, not being even partly evolved by us, deny us; and the heterosexual material equations, which, not reflecting our integers let alone our equations, defeat us. In employing the conditions, implications, and patterns that the heterosexual community has evolved in *their* own self-interests, *even amongst ourselves*, we defeat ourselves, we reduce ourselves to defensiveness, we exorcise ghosts of presumed guilts unscientifically imposed by heterosexual prejudice and ignorance, we tilt at the windmills of collectively contracted values, not socially evolved by us, which we cannot fulfill. We constantly attempt to verify ourselves through a language and a jurisprudence that, as Kinsey proves in his pamphlet, "Concepts of Normal and Abnormal Behavior," has with unscientific and unhistorical persistence ever sought to isolate and annihilate us.

Since I fancy myself a bit of a pedagogue, mine is the greatest error in this condoning, since I have insisted on the maintenance of my own pride even in the face of our mutual frustration of being unable to communicate. Therefore, by this tardy failure to recognize the key link of our personal and organizational weakness, I have contributed to the impedance and the undermining of all three of the Missions and Purposes.

The immediate harvest of my incorrect methods has been a wave of internecine resentments, which has blunted the initiative of every member, which has created factionalisms, and which has encouraged an epidemic of subjective rather than objective behavior on the part of several members besides myself. The end result, in its effect upon me, has been to separate my allegiances and actions from the collective anonymity of this guild. I have been guilty, as Steven [Konrad Stevens] pointed out a few weeks ago, of maintaining my pride by putting myself in a position with newer people of apparently knowing more than I ought, of playing an oracular part rather than a contributing part in the discussion groups to the intimidation of newcomers. This is distinctly an infringement upon section 1 of the membership pledge.

The general lowering of our second-order morale, the welter of subjectivity, and the helpless feeling of oscillation due to the inability to communicate have produced in me a slack and careless attitude toward committee work and toward the preparation of new papers and theses. This is a direct and serious infringement on section 5 of the membership pledge.

With all of your help, I should like in the next immediate period to seriously attack the horizons of our minority culture with a view to uncovering constructive approaches to this task. If you, my brothers, will agree to tear to shreds any postulates I may present that do not withstand the test of your collective logic, perhaps I can begin to learn a little humility, perhaps I can learn to contribute to, rather than retard, our morale and our will to grow.

Written in July 1952.

Notes

1. Stuart Timmons, *The Trouble with Harry Hay: Founder of the Modern Gay Movement* (Boston: Alyson, 1990), p. 153.
2. "I pledge myself (1) always to keep the interests of the Mattachine Society uppermost in my mind and to conduct myself in a way that will reflect credit upon myself and the organization. . . . (5) to participate actively and seriously in the work, responsibilities, and functions of the Society."
3. Lenin's famous "letter to Ivan Ivanovitch."— HH.

"The Feast of Fools"

IN 1953, HAY BEGAN to present the results of his historical
research and speculations at Mattachine meetings and discussion groups. No one since Edward Carpenter at the turn of the
century had attempted to synthesize the scattered references to
Berdaches in ethnographic reports and historical documents into
a comprehensive account of their role in Native societies. In fact,
thanks to his Marxist background, Hay was able to build on Carpenter's work.[1] For Carpenter, the "intermediate type" was nearly
always an isolated figure, a shaman or a priest, understood in
terms of his innate predispositions more than the social context of
his role and identity. Hay, however, takes the Marxist version of
history as a progression through a series of stages and inserts into
this model the missing role of the "homophile" as he understands
it. The result is a provocative revision of the canonical story of the
"rise of civilization" as Western scholars have imagined it since
the eighteenth century.

Marx and Engels adopted the terminology of the American
anthropologist Lewis Henry Morgan, who had defined the stages
of human progress as savagery, barbarism, and civilization. They
replaced civilization with capitalism and added a fourth, culminating stage of history—socialism. In the following essay, Hay
employs this framework to develop his version of Gay history.
Although the theory of progressive stages of civilization has fallen
out of favor today, the practice of categorizing societies in terms of
their means of subsistence remains a standard methodology for
comparative purposes in anthropology.

Also following Engels, Morgan, and many anthropologists of

the nineteenth century, Hay employs the theory of "primitive matriarchy," which posits matrilineal and matrilocal social forms as preceding the emergence of male domination. Hay, however, adds an important new element. In his reconstruction, the "Berdache institution"—an alternative gender status for those whose social differences are today termed homosexual—is one of the integral features of the "matriarchate." Since this institution was present in the "matriarchal" societies of Native North America, Hay sought and found evidence of its presence in similar societies in the prehistoric Near East and Mediterranean.

Although the claim that human society everywhere originated in matriarchy has been generally rejected, the "matriarchal theory" of social origins has by no means lost its influence in archaeology and anthropology. In the 1950s and 1960s, George Thomson, Robert Graves, Joseph Campbell, and others gave the theory new life. Today, the idea that women-centered societies did and do exist and the project of constructing a historical account of how men gained power over women continues to inspire the work of many feminists.[2] In fact, the "matriarchal theory" of social origins did not postulate women literally ruling men, but rather a principle of "mother right"—in which descent and inheritance passed through women rather than men—which often preceded the emergence of patrilineal and patrilocal customs. Where this principle existed, it was argued, women's status and independence were enhanced.[3] Today feminist anthropologists sometimes use terms like "matricentric" or "matrifocal" to describe societies (like the Zuni and Iroquois) that Hay, in the 1950s, termed "matriarchal." Nonetheless Hay's insights here into the relationship between alternative genders and the origins of social specialization remain provocative and potentially fruitful ones for future investigators.

The Homosexual and History . . .
An Invitation to Further Study

94

For lack of a better idea, I have entitled tonight's presentation "Remarks on the Homosexual and History: An Invitation to Further Study." All of the artifacts and activities I will mention tonight are excerpts derived from many divergent and unrelated anthropological studies, surveys, and expositions, and/or excerpts from reputable historical scholars on dance, folklore, and music, and from dissertations on the rise and fall of social forces in history. Since a proper coordination of the social history of the Homosexual in Society has yet to be attempted, some of my material organizations and coordinations must be regarded as speculation. But, even so, it is speculation carefully molded in the anthropological tradition of Lewis Morgan, whose nineteenth-century speculative reconstruction of American Indian clan or tribe culture out of similarities between the Iroquois Matriarchate and the Hawaiian group marriage culture was authenticated completely in the twentieth century by Boas, Benedict, and Densmore in the Americas, Herskovitz in the Caribbean, and Mead in Melanesia.[4] Leaning upon the coherent picture presented by these great scholars, I am tonight attempting a new correlation in assigning similar roles and developments to identical historical and cultural artifacts as they appeared earlier in the Mediterranean and later in Western Europe. If the logic of these speculations produces shock, well and good. If it produces controversy . . . this is even better. For out of controversy, we may begin to see the long-hidden outline of truth—and within that truth the real measure of the Homosexual's great contribution to society, to history, and to progress.

In the first place, it must be said that the greater part of the ignorance, prejudice, and superstition about Homosexuals is little more than a hundred years old. It begins when, in answer to that dreadful threat to traditional law and order known as "public education," moralizing historians of Macauley's stamp begin to pretty-up history for lower-class consumption and simplify it in edifying terms for the instruction of Females. Prior to that time, much had been written about Homosexuals. The average layman of today does not recognize it as such because most of it is clerical denunciation of folk resistance to the feudal domination of Church and State, and earlier it is monastic diatribes comparing superior Roman cultural tastes to those of more barbarian cultures. But the social artifacts are there and need only to be sorted out and assembled to give a picture vastly different from the garbled garbage currently popular in our literary journals.

Appropriately enough the letter of our legal troubles here in California is inherited straight out of the earliest known socially productive relationship, the food-gathering stage. The food-gathering relationship is that period in a given cultural development when a family or kinship group, the ancestor of what we today call a clan or tribe, must spend all of its waking time gathering edibles.[5] The art of fire is known but the art of cooking is only just dawning. Children and adults all gather anything edible that's not tied down—slugs, bugs, berries, digestible barks and grasses, roots, cereals, nuts, and fruit. The old people and the crippled, those who can no longer hunt and carry, are killed, fed to the dogs, or left behind to starve. There is never enough to go round, and all things gathered each day are equally shared in common. The basic task for survival in this period is the 100-percent reproduction of the family in order that each generation—in the face of a tremendous mortality rate—produce even more hands for the gathering than the generation before. In this period, then, in addition to the aged and the crippled, those who cannot—or will not—fulfill the urgent duty to reproduce are also killed or turned out to starve.[6]

The group we are concerned with tonight, of this food-gathering relationship, is a group in transition from the primitive level of food-gathering to the lower barbarian level of food-producing—a group who has begun to master the art of domesticating animals and has come to the concept of sowing cereals but has not as yet experienced the patterns and processes of a permanent village administration. This group is a series of families wandering in the northwest hills of Mesopotamia 3,000 to 5,000 years ago—a kinship group of Sumerian people under the leadership of an old man named Abraham.[7] The culture of the tribe of Abraham, as we now call this group, though reflecting the physical characteristics of pastoralism, was essentially a food-gathering social consciousness. The "book" of Leviticus, which incidentally was not consigned to written text until the approximate neighborhood of 50 A.D., reflects the historically established ritual myths and tenets of the food-gatherer's culture.[8] "Thou shalt not spill thy seed upon the ground," "Thou shalt not lie with a beast as with a woman," "Thou shalt not waste thy seed," etc., are but variations upon the theme that each production of sperm must produce a child else the family cannot survive. It is typical in this period for several kinship groups to combine and elect one elder or "patriarch" to remember the accumulated wisdom of former social experiences and to apply this wisdom to the administration of the combine or phratry. Thus the whole group, for the duration of the combine, accepts the applications of old wisdoms, or *revelations*, of the elected patriarch and, of course, his remembrances of the ancient wisdoms of his own familial ancestor heroes. Abraham's own ancestor hero was a gent named Jahweh, later to be called Jehovah. It is interesting to note that in most Hebrew folklore, Jahweh or Jehovah was not called God but rather the Lord God of Abraham.

Abraham's combine, then replete with their primal food-gathering culture, encounters stranger tribes as they near the fertile river valleys of Canaan. These valley tribes have entered a higher stage of productive relations wherein food is produced within a permanent social structure of which women are the centralizing forces. These kinship groups have ceased to be wanderers and pastoral nomads and have become village dwellers devoted to husbandry and agriculture under a newer social relationship called the Matriarchy.[9] Labor responsibilities are divided and even though food and shelter are still equally shared in common there is now and then an occasional surplus to be stored against hard times.

In these valley centers, Abraham's combine encounters men who do not share in procreative reproduction but who live together as a social unit. To the more primitive food-gatherer's culture this is untenable. This is anathema. This is the worship of false gods and of demons. How such a situation could come about is inexplicable to a people who had not lived through the pattern which produced it. It's always the guy who doesn't know about a situation who is the most hysterical inciter against it. If Abraham's crowd had settled in Canaan the first time through, and the Edomites had gone to Egypt instead, the California state laws, inherited straight out of Anglican Ecclesiastical law, which was borrowed lock, stock, and barrel from Ecclesiastical Holy Roman Empire law, which lifted it bodily out of the Hebrew Torah, today might hold a quite different text. One might comment, at this point, as did Dr. Kinsey to the California state legislature in 1951, that perhaps twentieth-century science would be a better base for social

legislation than the primitive survival taboos and exorcisms of a
backward people three thousand years ago in the deserts of Arabia.

98

The Matriarchal period of social history is perhaps the longest
enduring social productive relationship that we know about. Its
many independent beginnings and parallel relative patterns stretch
from the middle of the Neolithic era, perhaps 10,000 B.C., to Africa, South America, Australia, Polynesia, and parts of India in
1953 A.D., and thousands of its cultural patterns and complexes
are found as living breathing functions in nine-tenths of our world
today. The Matriarchy, which incidentally is the basic pattern of
European feudal villages from their discovery by the Romans to
the final breakdown of feudalism in the twentieth century, is that
period of food production that we might term as *ritual agriculture*.
When the family finally arrived at the discovery of the earth's yearly
regeneration of food-giving cereals, fruits, nuts, and edible tuber-
roots or vegetables, they also latched onto the concept that it was
similar to the fecundity of women. At the same time society had
gradually accumulated the understanding that the way to live in
harmony with nature was to imitate nature's processes as they
understood them. Thus the basic responsibility of superintending
the proper fertilization of the great Mother Earth is bestowed upon
those members of the family most obviously aware of the requirements of fecundity—namely the women themselves. Thus, the
woman is not only the head of the familial household, she is the pre-
dominant provider, and therefore the teacher and the councilor of
the village. The vital science of imitating nature, which now produces food enough for six months and sometimes for nine, is
woman's contribution. And its practice, its preservation, development, and its final application is her property.[10]

The average person today is not taught that the city-slave-state
empires of Greece and Rome were built on this social productive

relationship or that in methods of food production there were few differences between the labor techniques of the Roman latifundia and the Celtic village.

How many people here took Latin in school? What is the Latin noun for "farmer"? *Agricola, agricolae*—feminine. It is interesting to note that in fourteenth-century French clerical writing the word *agricole* still appears as a perfectly acceptable word. In this connection there are words common to our language of today that also need an airing for the full impact of their significance. The dictionary informs us that *agricola* not only meant "farmer" but it also meant "husbandman"—that the French word *agricole* also meant husbandman.

In an examination of the roots of husbandman we find that *hus* (Anglo-Saxon, Gothic, Icelandic) meant "house"; *bonde* (Anglo-Saxon, Gothic, Icelandic, Danish) meant "bound to" or "attached to," *hus-bonde* therefore means literally "bound to the house." In this connection it is important to note that in 1848, when the new Danish constitution was written, the *bonde* or serfs were freed. Thus, it would seem that Dr. Webster's meaning number four, "one who manages a household, a steward," would be the original meaning. As a house-serf, the *hus-bonde* might have overseen or directed the "field-*bonde*." Putting this data into what anthropologically has been established of the matriarchate, *husbonde* was either a man delegated to the needs of a given house or a slave of the woman's choosing assigned to her as property. And what might his work consist of? The putting in practice, under her direction and teaching, the recipes of work patterns for sowing, plowing, weeding, grafting, fertilizing, reaping, and gleaning, incorporated in songs and sing-song formulas, which the Catholic Church of Inquisition times would call incantation, pagan ritual, and witchcraft.

Why have I gone to such pains to give you these details of the European Matriarchal artifacts, you may ask? What's it got to do with us? It's a fair question. And the answer is this: Because the relation of the woman to the social production of ritual agriculture, the relationship of the man to the house, the development of the pairing marriage out of the group marriage system,[11] to be found in the root meanings of European words and in fragments of song and folklore, are *identical to the social Matriarchy recovered and analyzed here in the United States among the Iroquois, the Plains Indians and the Pueblo Indians of the Southwest.* The intersocial structure of the early Matriarchal European villages has, as yet, not been recovered. I am proposing, therefore, to superimpose certain characteristics of the American Indian Matriarchal village against the fragmentary European background that I have laid.

The anthropological findings of Bancroft, Boas, Benedict, Densmore, and Morgan show that in widely separated and independently developed Indian communities that practiced facsimiles of ritual agriculture, the combines of family units called tribes generally lived in large shelters or in closely connected shelters under the leadership of the tribal Mothers. When men married they moved into that one of the kinship shelters to which the wife belonged. The woman superintended the main production of food, which was the yield of husbandry and agriculture. The men were hunters or fishers, but their yield was chancy and seasonable. Therefore, though it took most of their time and energy, their food contribution was secondary in quantity to that of the women.[12] In their spare time, which was little, the men made bows, arrows, spears, and leather thongs. The women, when not tending to the needs of the family, the household collective, and the fields, tanned leather for shelter and clothing, made cloth, and later baskets and pottery.

Within this matriarchal village structure, we find a new type of

100

household, a separate household consisting of either one or two men. This household is called, anthropologically, the Berdache, or Bardache, a word applied to this phenomenon by sixteenth-century French and Spanish explorers. The Berdache, in contrast to the family households having no old ones or young ones to care for, could provide for their own needs in one-quarter of the time spent by the rest of the village. In their spare time, which was, by contrast to the rest of the village perhaps twenty-two days of the month, they, dressed in women's garb, gave the women a hand at pressing tasks, or they made many arrows, bows, moccasins, rugs, bowls, and tanned leather for thongs and tipi coverings. By the nature of their own householding, and by reason of their sharing in women's work, they learned the recipes and formulas by which ritual agriculture was maintained. In many cultures of Asia, Africa, and South America, the Berdache carried the responsibility as the medicine-men, or shamans, of their village cultures. In medieval Europe, Donald Webster Cory reports that Homosexuals were known as "witch-men."[13]

Thus, amongst the American Indians, the Berdache began to dress the everyday moccasin with pictorial designs representing the work-pattern recipe that must accompany its fabrication. He decorated tipi coverings with patterns of social history called wisdom. He began to make signs and designs to record the ritual festivals of dance, which were nothing more than the necessary natural imitations by which wind, rain, heat, and cold were summoned—which everyone must know and be able to perform if nature were to respond. He began to teach the children, because the women really didn't have the time, to do the stylized calisthenics which would prepare them for all the needed work patterns of their maturity.[14]

Thus, in the Berdache we see arise the great social division of labor which becomes the groundwork of industry as we know it today—the artisan and the cultural craftsman. Benedict and Densmore report that among the Southwest Indians, notably the Zuni, the Berdache is the organizer and the administrator of games and festivals. Games and festivals, in this social relation of ritual agriculture—equally true in the European feudal villages—were not times of fun and recreation. Rather, they were very serious and vitally important sociopolitical necessities through which everybody practiced and rehearsed, by formulas recorded in work-dance songs, the calisthenics of labor-patterns that would be needed in the coming season. Ruth Benedict reports that among the Sioux Indians of only a few years ago, a family group or, as we would say, a village, with beautifully decorated tipis and fine beadwork clothing was described as having as beautiful a household as a Berdache. She also reports that it was a common custom amongst the Plains Indians that if one village had two Berdaches and another village none, the lacking village would swap two family households in order to get one Berdache household.

It is important to mention at this point that, in the Balkan mountain areas, where nineteenth-century anthropologists recorded definite vestiges of the group marriage units or household collectives and where ritual agriculture still persisted—that in given villages of this area (such as Croatia, Serbia, Bulgaria, and Thracia) the mayors were men who were married to other men.[15] Again, the Berdache institution, playing an administrative role in a Matriarchal culture. There, the reasoning for Berdache mayors was simple. The Berdache, having no large family to maintain, and no sons to plan for, would obviously be the one least likely to graft, and the one most capable of impartial administration. The patron saint of this institution was Saint Medardus of the Greek Orthodox hierarchy of saints.[16]

Thus, in America, Asia, Africa, and Europe the Berdache was not only the initiator of arts and crafts as specialties, but he begins to prepare the organization of teaching through design, story-telling, singing, and organizing the practice of ritual—of these women's prerogatives and inventions—but also cultural patterns for which the women never had quite enough time. But this development of community tools and weapons, as a craft specialty of the Berdache, gives the men, in their leisure time from hunting, an opportunity to develop a new food-producing technique—the capture and domestication of animals. And with the coming of herds and the tribal competition for the rights to capture wild ponies, cattle, and sheep, not only does the man gain new equality with the woman as a provider—but in some climates he becomes the chief provider. Simultaneous with this evolution comes the concept of the elected hunter-protector, or chief, and, soon after, the beginning of war-chief dynasties.

The war-chief dynasties begin in many ways, in varying sections of the world. Some come out of the hunter-protector elections, as in North America. Others, such as in Mexico, Peru, and in the Mediterranean generally, out of the priest collectives who elect one of their number as the earth habitation of the solar spirit of fertility. But, whatever the origins, the ascendancy of the war-chief or the patristic culture brings a new development in the Berdache institution. In those areas where Patrism and the Matriarchy co-existed side-by-side, namely parts of Africa, Southeast Asia, Siberia, and most of Europe, the Berdache tendency among craftsmen, artisans, magicians, and ritual organizers was encouraged, or rather it was not discouraged, since it argued against certain vital techniques becoming monopolies of one family and thus giving that family special power and influence in the community. The Berdache institution required that craft knowledges in each genera-

103

tion be taught to a new group, thus in effect retaining the knowledges of survival as property of the community generally. But in those areas where Patrism gains the ascendancy, the story is a different one. Chieftains, in many parts of the world, at different times in history, found they could bypass their periodic elections by gaining monopoly over the sciences, the knowledges, and the crafts, without which the dependent communities could not survive.[17] Thus, state priestcraft, or State Berdache, appears as a means to the maintenance of dynasties. And the given ruling family actually designs their monopoly of the community's knowledges and patterns of survival as a State Berdache so that the scholars, scribes, medicine-men, astronomers, mathematicians, and master-craftsmen of the community having, as Berdache, no familial ties with the community and no issue can therefore *never organize a rival movement within the community nor can they ever produce a rival dynasty.*

It must be conceded that under State Berdache, as under its original form of tribal priestcraft, there was a percentage of recruits that were not Homosexually inclined. But the social patterns and practices of the Kiva,[18] and later the State Berdache, were generally known, and the element of choice as regards the recruit was usually present. At this point in social evolution, one can hardly find virtue in a choice of Opportunism over a choice of natural selection. Among the Kwakiutl of British Columbia, as among the Pueblo peoples, the candidate for admission to manhood must leave the land of the living—that is, the village of his childhood—and wander in the unknown to capture the dream vision of his destiny.[19] This dream is analyzed and given meaning by the priest-clan. And by their interpretation, the candidates become either warrior or Berdache. In both cultures, there are recorded cases of candidates rebelling against both the warrior decision and the Berdache decision and being allowed, after special ritual, to repeat their search for their visions.

The wide separation of theory and practice, which State Berdache practices produced in Egypt, in Babylonia, in Persia, in India, and in China[20] was largely responsible for the persistences of those backward superstitions and impregnable barriers to knowledge and social progress which rotted and destroyed these great empires.[21] It is vital to note that precisely in those slave-state empires where State Berdache was maintained as the integral factor of power, Berdache at any other level was forbidden on the pain of death. Note, please, that it is the Mediterranean—the cultural cradle of the Torah, of Plato, of Aramaic-Greek Christianity, of the Roman codex—where this denunciation of Berdache at any level other than ruling-class was nurtured and maintained. . . .

Thus, in the Patristic or Patriarchal societies, the Sumerian and Egyptian satrapies, and the city-state cultures, craft knowledge and theory were officially separated from practice and placed in the hands of the State Berdache or in the administration of an owning kinship group. Slave producers, therefore, could neither improve their methods nor eliminate cumbersome non-producing methods. They could never create a greater self-value and/or purchasing power within their own class. And being the only class whose increase in membership was the state's prime concern, the slave mass's alienation from the wealth they created eventually dragged the entire structure to ruin.[22]

The free tribal peasantry of Europe—the Goths, the Huns, the Slavs, the Franks, the Teutons, the Nordics, and the Celts—not having developed a chattel-slave structure and therefore not having had to torture themselves with theoretical justifications protecting those who had as against those who had not, were still developing the co-existence of ritual agriculture under the administration and teaching of the women, or the Sagas, and of herd-breeding and horse-stealing—which in those days were called "heroic exploits" by the men. The Folk or village Berdache, under these more democratic pre-conditions, taught their crafts to the family group as part of that group's communal responsibility.

We must understand that our democratic inclinations and traditions do not come out of the Mediterranean cultures of Greece and Rome, as our careless high-school histories imply. Rather, they stem from the Matriarchal village cultures spread westward over Europe by the Goths, the Franks, the Huns, and the Celts, beginning in the third century A.D.[23] It must be recalled also that priestcraft, as a Berdache specialty of dynastic ruling power, did not rise with these people. The organized science of their agricultural ritual and imitative magic, known to us as Druidism, remained primarily a property administered by the women. Thus, in the European tribal villages, as these people came into contact with the more advanced techniques and methods of Roman production, the arts and crafts teachings of the Berdache were cultivated as household practices of each family. The Berdache, in this area, begins to take over the burdens of group ritual—the organization of, the teaching of, and the rehearsing of group calisthenics to prepare for the great collective labors of group agriculture. When the villages, together with the thousands of refugee artisan slaves from Roman towns and plantations, enter together into feudal tenures during the seventh and eighth centuries, artisan families begin to appear in village towns and castle-towns. At this point, the Berdache take over the public responsibilities of teaching—by design, story, mimicry, and narrative song—the duties of political organizing and integrating by ritual, by invocations that were inventories of folk wisdom and past experience, refreshed to people's memories in a manner that we might call lining on the deacon.[24] In the European feudal village collective, still administered by the Matriarchal cul-

ture of imitative science, the Berdache evolve to the social responsibility of group coordinators rather than to the private ruling-
class servitude of subsidized specialists.[25]

For our sources of information and for indicators of further
study, in addition to the similarity to previously outlined patterns
of culture, we have the signposts of folk practices and folk words.
We encounter here the same initiation rites, as noted among the
American Indians, the Asiatics, the Africans, and the Mediterra-
neans, wherein the adolescent—cradled in the loving concern of
the hearth—is suddenly tried and tested by being sent into the unknown to brave all its threats and terrors. Upon coming through
this test, he (or she) suddenly finds himself an accepted adult in his
familiar home again, and everything that was frightful and topsy-
turvy is understandable and in its place again. This rite was in imitation of the seed, kept warm by the hearth in a protective basket
all winter. Then at the Vernal Equinox, March 25th, Old New
Year's Day in Europe until as late as 1755 in England, the seed was
suddenly thrust into unknown darkness, away from the friendly
sun and the blue sky and the faces of friends. But, when, pushing
through the best it knew how, its green head suddenly popped
through the crust of the earth—everything was right again, the
seed was a reproducing entity and surrounded once more by the
sun and sky and the familiar faces.

It was the vision that pulled the adolescent through, which revealed for a certainty whether he was what he seemed, or if he was
what he did not seem. This is the folk understanding of the word
"changeling"—he who is what he seems not to be. One explanation was that the changeling was a child who was swapped by the
fairies, the old people, the little dark friendly people who lived in
the forests and hills of the land before the village came there—
whose ways were different from the culture of the village. Be that
as it may, the changeling did not marry. He became known as the

Fool—in the sense that his appearance befooled or befuddled you into believing he was what he was not. In folk song and story, we find the Fool as the one who speaks out for the village against wicked laws and oppressive taxations. The Fool is the official spokesman because, being Berdache and having no household to provide for, were he to be struck down for his boldness, no family is left providerless.

In Welsh the word for fool is Bardh. The Bardhs of Celtic and Nordic tradition not only sang songs, but organized and led the festivals and rituals, taught the children and young people the history and wisdom of their traditions, and thus were mimes and actors as well as song and dance leaders. In Gaelic, the word for Bardh is Glee. The Glee men and Glee women were a vital part of the village culture of the British Isles. Glee also means to mock, to scoff, and to jest. Another word we run into in this period is the "Leman." In the Romances of the thirteenth-century feudal courts, Leman was assumed to mean mistress—for instance "yon lordling's leman." The ballads and stories about Leman, borrowed all of them from earlier folk dance-ballads and rituals, make it clear that the Leman was a favored servant or household member of a chief, a lord, or a king.[26] Yet the word derives from the Anglo-Saxon *leogh* (or *leof*) man—dear man. The Norman-French word—meaning also dear man—was *mignon* or, Anglicized, minion. There are speculations around that Leman may have originated as Gleeman, the king's Gleeman—which would bring up once again the Berdache role of the Fool in relation to ruling households. In Danish, the Bardh or Gleeman was actually known as the Singe-ful.

You will remember, earlier, that I mentioned that the Berdache had taken over some of the ritual responsibilities of the women as regards Matriarchal village administration. One of their most im-

portant responsibilities as Earth Mothers was the ritual of healing, child-birth, and prevention of household and animal diseases.
When the Catholic Church Empire, in its drive to break down
the anti-Christian resistance of peasant folk-culture, wrote down
the first description of the village Earth Mothers and their folk-
protecting magic practices, they described them as witchcraft and
the Earth Mother as a witch.

You might be interested to know that the word "peasant,"
paisan, derives from the Latin word *pagus*—pagan, meaning literally countryman as distinguished from townsman. Countrymen,
or pagans, or peasants, believed in the great Mother Earth who
brought forth everything they knew and needed for survival. They
believed that the great Mother was fertilized by the spirit of Life, a
precocious and rather unreliable Stud whom they referred to as
"The Earth-bound" (the earth-*bonde*, like *hus-bonde*, earth's man
or servant) or as Old Skraat[27] or as Old Providence. In Denmark,
to this day, Satan, the earth-bound spirit of fertility or carnality, is
known simply as *Jord*—Earth. And the wise-woman of the village,
the witch of the Church hysteria, the mid-wife—and today the
visiting nurse—is known equally simply as *Jordemoder*, Earth
Mother. According to Donald Webster Cory, the Homosexual in
addition to being known as the Fool was also known as the witchman. In America, in Siberia, in Africa the Berdache were also
known as witch-men, sorcerers, medicine-men, and shamans.[28]

Did the State Berdache ever appear in Europe? It certainly did,
imported by the "New Look" Roman Empire of the Papacy, complete with a God-via-Pope-given monopoly on all knowledge and
craft science—in the form of the monasteries and the priories or
abbeys. But the great scientific discoveries which were to birth the
growth of cities and trade did not come from the monasteries—but
rather in spite of them. And the middle class, frustrated in their at-

110

tempts to develop by the monasteries and bishop nobility, came to hate and fear the State Berdache and everything it represented. Yet during this period also we see elements of Folk Berdache in terms of the celibate fraternities of Lombard stonemasons, the Magister brotherhoods of master-craftsmen (the Gothic architects were appointed from this group), and the celibate orders of Cathar minstrels, a heretical sect banned by the Pope.

The Folk Berdache is attacked and undermined the first time by the State Berdache of the political papacy in its efforts to destroy the folk-village resistance to becoming the serfs of the monasteries. But it is essential to our understanding of the social attitude towards Homosexuals to see that this attack, though on a moral basis, was not geared on the "unnatural" level but on the witchcraft level instead. In parallel to this, we find an interesting paragraph in the decree of Ferdinand of Aragon of 1486, which, in alleviating some of the burdens of serfdom, such as declaring an end to the nobility's prerogative of the right of the first night, says also, "nor shall the aforementioned señors *use the daughter or the son of the peasant*, with payment or without payment, against their will."[29] So that apparently homosexual relations between lord and peasant lad were lawful and acceptable so long as consent was freely given.

To fully understand the reasons why the State Berdache attempts to undermine the Folk Berdache in the eyes of the middle class, we must consider a magnificent folk activity, which, led and organized by the Folk Berdache in their supreme role as organizers of the best interests of their sponsoring family villages, was one of the leading sparks in the great folk surges forward to birth the European nations—the Protestant Reformation—and finally the revolutionary overthrow of feudalism.

This activity can be entitled the *Feast of Fools*. The rite of initiation, beginning with the Vernal Equinox, March 25th, and lasting until approximately April 6th, by which the European folk had bravely attempted to maintain their social identity in the face of the feudal onslaught of Church and state, changes from the negative magic of destroying the enemy by curse and invocation—in the eleventh and twelfth centuries—to a new idea of crying out against and exposing the oppression. The rite of initiation, originally administered by the Berdache to both the young men and the young women, is now administered by the Berdache to the whole community. Everyone in that fortnight cried out against oppression, questioned the law and custom of the gentry, asked why things were so, and, true to the old imitation of nature in ritual magic, shot his wad—got his beefs off his chest—and came back into daily existence refreshed and reborn.

The Feast of Fools began at Vespers on the afternoon of the day of the Vernal Equinox with the chanting of the "Magnificat"—the one section of the New Testament that the Folk would ever accept—"He hath cast down the princes from their thrones and hath exalted the lowly and oppressed; the hungry he hath filled with good things, and the rich he hath sent empty away."[30] At this point, everyone changed places, clothes, and habitation with his opposite—the beggar with the bishop, the Fool with the lord or the sheriff, and so on all down the line. In this fortnight, the Fool, who represented this change every hour of his life, was the leader of the proceedings. Every custom, tradition, law, and decree was questioned, was turned upside down and inside out and fully exposed to the village collective. The young people, not yet socially perplexed with political and economic opposites, changed places and roles with each other, thus dramatizing the changeling characteristic of the Berdache. This dance is still to be found today, called variously the Guiser Dance and the Gooser Dance and is associ-

ated with the New Year.[31] In the Balkans, this spring dance was
performed by a celibate fraternity known as the Calusarie.[32]

112   Part of the Feast of Fools were mimicries or rude plays of satire
and mockery on the finding and questionings of the village. A ritual
section of the Feast were mimicry dances by masked performers in
a pattern known as a pyrrhic dance, wherein Might appeared to
triumph over Right—but through the magic of the Fool, who, in
his role of witchman, transforms that which is into its opposite, the
defeated or killed side rises once again from the dead. So did the
Church appear to overpower the folk and yet in the end the folk
would rise again to victory. This dance was known in France as Les
Mattachine, the Dance of the Fools, and in Mozarabic Spain as El
Matachin. Returning English Crusaders, seeing the same dance
being done in their own backyards of Scotland and Yorkshire,
called it the Moorish Dance or Morris. In later versions of the
dance, when the Fool had dispelled the darkness and the van-
quished had been reborn, he was rewarded by being given the
Bessy-Bride. The Bessy-Bride was also known sometimes as the
Maiden and at other times the Hoyden. Since all the dancers were
men, and in most cases a ritual celibate fraternity, the Bessy-Bride
or the Hoyden was a man. According to the reformed Anglican
morality of Shakespeare's time, the Hoyden was a boyish girl. But
prior to that time, and according to the root of the word, Hoyden
meant a girlish boy.[33] So, in the Morris or Mattachine dance, the
Fool, for his constructive and protective magic, is awarded the
partner of his Berdache by the appreciative community.

Thus the pyrrhic mime of Les Mattachine portrayed in vivid
drama, for all to understand and take courage from, the ancient
imitative ritual of initiation made militant and political—that the
lowly and oppressed would rise again from their despair and bondage by the strength of *their own faith* and *their own self-created*

dignity. And the people believed it—and three hundred years later they made it come true.

Then, you might ask, how could the social attitude towards the Berdache change so drastically to the discriminatory intolerance the Homosexual now enjoys? The answer is that in the flush and victory of its greatest achievement, the whole Matriarchal cultural structure—known as the folk—was transformed and, thus, disappeared as a social force in history. In the conflagration by which the feudal order and the absolute monarchies were forever overthrown, described sometimes as the greatest watershed in history, a huge social relationship beginning in the Stone Age comes to an end. The structure and the social forces of the ritual agriculture of the Matriarchate are consumed and vanish. Its cultural patterns and values remain to move forward as the traditions and inheritances of the new order, under the guidance and leadership of the Protestant Reformation and its central creed, "the sacred self-fulfillment destiny of each individual." We must remember, as Cory points out in his article in February's issue of *ONE*, that the United States was founded and given its cultural values by the Puritan principles of morality and property.[34]

As was pointed out earlier, the political Catholic Church undermined the Folk Berdache in the eyes of the rising town middle classes in an effort to woo the larger town corporations away from the anti-church and anti-state practices of the Feast of Fools. The Protestant middle class itself finishes the undermining—not only of the Folk Berdache but of the papal State Berdache as well. Their hatred and justified fears of the papal Berdache of the "barracked monks" of the Inquisition was closely seconded by their need to create a free labor market in order to develop their middle-class democracies. This they could do only by crushing the scattered remnants of folk culture resistances, the pivots of which were as before

113

the wise Earth-Mother, or the witch, and the traveling circuit organizer and teacher—the Bard or Fool. It is out of this final attack
that we find the Salem witch-hunts of 1692. And this time, because
there is no longer a strong self-reliant village culture to give him
roots and function, the Berdache is attacked on the morality issue.
He is attacked and put to flight on the paterfamilias core of Protestant political conviction—that God, through Calvin and Luther,
was revealed as ordaining that Man was contrived and fashioned
to produce for himself and to the extent that he so produces so shall
his labors be judged. The Berdache who never produced for himself but primarily for others is condemned as a loiterer, an idler, a
profligate, a wastrel, a cohabitator with Satan—and is put to flight
as thus unnatural in the sight of God and God's chosen elect. Even
to this day, the Homosexual Minority as a group is attacked and
put to flight on this same morality red-herring. And so long as the
Minority continues to argue and wrestle with this false issue, so
long will they still be on the run.

What else can the Minority do? Well, if nothing else, they can
take a leaf from their long and productive history. They can learn
to realize in all previous economies where the Berdache was an accepted institution, it was so because the Berdache, like the Alba-
nian Berdache mayors, having no household and children to care
for, could devote most of their time—aside from filling their own
two bellies—with the social, economic, and educational needs of
their communities generally. The Minority today must take stock
of the communities in which they live and find the services they can
undertake that the community needs and that familial households
have not the time to do. They must once again take the initiative to
produce that area of social—even if grudging, at first—recognition of their capacity for needed community contributiveness.

114

They must erect for themselves a self-disciplined platform upon which they can be recognized as functioning members of society. As Ruth Benedict says of the Berdache in Zuni, even today, "Their response is socially recognized. If they have native ability, they can give it scope; if they are weak creatures, they fail in terms of their weakness of character, *not in terms of their inversion*."[35] The Homosexual must once again set as his goal the winning of the complete trust and faith of his fellow citizens—which he achieved eight hundred years ago at *the Feast of Fools*.

> Written in 1953. Based on lectures presented at the Laguna discussion group, October 1952 and March 1953.

Notes

1. See p. 188, n. 6.

2. See chapters by Karen Sacks and Joan Bamberger in *Woman, Culture and Society*, ed. Michelle Rosaldo and Louise Lamphere (Stanford: Stanford University Press, 1974); Eleanor Leacock's introduction to Frederick Engels, *The Origin of the Family, Private Property and the State in the Light of the Researches of Lewis H. Morgan* (New York: International Publishers, 1972); and Peggy R. Sanday and Ruth G. Goodenough, *Beyond the Second Sex: New Directions in the Anthropology of Gender* (Philadelphia: University of Pennsylvania Press, 1990).

3. Robert Briffault, *The Mothers: The Matriarchal Theory of Social Origins* (New York: Macmillan, 1931), p. 180; see Engels, *The Origin of the Family*, p. 266.

4. It would perhaps be more correct to say that these anthropologists built on foundations laid by Morgan in the systematic analysis of kinship.

5. Hay has in mind examples like the Seri Indians of Baja California and the tribes of the Kalahari Desert of Africa, who pursued a truly marginal existence. However, field studies by anthropologists have found that generally speaking agrarian peasants work the hardest and horticulturalists slightly less, while food-gatherers have the most leisure time.

In fact, hunter-gatherers often have a better diet than horticulturalists (Charlotte G. O'Kelly and Larry S. Carney, *Women and Men in Society: Cross-Cultural Perspectives on Gender Stratification*, 2d ed. [Belmont, Calif.: Wadsworth, 1986], pp. 6–7, 86–87).

6. Abandonment and infanticide, assumed to be commonplace by many Victorian anthropologists, have been shown to be relatively rare practices, limited to periods of economic and environmental distress.

7. Abraham is customarily assigned the date of ca. 1996 B.C.E., although this is probably too early. "Ur of the Chaldeans" is presumably the region of southern Mesopotamia during the final renaissance of the Sumerians. See Robert H. Pfeiffer, *Introduction to the Old Testament* (New York: Harper and Brothers, 1948).

8. By this Hay means that, except for the scroll kept at the temple at Jerusalem, Leviticus remained for all purposes oral law until the Diaspora.

9. Although scholars would no longer term Canaanite culture matriarchal, there were significant differences in religious belief, gender roles, and sexuality between the culture of the Canaanite settlements and that of the nomadic Hebrews. See Robert H. Pfeiffer, *Religion in the Old Testament: The History of a Spiritual Triumph* (New York: Harper and Brothers, 1961).

10. That women were the original farmers is often speculated but difficult to prove (see George Thomson, *Studies in Ancient Greek Society: The Prehistoric Ægean*, rev. ed. [London: Lawrence and Wishart, 1954], pp. 41–42). Cross-cultural surveys show that women's participation in production and their social status is significantly higher in horticultural societies than in agrarian societies, where men dominate agricultural production and women tend to become a surplus labor force in times of hardship or population decline. In societies like the Pueblos of New Mexico, where men grew the staple crops of wheat and corn and women tended smaller garden plots, all the processes of agriculture were conceptualized in terms of female reproduction. For an overview of gender roles during Europe's Middle Ages, see O'Kelly and Carney, *Women and Men in Society*, pp. 108–15.

11. For the theory of "group marriage," see Thomson, *Studies in Ancient Greek Society*, pp. 69–70; and Leacock in Engels, *The Origin of the*

116

Family. Many of the practices once cited as instances of "group marriage" would be termed "serial monogamy" or "open marriage" today.

12. This is often true in hunting-gathering tribes and sometimes among horticulturalists, when women are active in agricultural tasks.

13. Donald Webster Cory, *The Homosexual in America: A Subjective Approach* (New York: Greenberg, 1951), p. 22.

14. Although the description of Two-Spirits as religious and economic specialists makes sense from the historical materialist perspective, to my knowledge no Marxist anthropologist or archaeologist made this connection before Hay. Engels's influential *The Origin of the Family*, while purporting to be a demonstration of historical materialism, has surprisingly little to say about the productive relations and division of labor in precapitalist societies.

15. Hay had learned about this custom in the 1930s. Institutionalized romantic friendships between males were once common in the Balkans (Louis Crompton, *Byron and Greek Love: Homophobia in 19th-Century England* [Berkeley: University of California Press, 1985], pp. 133 ff.; John Boswell, *Same-Sex Unions in Premodern Europe* [New York: Villard Books, 1994], pp. 267–79).

16. See p. 76, n. 5 above.

17. This reconstruction of the origin of crafts and the emergence of kingship and state formations follows that of Gordon Childe (*Man Makes Himself* [New York: New American Library, 1951] and *What Happened in History* [Baltimore: Penguin, 1964]).

18. Kivas are semi-underground ceremonial chambers employed by Pueblo Indians.

19. The vision quest is an element of many tribal cultures in North America, including groups like the Kwakiutl, but it has no role among the Pueblos—an error Hay would later be able to correct from direct contact with Pueblo Indians.

20. Here, by "State Berdache," Hay has in mind (among other examples) the frequent use of eunuchs in administrative functions. See, for example, Kathryn M. Ringrose, "Living in the Shadows: Eunuchs and Gender in Byzantium," in *Third Sex, Third Gender: Beyond Sexual Dimorphism in Culture and History*, ed. Gilbert Herdt (New York: Zone Books, 1994), pp. 85–109.

118

21. That the separation of theory and practice leads to social disintegration or stagnation is a Marxist axiom frequently applied to ancient societies (see Childe, *What Happened in History*, pp. 184 f.).

22. Classical Marxist theory characterized slavery as "the first great social division of social labour" (Engels) and Greece and Rome as slaveowning societies—i.e., societies whose production was dependent on slave labor. Such societies were doomed to stagnation and collapse because they provide the work force no incentive for improving the methods of production. See, for example, a work Hay encountered in Communist Party classes in the 1930s, A. Leontiev, *Political Economy: A Beginner's Course* (London: Martin Lawrence, 1935); as well as Karl Marx, *Pre-Capitalist Economic Formations* (New York: International Publishers, 1965), p. 124; and Engels, *The Origin of the Family*, pp. 206–11. Childe provides a modified Marxist account of the decline of Rome (*What Happened in History*, pp. 266–69 and chap. 12). More recently, the characterization of Roman social stratification in terms of class and its dependence on slave labor have been questioned by Géza Alföldy, among others (see *The Social History of Rome*, trans. David Braund and Frank Pollock [Baltimore: Johns Hopkins University Press, 1988]).

23. Here Hay drew on Engels's essay "The Mark" (in *Socialism Utopian and Scientific*, trans. Edward Aveling [New York: International Publishers, 1935], pp. 77–93), *Peasant Wars in Germany*, trans. Moissaye J. Olgin (New York: International Publishers, 1926), and *The Origin of the Family*, chap. 7.

24. As Hay later wrote, "By 1660 the majority of the New England congregations could no longer read music: hymn singing in Church was known as 'lining on the Deacon.' The Deacon would do-re-mi his way through a line (more often than not off-key—this is when he wasn't literally carrying the tune in a bucket) and then the congregation would copy right along after him" ("What Wonderous Love Is This," mimeograph).

25. This is the fundamental distinction Hay makes between the "folk" and "state" versions of the Berdache institution.

26. See, for example, James Carney, *The Irish Bardic Poet* (Dublin: Dolmen Press, 1967).

27. On the hermaphroditic figure of Skraat or Scrat, see Will Roscoe, *Queer Spirits: A Gay Men's Myth Book* (Boston: Beacon, 1995), pp. 130–32.

28. Cory summarizes historical and cross-cultural data on homosexuality (Donald W. Cory, *The Homosexual in America: A Subjective Approach* [New York: Greenberg, 1951], pp. 15–19).

29. Quoted in Engels, *The Origin of the Family*, p. 116.

30. Luke 1:52–53.

31. According to Lewis Spence, in the Scilly Isles "'goose-dancing'. . . seems to have taken the form of a general round dance, the youths being dressed as girls and the girls as young men" (*Myth and Ritual in Dance, Game, and Rhyme* [London: Watts & Co., 1947], p. 144).

32. According to Evelyn K. Wells, "The Rumanian Căluşari dancers, a remarkable survival of ancient belief and practice, are annually excommunicated. For six weeks every spring these men in women's costume, led by a masked man and carrying flowering garlic, dance through the villages. Their dance has power to heal the sick and perform other miracles" (*The Ballad Tree: A Study of British and American Ballads, Their Folklore, Verse, and Music* [New York: Ronald Press, 1950], pp. 178–79).

33. The *Oxford English Dictionary* defines "hoyden" as "1. A rude, ignorant, or awkward fellow; a clown, boor; 2. A rude, or ill-bred girl (or woman); a boisterous noisy girl, a romp."

34. Donald Webster Cory, "An Address Delivered to the International Committee for Sex Equality . . . ," *ONE* 1(2) (February 1953): 2–11.

35. Ruth Benedict, *Patterns of Culture* (Boston: Houghton Mifflin, 1959), p. 264. Emphasis added–HH.

"Music . . . man's oldest science of organization"

ALTHOUGH HAY'S INVOLVEMENT in Mattachine and his Marxist teaching occurred in distinct compartments of his life—Gay and Communist, respectively—they largely overlapped in time. In fact, Hay's research in European folk music directly contributed to the development of the cultural minority thesis that helped launch Mattachine, and it became the foundation for his subsequent research in Gay history.

Other Marxist musicologists, like Sidney Finkelstein, had applied Marxist principles to music but only to the extent of acknowledging class relations in the history of Western music and praising certain popular forms like jazz music or folk songs. Yet the relationship of folk music to daily life tasks in the areas of work and religion was commonly acknowledged by Marxist and non-Marxist historians alike. Hay's approach to the study of folk music was unique, however, in treating it as an example of dialectics in action—the same way Marxism viewed science, as a comprehensive system of knowledge and communication. Somewhat parallel to the work of Claude Lévi-Strauss, the French anthropologist who developed structural anthropology, Hay sought to derive the "message" of folk music from an analysis of the musical form itself. In the following selection, he identifies five basic forms and relates each to tribal modes of social organization.

In cultures without written records, Hay argues, music serves not only to *preserve* information, it provides the means of *imple-*

menting knowledge as well, through songs and dance steps that organize work functions. For this reason, it was impossible for the folk to separate the tasks of planting and harvesting from the rituals that had always surrounded these acts. Consequently, European tribal villagers clung to their pre-Christian customs and cultural forms, including music, not only to preserve their social identities, but because these forms were indispensable to their modes of production.

The capacity of a folk song to convey information above and beyond its lyrics becomes apparent when folk culture and identity are subject to repression. Hay's favorite example is how a certain tune, later to be known as "Bergen op Zoom," was used in 1622 to organize Netherlands freedom fighters from villages that did not understand each others' languages. They all had their own words for the song, but its rhythms were everywhere associated with the same dance steps, which included, at one point, the formation of a double file—exactly the organization needed to start the soldiers on their march to rescue the town of Bergen op Zoom from the Spaniards. The song was also used by the Dutch resistance during World War II.[1] At Hay's suggestion, the Mattachine organizers adopted it for their membership initiation ceremony.

The following selection from Hay's 1955–1956 lecture notes, the last occasion he offered the course, represents his most concise presentation of his theory of the origin and history of folk music. Where possible, I have provided information on the musical examples Hay mentions in the footnotes.

Music . . . Barometer of the Class Struggle

SESSION I. MUSIC AND SURVIVAL

"Music . . . man's oldest science of organization"
"From food-gatherers to slave-holders; from
hunger to magic—origins and social concepts."
"Where men and women organize"; "Come all ye
out of the wilderness"; "The falcon hath taken my
make away."[2]

A. Detoxification of the audience.
   1. The question "What is music?" is like asking "What is
      Herzegovinian?"
      a. To all of history and to two-thirds of the world today,
         *music is a language, an encyclopedia of patterns, a
         science—of organization.* A method of communi-
         cating, organizing, educating, mobilizing in ways
         beyond the scope of language or static illustration.
      b. *But it talked to you only because you knew its pat-
         terns and no matter where you encountered the pat-
         tern you recognized it.* (Illustrate by using "Cotton-
         eyed Joe"[3]—re-arrange patterns; "Blue Danube"—
         how it organizes a crowd of 1,000; how the non-
         dancer with the help of a well-wisher can get the
         swing of it quickly in a crowd.)
   2. If music is an encyclopedia of social organization, edu-
      cation, and mobilization, then it must have been, and is,
      completely comprehensible to all of the people.
      a. Ask how many people remember the algebraic bi-

nomial theorem—ninth grade. *You don't remember
it? . . . Why? Because you don't use it,* and you
haven't time to clutter up your mind with a lot of patterns you can't use.

b. The vast majority of music that we know is the social
production of the world's people—and 90 percent of
it was never written down. Yet the forms, the patterns, the melodic ingredients have been remembered and passed on, as we shall see, for at least
5,000 years. Why? Because they were used, were
needed, were vital, were basic to survival. Most folk
collectors find that folk singers can remember neither words nor tune without doing the "movement."
Thus the form and pattern of the dance-song are
the production-tools of the work required—and
not products of the fun. And the people preserved
these patterns as long as the work these patterns produced was necessary to the struggle of daily existence—from mumble-mumble B.C. to 1850 A.D. in
Nebraska.

3. In the social history of humanity, the period of man's
fight for survival on a twenty-four-hours-a-day level ex-
tends roughly from the appearance of the communal
family to the disappearance of the "folk" as a productive force in history—we might say 10,000 years, from
mumble-mumble B.C. to roughly 1750 A.D. in Britain,
1850 in Europe and North America, 1950 in Asia, and
no date as yet for Africa and South America. *Who are
the folk?* Webster says "a group of kindred people, forming a tribe or nation; generally used with reference to a

124

primitive stage of political or social organization, especially to that of people just emerging from the tribal state." An examination of history in terms of political economics shows that the Feudal village was politically, economically, and culturally a final form of the tribe or clan. Understanding then that the folk-village of Feudalism, the central social organization of approximately 95 percent of society, is the last manifestation of clan, phratry, or tribal organization, we must recognize that its culture is a closely knit, clearly intercommunicating group or collective culture. We must recognize that its struggle for survival was a group or collective struggle to perpetuate itself and maintain its identity. And this group culture makes its greatest contribution, as we shall see, in the complete overthrow of Feudalism by the Democratic coalition revolutions—and like the other contradicting forces in that qualitative change, the folk community together with its culture is consumed and negated.

4. In a discussion of this sort, the lecturer is expected to ask himself—how do you suppose Music was first thought of? And somebody nearly always says—from the birds singing on a lovely sunny day. How many of you have been to the County Museum and looked at the animals sucked out of the Brea Tar Pits? Can you get a clear picture of dinosaurs, mastodons, or giant ground sloths humming happily to themselves? Can you picture Mama humming a little hum to herself that she learned from the little tune the wooly mammoth hummed the day he trampled father into jelly? How many have been in the jungle areas, or seen travelogues of same? Did

you ever hear such a cacophony of noise in your life? Like 7th and Broadway the weekend before Christmas! Three-quarters of the world's birds make at most three notes. And few of those correspond to our spiritual poetic concept of tones. Also birds don't sing just for the hell of it. They are performing work patterns basic to their survival. When the fight to survive from day to day is man's concern, he hasn't time to sit around listening to birds who aren't sitting around either. *From where would he get such a concept? The jungle and its racket were there before he was. Where would he get the concept, the idea, to concentrate to the finite level necessary to hear one single melody out of all that tumult?* The power of concentration was hardly learned over a long, long historical period—as witness the fact that even today, ten minutes of concentration is considered a severe strain for most adults. *No, we must look at quite different social aspects for the origins of music.*

B. Demonstration of the possible origins of music.
  1. Social consciousness of prehistoric group survival.
     a. The food-gatherer's family and its life.
     b. Mama and Jr. who wandered thirteen trees—scaring the skunks.
     c. Poppa and the deer-trap which caught the young elephant, still alive.
     d. Crossing the river—and the saga of the big log.
     e. The animals that ran for their lives when Momma screamed—and chants against fear.
  2. The forms that evolve out of the familial primitive group.
     a. Unorganized shouting out against fear organized

126

into *collective chants* against the unknown—into chants of what is known, defiantly paired against the unknown:

(i) Play Chiapayeka processional;[4]

(ii) Demonstrate unison at the fifth (Quechua spinning song);

(iii) Play Bantu chant of praise (in fifths);

(iv) Women and children or girls in thirds (matriarchate), Ashanti.

b. Division of labor between men and women in familial group representing different physical responsibilities within the whole—*group statement or suggestion and group response*:

(i) Transitional form—processional into group suggestion and group response (Chant Bahutu);

(ii) Play Foliada II;

(iii) Play Quelli Quelli Quer;[5]

(iv) The next variation—group statement and solo comment (Mambutu Pygmies; Mossi Chant [Long John]; Ashanti).

c. Within the division of labor comes the handing out of specific responsibilities which one person must assume so that the others can work around him or her. In this social consciousness the responsible focal job is done on Monday by Joe, Tuesday by Pete, and so on through the whole group. In this cultural pattern we find the form of *solo suggestion and group response*:

(i) Transitional form—solo and group into group and group (Hebrew Yemenite ceremonial song[6]);

(ii) Tanganyika; Ashanti.

d. From the sharing of pivot jobs by each member of the group in turn, we evolve to the recognition that certain people in the family or tribe are always better at certain tasks, or more able to take old patterns and adapt them to new needs, than others. So evolves the elected group leader—the teachers who finally become the elected chieftains, and the wise ones who become the law-interpreters (prophets, magicians, priests, and judges):

127

(i) *The elected teachers of new ways in survival*—solo statement and group repeat (Sudanese safari song;[7] Ashanti muezzin call), solo statement and variation with group repeat (Macumba[8]), mixture of both solo suggestion and group response and solo statement and group repeat (Gahztekh song, Soviet Armenia;[9] Mano work song, Liberia);

(ii) *The teaching of past wisdom and experience as knowledge that children and adults alike must remember every day to survive*—leader and chorus (Accra, children songs; Haiti; song of Ramadan;[10] Macumba). In this last development, all the previous ingredients are utilized at a higher level—solo statement and group response in leader and chorus form (Samba Caboclo Do Matto; Fanti Jamboree, Ashanti).

e. In addition to the driving requirements of everyday needs was the need to review and revive the general overall wisdom of the past and the specific deeds of accomplishment. *At this point the fifth great form of musical organization appears*—the personification of the group, the group's achievements and discoveries as the wisdom of a single mythological wise-woman—or the exploits of a legendary hero—the saga, which means the *seeress* or wise-woman, an epic solo chant—and the chanson de geste, a heroic chant of mighty hunters and great warriors as told by men. *But it is vital for us to understand that this personification is not presented as an example to be followed by individuals*—such interpretations are our mis-inheritances from the distortions of the Renaissance and romantic apologists of history.

3. The familial group or clan in contact with other groups—*slavery*.
   a. What happens to the marsh culture when enslaved to a steppe or plateau culture:
      (i) Leader-and-chorus in new usage—overseer;
      (ii) Solo suggestion and group response in new role—slow-down.
   b. Appearance of Ritual and its political meaning of Freedom by return in memory to the Golden Age when *they were free*:
      (i) What happens to old work patterns and protective patterns under new physical and geographic conditions of existence—the emergence of pantomime and stylization (play Ibo Dance).
   c. Magic of ritual and invocation has its effect on dominant culture too—and becomes a part of its political identification with survival:
      (i) Rites of fertility and fecundity and their real social importance;

(ii) Midsummer rites of European survival come out of this heritage;

(iii) Play Chorale—Chant Mambetu as an example of all the ingredients developed and poured into composite of invocation, chant of praise, leader and chorus repeating wisdom and knowledge, and dance displaying and perfecting the physical techniques of their survival.

Lecture notes for "Music . . . Barometer of the Class Struggle," 1955–1956.

Notes

1. The tune was originally an English sailors' song (János Maróthy, *Music and the Bourgeois, Music and the Proletarian*, trans. Eva Róna [Budapest: Akadémiai Kiadó, 1974], p. 279).

2. "Come all ye out of the wilderness, and Glory Be" is the refrain from the Appalachian "Seven Joys of Mary," a folk version of the Magnificat (Victor #2018-A). "The falcon hath taken my make away" is a refrain from "Down in Yan Forest" (Victor #2120-A), a pre-Christian carol with elements of the Parsifal legend. The "make" is the baby who comes back on his own feet as an adult.

3. ASCH 348-3A.

4. Yaqui unison singing, General #5013A.

5. Gallegan antiphonal song, Disc #60468.

6. Folkways #1434B.

7. Disc #1511A.

8. Macumba de Ochoce, Brazil, Col. #36503.

9. Disc #1505B.

10. Arabic, "Song of the Month of Fasting," Folkways #1435A.

Mattachine Documents

THE FOLLOWING ARE SOME of the key documents created by
Mattachine between 1950 and 1953. First is the statement
of missions and purposes developed by the founders in the spring
of 1951 and formally adopted in July. It remains one of the seminal declarations of Queer liberation.

Anyone who has worked in community-based organizations
will appreciate the practical advice on conducting groups contained in the second document, a hand-out prepared for Mattachine discussion group facilitators. It could be used today in any
number of grassroots organizations and projects.

The final document is a leaflet prepared by the Citizens' Committee to Outlaw Entrapment, the organizational front created in
the spring of 1952 to coordinate the legal defense of Dale Jennings, who had been entrapped by the Los Angeles vice squad. In
the period of a few months the Committee distributed thousands
of mimeographed leaflets in the Los Angeles area by leaving them
on buses, handing them to "sympathetic" customers at places of
work, and so forth. The following hand-out, designed to be kept
in one's wallet for quick reference, was the most practical of these,
offering advice to Gay men on what to do in case of arrest. It
underscores the level of police harassment and legal persecution
that male homosexuals faced in the 1950s.

Mattachine Society Missions and Purposes

To Unify—While there are undoubtedly individual homosexuals who number many of their own people among their friends, thousands of homosexuals live out their lives bewildered, unhappy, alone—isolated from their own kind and unable to adjust to the dominant culture. Even those who may have many homosexual friends are still cut off from the deep satisfactions man's gregarious nature can achieve *only* when he is consciously part of a large unified whole. A major purpose of the Mattachine Society is to provide a consensus of principle around which all of our people can rally and from which they can derive a feeling of "belonging."

To Educate—The total of information available on the subject of homosexuality is woefully meager and utterly inconclusive. The Society organizes all available material and conducts extensive researches itself—psychological, physiological, anthropological, and sociological—for the purpose of informing all interested homosexuals, and for the purpose of informing and enlightening the public at large.

The Mattachine Society holds it possible and desirable that a highly ethical homosexual culture emerge, as a consequence of its work, paralleling the emerging cultures of our fellow-minorities—the Negro, Mexican, and Jewish Peoples. The Society believes homosexuals can lead well-adjusted, wholesome, and socially productive lives once ignorance and prejudice against them is successfully combated, and once homosexuals themselves feel they have a dignified and useful role to play in society. The Society, to these ends, is in the process of developing a homosexual ethic—disciplined, moral, and socially responsible.

132

To Lead—It is not sufficient for an oppressed minority like the homosexuals merely to be conscious of belonging to a minority collective when, as is the situation at the present time, that collective is neither socially organic nor objective in its directions and activities—although this minimum is in itself a great step forward. It is necessary that the more far-seeing and socially conscious homosexuals provide leadership to the whole mass of social deviants if the first two missions (the unification and the education of the homosexual minority) are to be accomplished. Further, once unification and education have progressed, it becomes imperative (to consolidate these gains) for the Corporation to push forward into the realm of political action to erase from our law books the discriminatory and oppressive legislation presently directed against the homosexual minority.

The Society, founded upon the highest ethical and social principles, serves as an example for homosexuals to follow, and provides a dignified standard upon which the rest of society can base a more intelligent and accurate picture of the nature of homosexuality than currently obtains in the public mind. The Society provides the instrument necessary to work with civic-minded and socially valuable organizations, and supplies the means for the assistance of our people who are victimized daily as a result of our oppression. Only a Society providing an enlightened leadership can rouse the homosexuals—one of the largest minorities in America today—to take the actions necessary to elevate themselves from the social ostracism an unsympathetic culture has perpetrated upon them.

Written April 1951 and ratified July 20, 1951. Published in Marvin Cutler, ed., *Homosexuals Today: A Handbook of Organizations and Publications, 1956* (Los Angeles: ONE, Inc., 1956), pp. 13–14.

A Quick Guide to Conducting Discussion Groups

I. INTRODUCTION (read to the group or tell in your own words): The Mattachine Foundation, a California Corporation, has the following aims: (1) To aid in research on sexual deviation, (2) To promote understanding of sexual deviates amongst themselves, and (3) To develop public understanding of the social problem of sexual deviation. These discussion groups, open to homosexuals and sympathetic heterosexuals, are for the purpose both of giving people an opportunity to exchange ideas and of collecting for the Foundation information on the lives, ideas, feelings, and problems of homosexuals. Besides these discussion groups, there are action committees to give all interested people a chance to work and help the Foundation carry out its program.

II. THE DISCUSSION:

A. Subject.

The subject for discussion should be selected by the group at the previous meeting. Usually a specific subject results in a more interesting discussion. Examples of subjects that have proven good:

1. Why are there so few successful homosexual "marriages"?

2. What causes swishing?

3. Is there a homosexual culture?

4. Should homosexuals try to pattern their "marriages" after the heterosexual ones?

B. *Remember*—any information about how homosexuals live and solve their problems is interesting and valuable.

III. THE MODERATOR SHOULD:

    A. Throw out questions and ideas if the discussion lags.

    B. Give everyone a chance to talk by curtailing those who tend to monopolize the time and encouraging others to enter the discussion.

    C. Attempt to keep the discussion going in some general direction, not in all directions.

    D. Try to summarize the discussion briefly at the end.

IV. THE MODERATOR SHOULD NOT:

    A. Talk too much.

    B. Take advantage of his position to advance his own ideas.

V. BE SURE TO:

    A. Announce and explain the action committees before the break.

        1. Dossier committee [collecting information on legal cases].

        2. Mailing and mimeograph committee.

        3. Committee to edit discussion group reports.

        4. Committee to gather information from newspapers, magazines.

    B. Have someone take notes.

    C. Pass out slips of paper and pencils to everyone and let them, if they choose, give names, address, and phone number and indicate whether they want to be on the mailing list and what projects they would like to work on. This is done during the break. Appoint people to help you do this job.

    D. Have literature about the organization available.

    E. Decide on place of next meeting before people start leaving.

Undated.

Your Rights in Case of Arrest

1. If an officer tries to arrest you, he should have a warrant unless   135
   a misdemeanor (minor violation) or a felony (serious offense)
   has been committed in his presence or he has reasonable
   grounds to believe the person being arrested is guilty.
2. If he has no warrant ask what the basis of arrest is. If it is not
   explained as in No. 1 above, go along but under protest made
   before a witness if possible. DO NOT RESIST PHYSICALLY.
3. GIVE NO INFORMATION! You may, but do not have to, give
   your name and address. Do NOT talk to any policeman.
   Q: *"Why did you commit this crime?"*
   A: "I'm not guilty and I'd like to speak to my attorney,
   please."
   Q: *"How long have you been a lewd vagrant?"*
   A: "I'm not guilty and I'd like to see my lawyer before making
   a statement."
   Q: *"Have you been arrested for this before?"*
   A: "I'm not guilty and my attorney would rather I speak
   through him."
   Q: *"Nice day, isn't it?"*
   A: "I'm sorry but I'd like a lawyer's advice before making a
   statement."
4. Deny all accusatory statements by arresting officers with, "I'm
   not guilty and I'd like to contact a lawyer." Otherwise your silence before witnesses can be construed in court as assent.
5. If an officer insists on taking you to jail, ask when you are
   booked (registered) what the charges are.
6. Insist on using a telephone to contact your lawyer or family.
7. DO NOT SIGN ANYTHING. Take numbers of arresting officers.

8. You have a right to be released on bail for most offenses. Have your attorney make the arrangements. Or you can ask for a bail bond broker. For a fee, he will post (deposit with the police) the amount needed for your release.
9. Under no circumstances have the police a right to manhandle, beat, or terrorize you. REPORT ALL SUCH INCIDENTS.
10. If you do not have an attorney by the time you are required to plead guilty or not guilty, remember this:
    a. You are entitled to a copy of the charges made against you.
    b. You are entitled to have a lawyer. Ask for a postponement until you get legal representation.
11. PLEAD NOT GUILTY.
12. Ask for a trial by jury unless your lawyer advises otherwise.
13. You are not required to testify against yourself in any trial or hearing.
14. If you are questioned by a member of the FBI, you are not required to answer. Immediately consult an attorney so that your rights may be adequately protected.

Citizens' Committee to Outlaw Entrapment, Spring 1952.

136

Homophile

1953–1969

F ACED WITH THE PROSPECT of a split within Mattachine
over the issue of anti-Communism, Hay and the other Mattachine founders decided to resign in the spring of 1953 in the
hope that a unified movement would survive them. But the new
leaders of Mattachine repudiated the principles, goals, and methods of the original movement. Informal discussion groups, which had
served to foster self-esteem and build identity, were replaced with educational forums in which heterosexual psychiatrists expounded
their theories on the cause and cure of homosexuality while well-
dressed Queers nodded in approval. The original name was retained
but its origin revised—the Mattachine was now a medieval *court*
jester, who "lived and moved in the circles of the nobility."[1]

The years following Mattachine were often lonely and isolated
ones for Hay, but they yielded a rich harvest in terms of research
and study. Despite a full-time job, he managed to spend hours
every night (and often at work) reading and writing, while on
weekends he slipped into the stacks of the research library at the
University of California's Los Angeles campus. Hay originally
intended to report the results of his research in a book-length
work—"The Homophile in Search of an Historical Context and
Cultural Contiguity"—and at one point he typed up a chapter
outline for it. Its scope was nothing less than a universal history,
not of homosexuality, but of the "Berdache institution"—its representatives among Native Americans and other tribal people; its
origin in the ancient Near East and Mediterranean where it developed into a priesthood; its history following the male takeover of
matrifocal institutions; the distinction between "state" and

140

"folk" Berdache that resulted; and the continuing manifestations of these patterns up to the eve of the modern era in Europe. These findings are summarized in the essay included in the following section, "Christianity's First Closet Case" (pp. 218–37).

Although the projected book was never written, Hay produced three major papers in this period, which appeared in publications of ONE, Inc. In 1957, what was intended to be the opening chapter of his book was published under the title "The Homophile in Search of an Historical Context and Cultural Contiguity." A second essay, "The Moral Climate of Canaan at the Time of Judges" (1958) was an extended analysis of Hebrew and Canaanite cultures at the time that the religious functionaries called *qedeshim* served in ancient Near East temples. In 1963, Hay published an analysis of a long-forgotten report on Pueblo Two-Spirits.

Hay's political exile ended with the onset of his relationship with John Burnside, who shared his political, social, and cultural outlook to an extent that proved exhilarating for both men. Whereas Hay's previous lover had discouraged him from maintaining contacts with the homophile movement, Burnside was already active in ONE, Inc. when the two met. In 1965, they helped form the Southern California Council on Religion and the Homophile. The following year they participated in one of the country's first Gay demonstrations—a fifteen-car motorcade through Los Angeles protesting the military's exclusion of Gays—and they traveled to San Francisco to attend the second national planning conference for the North American Conference of Homophile Organizations and participate in a symposium with local religious leaders. Two pieces in this section represent the evolution of Hay's political thinking in the 1960s—his letter to *The Ladder* in 1961 (pp. 150–60) and his "Open Letter to All Homophile Organizations," published in 1967 (pp. 168–74).

Burnside encouraged Hay in another area, as well. Both men were interested in questions of the origin and nature of Gay desire and personality. Burnside, a trained engineer and a successful inventor, was aware of recent works in the fields of biology and genetics that the two were able to draw on in forging answers to these questions. In the 1950s, Hay's writings had been remarkably free of speculations concerning the origins of homosexuality at the individual level. As a Marxist, he rejected psychoanalysis on principle and was predisposed to favor "scientific" explanations after the models of the "hard" sciences. His attitude toward the etiologic question is summed up in a talk he gave in 1969: "The Homosexual Nature, as the psychic architecture of an existential Minority from the dawn of history through the present and into the future, needs neither to be explained nor defended. It requires only to be acknowledged and its particular potential—for the expansion of human consciousness—re-evaluated."[2]

At the same time, precisely because Hay premised his approach to Lesbian/Gay history on presence rather than absence, he needed a way to put the etiologic red herring to rest. Postulating genetic factors provides a parsimonious and morally neutral answer to this question. Once an origin in the realm of inborn or "natural" sources is predicated—even at the most minimal level of a diffuse and non-specific tendency that tips the individual constitution from the polymorphous sexuality of the infant, as posited by Freud, toward homosexuality (and, indeed, Freud himself allowed for such a "tipping of the balance")[3]—the focus of discussion automatically shifts to the *nature* of these traits, that is, the nature of homosexuality itself. From Hay's point of view—that is, from the standpoint of developing a political theory for a broad-based social movement—a tentative answer to etiology is better than no answer at all.

Two works that influenced both Hay and Burnside were Konrad Lorenz's *King Solomon's Ring* and *On Aggression*, published

142   in English in 1952 and 1966, respectively.[4] Lorenz argued that "love" (i.e., pair bonding) arose in aggressive species as a ritualized redirection of aggressive impulses between species members. The more aggressive a species, the greater the need for love as a safety valve. In a remarkably nonjudgmental account, Lorenz describes the occurrence of homosexual bonding among his favorite animal subjects, the Greylag goose:

> If such a young gander makes his triumph-rite proposal to another male and is accepted, they each find, in respect of this all-important ceremony, a far better partner and companion than they would have done in a female. Since intraspecific aggression is far stronger in ganders than in geese, the inclination to perform the triumph ceremony is also stronger and the two friends stimulate each other to acts of courage. No pair of opposite sex can compete with them; thus such gander pairs always attain very high, if not the highest, places in the ranking order of the colony. They keep together for life just as faithfully as a pair of heterosexual individuals. (196)

Lorenz concludes that we "cannot regard the 'homosexual' triumph bond of two ganders as something pathological, the less so since it also occurs in wild geese in the natural state" (199). At the end of the chapter, he notes that if highly complex behaviors in humans and in Greylag geese are similar, "We can be sure that every one of these instincts has a very special survival value, in each case almost or quite the same in the Greylag and in man" (218). Thus, Lorenz provided Hay with evidence that not only supported the thesis that homosexual bonding involves inherited traits but also that these traits contribute to the survival of the human species as well.

In the 1970s, Hay and Burnside found additional support for
their theory of Gay origins in the works of sociobiologist Edward
O. Wilson. Wilson speculated that genetic factors underlay "the   143
adoption of certain *broad* roles," and he offered an explanation
for how such a trait was transmitted—since homosexuals marry
less frequently and have fewer children. Referring to the examples
of Berdaches and shamans, Wilson speculated that the value of
such individuals as "helpers" may have led to the genes favoring
homosexuality being sustained by kin selection—indeed, there
are many reports of Native American families encouraging and
favoring children with Two-Spirit tendencies. Individuals in such
roles could, in turn, help perpetuate both genetic and social diversity by aiding heterosexual friends and relatives who have non-
aggressive traits to reproduce and helping to ensure that children
with non-aggressive traits survive to reach adulthood.[5] Wilson
makes a qualification often overlooked by his critics: "If such
genes really exist, they are almost certainly incomplete in pene-
trance and variable in expressibility, meaning that which bearers
of the genes develop the behavioral trait and to what degree they
develop it depend on the presence or absence of modifier genes
and the influence of the environment."[6] Hay would emphasize
that whatever biology underlies homosexuality, it must involve a
complex or *constellation* of traits rather than a single factor in a
linear model of causation.[7]

From these sources—history, paleontology, ethology, genetics,
and neurobiology—Hay and Burnside constructed an account of
the historical and individual origins of homosexuality, which is
contained in two jointly authored pamphlets: *The Circle of Loving Companions* (1966) and *A Contribution to the Principles of
Gay Liberation* (1975). While essentialist, in that their account
relies on biological factors, it is more complex than other biologi-

cal models of homosexuality I am aware of, including those of
recent researchers like Simon LeVay, because it draws on models

144   from more than one field. Further, instead of defining homosexuality in strictly sexual and behavioral terms, they define it in cog-
nitive and cultural terms. Rather than a technical discussion of
how genes determine behavior, they offer a genuinely cultural and
sociological account of Gay identity development. "To be homosexually oriented," they wrote in 1975, "is to find oneself absolutely at odds with the culture, with the relentlessly and blindly
heterosexual home, school, and society, at the deeply primal levels
of sex and sexual love." Cast out by family and society, Gays have
no choice but to find their own way toward self-understanding
and self-acceptance. "The struggle to wholeness, to reach a level
where Gay love is embraced as a true human value, means the
attainment of a high level of consciousness." Thus, what begins as
an unformed disposition toward non-aggressiveness, favoring
homosexual orientation, ends in a special form of consciousness.
It is this consciousness, not the genes, that is the source of the
social contributions of Gays.

In the late 1970s, Hay incorporated the findings of Roger Sperry's work on the bicameral or dichotomous structure of the brain
into his understanding of consciousness. Sperry found that each
hemisphere of the brain had discrete functions—the right special-
ized in visualization, spatial and object recognition, music, intuition, and emotion; the left was the site of verbal, mathematical,
and analytical skills. Sperry concluded that consciousness was
both "hardwired," in the sense of being an integral part of the
brain's process, and "a higher emergent entity that's more than
just the sum of its right and left awareness and supersedes this as a
directive force in our thoughts and actions."[8]

The idea that neural networks could be inherited led Hay to

speculate that Gay consciousness might indeed have a neurological basis in a distinct psychic organization perhaps involving the relationship of right and left hemisphere functions. He linked the idea of an innate psychic structure to one other Lorenzian concept, that of "triggering." This is the ethological phenomenon whereby an innate behavioral pattern remains dormant until "triggered" or "released" by specific external stimuli. In the case of newborn chicks in an incubator this could be the tapping of the incubator floor, which serves to trigger pecking and feeding behavior; in humans, exaggerated proportions between the cranium and face, whether in human infants or animals, tend to trigger parental care responses.[9] Hay believes that in the case of Gay men our first intense sexual contact can have a similar effect: "At the instant of first eyelock, it was as if an invisible arc of lightning flashed between us, zapping into both our eagerly ready young bodies *total systems of knowledge*. . . . Now, through that flashing arc of love, we two young faeries knew the *triggered* tumult of Gay consciousness in our vibrant young bodies."[10]

145

Hay's account of Gay roles and identities still remained historical and materialist. For Hay, even if certain human talents, behaviors, and psychological patterns are distinctly Gay, or concentrated in those who call themselves Gay, this does not mean that they are always developed, and it certainly says nothing about the ethics of the ends to which they are applied. It is also likely that if there are genetic "Gay traits," not all individuals today who are homosexual or even identify as Gay have them (and, conversely, not all who carry the traits practice or identify as homosexuals). However, the assumption of Gay presence as a normal state of human society leads Hay to ask not whether society "constructs" homosexuals, but whether it makes possible the expression of homosexual traits (e.g., sexual difference, gender

146

difference) or whether it prevents their expression. If the "channel" for expression exists, then Queer "roles" and "identities" will be invented. These constructions will reflect the praxis of individual and society—they will be neither freely chosen nor predetermined.

These insights into the origins of Gay desire and sexuality began to show up in Hay's writings in the late 1960s, in particular, the essay "The Homosexual's Responsibility to the Community" included here (pp. 162–66), and they found a receptive audience among the young activists who joined him in founding the Los Angeles Gay Liberation Front. In the 1970s, they became the springboard for his writings and efforts in launching the Gay men's spirituality movement.

Notes

1. Marvin Cutler, ed., *Homosexuals Today: A Handbook of Organizations and Publications, 1956* (Los Angeles: ONE, Inc., 1956), p. 43.

2. "Homosexuality and Religion," unpublished manuscript, July 27, 1969.

3. Kenneth Lewes, *The Psychoanalytic Theory of Male Homosexuality* (New York: Penguin Books, 1988), pp. 80 f.

4. Konrad Z. Lorenz, *King Solomon's Ring: New Light on Animal Ways* (London: Methuen, 1952) and idem, *On Aggression*, trans. Marjorie K. Wilson (1963; New York: Harcourt, Brace and World, 1966). The quotes that follow are from *On Aggression*.

5. Those who would point to individual examples of competitive and aggressive Lesbians and Gay men are missing the point. "Non-aggressiveness," or "love," from Lorenz's perspective is redirected aggression, in which the object of aggression and rivalry becomes the object of love. Committed homosexuality is not incompatible with continued manifestations of this human capacity for aggressivity, and, indeed, the sexual activity of many homosexuals speaks to the intensity of the original drive. Homosexuality does not automatically make one less aggressive or com-

petitive, but it does create the possibility of developing non-aggressiveness and cooperation through the social experience of loving and identifying with one's similars.

6. Edward O. Wilson, *Sociobiology: The Abridged Edition* (Cambridge, Mass.: Harvard University Press, 1980), p. 279; see also idem, *On Human Nature* (Cambridge, Mass.: Harvard University Press, 1978), pp. 142–46. See Stephen O. Murray's critique in *Social Theory, Homosexual Realities* (New York: Gay Academic Union, 1984), p. 63. Sociobiology has acquired the status of opprobium in some circles because of the sharp feminist critique of any theory that hints at women's social role having a "natural" or genetic basis. However, the implications of sociobiology and the political stakes involved in its claims are different for Gays and Lesbians. Any theory that suggests that we *are* a part of nature and that our presence is a socially valuable adaptation of a naturally occurring human difference pulls the rug out from under the claims of our most virulent opponents.

7. So concludes James D. Weinrich, a biologist strongly influenced by sociobiology, who visited Hay in the 1970s (see Weinrich, *Sexual Landscapes: Why We Are What We Are, Why We Love Who We Love* [New York: Charles Scribner's Sons, 1987] and John A. W. Kirsch and James D. Weinrich, "Homosexuality, Nature, and Biology: Is Homosexuality Natural? Does It Matter?" in *Homosexuality: Research Implications for Public Policy*, ed. John C. Gonsiorek and James D. Weinrich, [Newberry Park, Calif.: Sage Publications, 1991], pp. 13–31). See also the special double issue, "Sex, Cells, and Same-Sex Desire: The Biology of Sexual Preference," *Journal of Homosexuality* 28(1/2, 3/4) (1995).

8. "Interview: Roger Sperry," *Omni* (August 1983): 69–100, esp. p. 74. In his copy of this interview Hay underlined Sperry's comment: "In Marxism, what counts in shaping the world and human affairs are the actions man takes to fulfill his material needs. But this overlooks the key principle of downward causation. . . . The higher idealistic properties that have evolved in man and society can supersede and control and take care of these more primitive needs" (p. 98).

9. Lorenz's more technical term for this phenomenon is "innate releasing mechanism" (Konrad Z. Lorenz, *The Foundations of Ethology* [New York and Vienna: Springer-Verlag, 1981], pp. 153–75).

10. Harry Hay, "A Separate People Whose Time Has Come," in *Gay*

148

Spirit: Myth and Meaning, ed. Mark Thompson (New York: St. Martin's Press, 1987), pp. 279–91, esp. p. 286. See also "Toward the New Frontiers of Fairy Vision," herein. Most of the scientists investigating biological correlates of homosexuality remain trapped within the binaries of male/female and normal/abnormal, and the medical-psychiatric definition of homosexuality in terms of sexual object choice. For LeVay and others, homosexuality is always-already some combination of male and female. See Simon LeVay and Dean H. Hamer, "Evidence for a Biological Influence in Male Homosexuality," and William Byne, "The Biological Evidence Challenged," *Scientific American* (May 1994): 44–49 and 50–55.

"A Homophile Bill of Particulars"

FOR ITS JANUARY 1961 Midwinter Institute, ONE, Inc. proposed that the participants debate and adopt a "Homosexual Bill of Rights." This document proved to be the source of bitter controversy within the fledgling homophile movement. Representatives from the Lesbian organization Daughters of Bilitis (DOB), founded in 1955, attacked the "Bill of Rights" for adopting "a demanding attitude toward society." In the opening session they moved that the entire program be canceled. Dorr Legg, writing in *ONE* magazine, accused the women of being "brainwashed."[1] Meanwhile, the tenuous national network of Mattachine Society chapters was collapsing because of the mismanagement of the leaders in San Francisco. It was a definite low point in the history of the post-1953 homophile movement.

The debate over the Homosexual Bill of Rights revealed the fault lines in the movement and the internal constraints on the emergence of genuine activism. ONE's proposal for a Homosexual Bill of Rights was a bold step at the time, but for Hay, of course, not bold enough and based on the wrong principles. In this article, published in DOB's magazine, *The Ladder*, Hay challenges the positions of both ONE and DOB, arguing that the notion of specific "rights" for a minority is inimical to democratic principles—rights are indivisible, that is, extended to everybody equally. Instead, Hay argues for a "bill of particulars"—a kind of political wish list of social changes that Lesbians and Gays should demand but be prepared to modify when the opportunity to negotiate arises.

Hay demonstrates a level of political analysis and strategy far in

150

advance of the accommodationists who then held the leadership roles in the homophile movement. The key challenge of the movement, he argues, is overcoming the prejudice against homosexuality. Trying to downplay, minimize, or sanitize homosexuality fails to address this prejudice. For this reason, Hay opposes the strategy of defending homosexual acts because they are based on "mutual consent," much as he opposes the strategy of claiming legal protection for Gays and Lesbians on a presumed right to privacy. Neither of these approaches challenges the fundamental public perception of homosexuality—not as a mode of personhood or an emotional orientation whose fulfillment is central to the Gay person's happiness, but as the social and moral equivalent of prostitution and adultery, which are victimless crimes between consenting adults performed in private. Those who view homosexuality in the same context as prostitution are hardly likely to welcome the presence of Gay men and Lesbians in their daily lives. Anti-Gay prejudice is unchallenged.

The fault lines of 1961—between accommodation and confrontation, between minimizing homosexuality as a minor variation and redeeming it as a social identity—are today deep ruptures in the Lesbian/Gay movement. What is at stake in the various positions represented in these debates remains poorly understood. Three and a half decades later, Hay's analysis still offers clarifying insights into these issues.

Letter to *The Ladder*

I am generally elated with the tenor of your group's position at ONE's 1960–61 Midwinter Institute as regards the Homophile

"Bill of Rights" issue and, at the same time, signally dismayed by
your apparent unconcern for substantially materializing your reasons. Shallying between the GO and NO-GO termini of whether to
invoke an exchange of correspondence in and around this, I am
now of the opinion that a strengthening and broadening of your
position is very much an order of the day. My opinion is even more
confirmed by the recent abysmal developments in the Mattachine
Society II (*The Ladder* 5[9] [June 1961]: 13).

Perhaps a word or two of self-identification might be useful. As
first founder of the Mattachine Idea (the "closed" Society I, with
its open-face Foundation as opposed to the subsequent "open" Society II), the writer did not associate further with the name after
the factional eruptions of May 1953 dissipated the first Society and
gutted the Foundation despite his desperate and vehement opposition. My association with ONE, Inc. over the last eight years might
loosely be described as that of—more often than not—a loyal opposition. In education, for instance, the writer has up to now
agreed with their directions but not with many of their positions
and/or postulates.

But now I stand in the very strongest opposition to their Homophile Bill of Rights—not only the position but the very approach
and direction. At the moment the core of my protestation is equally
compounded by what I deplore as the "red herring" type of rebuttal (yours), instead of a direct and open counter-offensive.

Being unable to attend this year's Institute I have been dependent upon those notes which have been reported by *ONE Magazine* from time to time. It is possible that in missing your reports (*The Ladder* 5[6] [March 1961] and subsequent issues) our
impressions of your opposition do great disservice to your efforts.
But hear me out, and if I do no more than reiterate what you have
stated I shall most humbly apologize.

The reason I suspect that your stated opposition contented itself with things *less* than a coming to grips with the primal error—that of a Bill of Rights specifically favoring *any* minority—is because *ONE Magazine*'s defense seems to have taken shape on deviational levels far from the basic postulates of the conflict. In effect, their rebuttal is one of taunting. "Wassamatta," they hoot, "after so many years of open publication and yearly open conventions are we to believe that Homophiles are *afraid* to stand up for their rights?" This particular herring, I believe, is one counter to your negative assertion that a stratagem such as the Minority Bill of Rights in itself (let alone its projection) would set the Homophile movement back many years. I contend that being afraid to stand up for our rights, equally with the fear of being "set back," are definitely not the issue in any way, shape, or form.

The issue is, in a nutshell, that a Bill of Rights specifically drawn up for *any* minority (whether political, racial or social) is wholly undemocratic and thus wholly UNAMERICAN. Civil rights, or more correctly in constitutional terms, *civil privileges*, in a Republic engendered upon and devoted to the preservation and constant extension of the democratic processes, *are, and must ever be, indivisible*. Civil privileges, being both a collective responsibility as well as the individual's benefice, devolve upon *all* the obligation to apply them to each alike, without reservation, *or to none*!

Two of ONE Institute's presumed "rights" come to mind vividly exposed in this context: (1) The right of Homophiles not to have to pay educational taxes to care for the excessive inseminations of Heterophiles; and (2) the right of Homophiles to establish Homophile neighborhood concentrations and live in them if they so choose.

In demolishing the latter postulate one need go no further than to note that "restrictive covenants" in the matter of real property are now unconstitutional in most non–Jim Crow states and soon may be the rule in all American states—we hope.

In regard to the first item, the dreadful and divisive character of its concept immediately becomes apparent when we realize that such an equity would protect Protestants from having to pay taxes for the public education of Catholics or Jews; would protect whites from having to pay taxes for the public education of Asians, Amerindians, Mexican-Americans, or Negroes; would protect wealthy employers from having to pay taxes for the public education of unionists; would protect landlords from having to pay taxes for the public education of renters.

As I see it, the planners of ONE's Midwinter Institute failed to distinguish between the "political fiction" of the inalienable rights (which are polarities of an elective intellectual climate only) and the political entities (derivative of such a climate) of the conferred civil privilege. They further equated the inalienable right fiction with the "DEMAND tactic" by which a militant minority or faction *negotiates* an armed truce to an advantage. The conflicting factors of each of the above propositions should never, under any circumstances, have been presumed to be either equivalents or interchangeable. In terms of everyday political exigencies the popularly current myth of "inalienable rights" is no more than the constantly reiterated posits of our founding fathers' "self-evident truths." As such, then, "inalienable rights" must be seen to be a valid concept *only* when comprehended as inseparable from "duties owed." All other political sacra are "civil privileges" voluntarily and collectively *conferred* in convention by the democratic process. And precisely because they are conferred they are equally collectively revocable.

Had ONE Institute seen its project in terms of a "Bill of Particulars" this would have been a horse of quite another shape. A "Bill of Particulars," to encompass a basis of negotiations when the time comes to integrate the Homophile minority (as a socially decent and contributive element) into the parent community, is a projection with which none of us would wish to quarrel. Indeed, a "Bill of Particulars," giving voice and cognizance to the diverse methodological motivations and colorations characterizing the provenance of necessary morality within our minority, collated and prepared for extensive discussion and selective public dissemination, might prove to be of significant value to our parent community at this time. Especially so as that community's more sober and serious press currently editorializes on the need to seek a reconstitution of its own all-embracing system of ethic from which to derive a more contemporary manual of moral discipline.

As regards setting brakes on our actions, purportedly in the interests of maintaining fraternal rapport with "friends" in our communities, national or regional, the Homophile minority by now should have accrued sufficient political maturity to have dispelled any such illusions. As the brief but messy essay into politics enjoyed by the Mattachine Society II so ably demonstrated,[2] and as the Negro people have so painfully learned, national and/or social *minorities have no friends*—other than the infrequent materializations (remorsefully-flashed or conscience-stabbed into temporary or fitful existence) of their fellow-travelers. They do have, from time to time, temporary allies, each motivated by their own (and usually adverse) self-interests.

It is true that there are numerous forces and combinations within our society, some not without considerable influence, who have voiced, and may continue to do so, an interest in our being heard. But we should err disastrously were we to initial them as "friends." When a new political party desires to be put on the ballot it must secure petitions containing a minimum of 50,000 signatures. These signatories, by and large, are neither "friends" nor even well-wishers. They are simply earnest or decent people who believe in the democratic principle of fair play; who believe that every sincerely motivated contender has the right to be heard.

As the progress of the Wolfenden Report from committee to the floor of Commons in the British Parliament demonstrated, there were many who warmly supported its right to be debated on the floor *precisely in order to vote against it.*[3]

Insofar as our being heard is concerned, we should realize that (in keeping with the experiences of all our predecessors in crusades for social reform) we must set as a basis of negotiations *two* loaves in the earnest hope of getting *one*, but settling for *half* as the first step in an inevitable escalation process. In such a negotiation, even as the "Integration" forces of government have discovered and as the emerging nations of Africa and Asia experience with each new day, it will be precisely our "friends," our self-seeking allies of other occasions, who will be the first to moan that even our minimum "half loaf" is ten times too much for us to ask—and has been brought up twenty-five years too soon!

In the matter of a Homophile orientation toward the collective obligation to apply civil privilege to each without distinction, the notion inescapably arises that the solution to our problems—not only in the U.S. but in any nation—is a constitutional one.[4] Concomitant to the notion runs a conviction that such constitutional privilege/obligations must state their premises in primal Homophile values—even as the privilege/obligations insuring definitive security and status to currently acknowledged and accepted national and social minorities spell out such securities and limitations in the Thirteenth through Fifteenth Amendments in such a way as to tacitly insure them, equally and specifically, in terms of the first ten.

To be specific, in Homophile terms, I am firmly convinced that a state-by-state jurisprudential insertion of a "mutual consent" clause—even were such a projection practicable—does *not* solve the contradictions oppressing our minority. I believe that the essential compromising opportunism and negativeness of the "mutual consent" position (as applied to the Homophile minority problem) was wholly exposed by the career of the Wolfenden Report and the consequential debate which buried it.

The significant coupling within a "presumably" liberalizing amendment, which our minority editorials here in the U.S. seem to have overlooked, between importuning and the common garden-variety of Homophile contracting for mutual consent, markedly reveals the startling realization that, to the humanistic English "establishment" (which of course includes the Church), the social aspects of practicing homophilia and prostitution are seen as parallel phenomena or procedures!

The categorical grouping cited above, afforded us in the Wolfenden symposium, is to a large extent a product of our own unwittingness. A doing, I might add, that the writer managed to keep *excluded* from the First Mattachine Movement but which has flowered all over the place in the Second Mattachine and its affiliates. This grouping inevitably derived from the tendency of eight years or so of "toleration, folks, pretty please?" editorials in our several magazines. These editorials cited, in support of their claims that the level of moral opinion was now liberalizing itself, the numerous addictions to casual adultery presumably now found tolerable within large sections of our national community. Be our common conventions of morality as collapsed nationally or internationally as they may, the fact remains that Occidental jurisprudence still collates ADULTERY as an aspect of PROSTITUTION and, co-axially, prostitution as an aspect of adultery.

The Homophile minority code, per se, is concerned *neither* with prostitution nor adultery, and must not be—at least in its initial conceptualizing. Heterophiles certainly have the right to establish an "A to B" morality gamut from "A," conjugal continence, to "B," celibacy. But we cannot so tailor our social requirements because, (1) we are neither Heterophiles nor, (2) may we expect to accrue the social expectancies, and in return rewards, of Heterophiles.

In certain aspects of our inclinational patterns we might *appear* to parallel Heterophile templates, true! But since the Homophile social patterns most liable to accrue the best levels of our social contributions deviate rather sharply from those attributable to the conventions of Heterophile morality, we must dedicate ourselves to the educational task of broadening community morality to honestly assess the *necessary requirements of both* the Heterophile and the Homophile.

Granted that the resulting morality must be all-inclusive and indivisible; yet the state and local jurisprudence must contain allowances for *particulars* even as are granted religious (such as Christian Scientists, Jehovah's Witnesses), national, and social (such as trade unions) minorities currently. Such *particulars*, in my opinion, more correctly should have been and should be the first concern of the Homophile movement minority publications and conventions of today and tomorrow.

In this direction, a resolute cleansing of our own conceptions and intellectual processes or moral evaluations would seem to be in order. Number one on such a list would be, I think, the rooting out of the mechanical and wholly fallacious habit of comparing and/or evaluating our minority patterns of behavior in terms of Heterophile values and/or conventions.

Homophile promiscuity, for example, may not be adumbrated with that form of behavior excoriated by the Heterophile community. It does not carry the same connotations of disaster and dissolution with us as it *must* with them, for reasons too obvious to further discuss.

That Homophile promiscuity is wasteful of time and energy which might be much more profitably spent is a *sentiment* not necessary for us to belabor. But immoral, in the spiritual and social criminality of the heterophilic infraction's intent, *it is not!* Homophile promiscuity, then, simply becomes for us one of our several mean-average deviant behaviors FOR WHICH WE MAKE *NO* APOLOGIES. Occasional *multiplicity* of sexual expression, as a casual variation of "otherwise devoted couple" behavior, might be another such. Yet such deviances as these, and others, construed from our minority behavior values, cannot in any way be measured or weighed in current heterophilic moral "koine" (or should we say coinage?) because neither the socially evaluated purpose nor objectives of heterophilic sexual behavior were ever construed to correspond with our expectations—or vice versa.

Thus we must realize—all our Heterophile sympathizers and fellow-travelers notwithstanding—that without sharing *as Homophiles* the indivisible civil privileges of the sanctity of private conscience, the invincibility of the home, the privileges of free assemblage and territorially unrestricted association, the privilege of socially acceptable free speech, that without the privilege of being able to freely assert ourselves *as a group* and being socially received with the same dignified and decent hospitality extended to any and all other minorities, *we have nothing!* And until we have begun to consolidate around such a conceptual program, *as a minority*, we have accomplished nothing!

It is on this latter point where our success or failure swings; it is on this latter point that all the Wolfenden well-meaningism *failed*, and most surely will founder again. A general bill of "mutual consent when privately enjoyed" is neither gain nor security for us if, at the same time, we are forbidden to seek or associate beyond our front doors. France had just such an unspecified "mutual consent when privately enjoyed" clause for 150 years, *generally*. And for the same length of time the French Homophile lolled in the enervating illusion that the "double standards" of the bourgeois-formulated marriage contract applied to him also. So that when, in the last two years, De Gaulle tacked on a specific Homophile exclusion clause to certain liberties in this category our minority was not prepared to receive, let alone socially resist, such an onslaught.

A full *Bill of Particulars* upon which to negotiate a general liberalization of our national social code, and to amend local or regional "prejudices" currently lodged in criminal equities, reflects no more than the traditional bargaining position of demanding two loaves with the firm conviction to accept no less than one. Although (in small print) half a loaf *could* be entertained as a "good faith" commitment at the armed truce concluding a first engagement.

But however half-loafey our first temporizings may be, even those initial small gains *must be firmly rooted and couched in terms of acceptable Homophile values*—or we've achieved *nothing*!

> Signed Henry Hay. Published in *The Ladder* 5(10) (July 1961): 16–23.

Notes

1. Del Martin, "Editorial—How Far Out Can We Go?" *Ladder* 5(4) (January 1961): 4–5; W. Dorr Legg, "ONE Midwinter Institute: A Report," *ONE* (April 1961): 7. See also W. Dorr Legg, ed., *Homophile Studies in Theory and Practice* (San Francisco: ONE Institute Press and GLB

Publishers, 1994), pp. 38–39, 185–87, 368–70, 442–45; John D'Emilio, *Sexual Politics, Sexual Communities: The Making of a Homosexual Minority in the United States, 1940–1970* (Chicago: University of Chicago Press, 1983), p. 123.

160

2. This is a reference to the 1959 San Francisco mayoral campaign, in which Democratic candidate Russell Wolden accused incumbent George Christopher of welcoming homosexuals to the city, singling out the presence of the Mattachine Society as evidence (D'Emilio, *Sexual Politics*, pp. 121–22).

3. The government-appointed members of the Wolfenden Commission issued an unexpectedly liberal report in 1957 recommending repeal of sodomy laws. These recommendations were adopted in 1967 (Barry D. Adam, *Rise of a Gay and Lesbian Movement* [Boston: Twayne, 1987], pp. 67, 74).

4. An opinion now borne out by the existence, in the new constitution of South Africa, of a clause banning discrimination *of any sort* against members of the Gay and Lesbian minorities—HH.

"Calling one another into being"

T HE IMPACT OF THE COUNTERCULTURE is clearly apparent in the ideas and language Hay uses in this short essay. Despite its prosaic title, it represents a watershed in his intellectual development. This is apparent from the opening sentence. The defensive concern with Gay male sexuality, the preoccupation with "promiscuity," are gone. In their place, Hay asserts the central tenet of sexual liberation—that sexual expression is central to individuals' psychological well-being, while repression is stultifying and unhealthy.

In 1967, this new vision of sexuality had many exponents, who often cited the works of Wilhelm Reich and Herbert Marcuse. For Lesbians and Gay men, sexual liberation made possible a quantum leap in politics and identity. Sex had always been a problem in the homophile movement—now it was the answer to nearly everything. Gay sex was not only revolutionary in and of itself, it was the path to psychological and spiritual integration. For Hay, however, the freedom to assert Gay sexuality was a means to an end, not an end in itself. It meant that now Gay *relationships*, in all their dimensions, sexual and nonsexual, could be affirmed and explored. This, for Hay, was the brave new world opened up by sexual liberation.

In earlier writings, Hay had sought to connect evidence of the "Berdache institution" with contemporary homosexuals in strictly historical materialist terms, by pointing to their common relationship to a gendered division of labor and society's inherent need to reproduce itself. Here he identifies a commonality between past and present based in the psychological and social experience of Gayness itself—not sexual desire as such, but the experience of being an "outsider" that results whenever one differs significantly from a social

norm. It is this outsider vision, in Hay's view, that led to the institu-
tionalization of roles like that of the shaman and Two-Spirit.

162   Although he draws on the same historical examples he used in the
1950s, Hay now abandons the pretenses of scholarly discourse and
uses this evidence instead to construct an avowedly mythological
account of Gay origins. There are, after all, some truths that only
mythology and mythological images (and literature and art) can convey. In this essay, the validity of Hay's "origin myth" is a function of
its resonance with the contemporary Gay experience of being an
"outsider," as well as its accuracy as a reconstruction of history. It is
on these terms that Hay hopes his readers will judge the historical
accounts he offers—namely, the extent to which his stories capture
the truth of their own personal history.

With this essay, Hay's perspective can be called truly "Gay-
centered." That is, rather than deriving the presence of homosexuals
from features of the social system, he now accounts for homosexuals
first, *then* the features of the social system that have evolved as a
result of that presence. Also apparent is the influence of Lorenz,
whose work inspired Hay to seek deeper meanings of homosexuality
in human evolution. Hay also introduces here the phrase "subject-to-
subject" (later subject-SUBJECT) to describe the kind of "responsible
caring relationships" that social equals can form, which he contrasts
to heterosexual relationships, where the partners are unequal and
perceive their counterparts as "other."

The Homosexual's Responsibility
to the Community

We are coming more and more to realize that the morally
healthy person is he who is capable of realizing his sexual nature to

its fullest potential for growth. Contemporary modes of discourse quite agree that such realizations require persons to be able to relate to one another on a subject-to-subject basis.

At this point modern western man finds himself singularly unsupported by his cultural traditions and by his socio-political sanctions. His ancient world basis of matriarchy—wherein women related to men as objects—was expropriated (rather than resolved) at the ruling-class level by Patrism, wherein men treated women as objects. Judaeo-Christianity, going the brutal Patrist expropriators one step further by subjugating not only women but their children as well as objects, in the intervening two millennia succeeded in corrupting almost the entire population of Western Europe to this betrayal of Species instinct to social bonding we currently refer to as male superiority—male chauvinism—or more simply the almost total comprehension (by men) of women as *objects* . . . Playboy "Bunnies" at the least . . . and captive Lady Governors at the best.

When the earnest ordinary man now turns in deepest sincerity to his woman mate to seek the way of marital friendship and loving companionship, the sickening flood of traditional male-chauvinist accretia pervading every pore and interstice of law and custom appears to subvert his every turn. Audacious voices calling faintly along the wind whisper the Sesame he seeks . . . sexual love between himself as subject and his mate *as subject*. But how is he to perceive such a relationship, let alone achieve even its first step? To do so would seem to mean that our earnest ordinary man must UNlearn 2,500 years of male-chauvinism and UNlearn 2,000 years of Christianity's equating sexual integrity with "EORTHE," earth, filth, evil, Satan.

Unable to find guidance or sustenance from his traditional institutions or from the monstrous social sanctions he is persuaded unwittingly to maintain, is our ordinary man condemned—in his quest—to stumble blindly and alone?

164   Interestingly enough the answer is NO. For it is also in the tradition of the Mediterranean basin, and in the tradition of the waves of expanding populations who successively swept westward over Europe out of the primitive-gardening heartland of the Oxus basin, that persistently there would appear a tiny percentage of persons unsuited to the instituted polarities of sexual specialization conducive to the long-prevailing social objective of population expansion. This tiny percentage of deviant persons might indeed have been apprehended as thwarting (in infinitesimal measure) this institutional polarity which could have become—as did similar inbuilt or instinctual mechanisms in other animal species—an "over" specialization. Permitted to subsist on the fringes of the horde or just "outside" the village-camp, providing he could survive the continuous onslaught of the supernatural powers who harried the no-man's land beyond the village gates, and providing he could develop a rapport with the spirits who equally sojourned there, the deviant outcasts were themselves institutionalized as messengers, intermediaries, interpreters, expendable surrogates, and even far voyagers, between the vast and fearful unknowns of the infinite psychic universe and the microcosm of the material communal reality.

It would be true to say that—traditionally—the Homosexuals have lived outside the village, have been thrust "outside" the protecting sanctions, and "outside" the scope of benevolent and supportive institutional rewards of praise and status. Yet that traditional "outside" place of exile must be understood as a defined and special place . . . a consecrated institution in itself . . . the Temenos, the Acropolis, the Sacred Cave or Cleft, the high places, the riverside, the cross-roads, the ford, the burial place, the Temple. The Homosexuals' "outside place" has always been a special, though proscribed-for-the-unconsecrated section, of the village space . . . a space to be inhabited by what might be seen as one of pre-history's early non-productive Specialists. Begrudged a subsistence, but quite counted upon in turn to repay in selfless thankless servitude, the deviant was expected to observe, and predict, with objective detachment, potential ways and means of easing the convulsive interflows in the subject-to-subject relationship between Gods and men.

It should surprise no one, now that the newest scientific mode of discourse known as Ethology has come of age, that these institutionalized "outsiders"—severely regimented as to social and sanctional space, specifically exempted from the social bondings of marital and reproductive institutions with all their joys as well as their exactions, and *proscribed from engaging in sexual acts deemed sacred, whose practice outside ritual must be seen to have been preemptive and thus* ANATHEMA *to the common weal*—should turn in upon themselves to discover higher reaches of personal and intimate inter-relationships . . . those of sexual and psychic love *between equals* on a subject-to-subject basis. Only here—in the ancient world—could love *between equals* have been explored; and out of the Homosexual's endless bondage to service we may say that the concepts and precepts of conscious love—love neither subordinate to nor subservient to the inbuilt instincts for continuum—were evolved, love not only for a particular and intimate other but love for fellows equally dedicated and devoted.

As Ethology teaches us, once a given instinct—such as that re-direction of aggression known as social bonding—is established in support of whatever function of natural selection, that instinct evolves an independent direction and development of its own. True Homosexuals today, enduring the ceaseless ignorant drivel of psychiatry, and knowing that none of such exorcisms in any way even begin to touch the core of that singing glory they carry within themselves, must now at last recognize that overpowering call *within*—as just such an instinct.

The Rev. Cecil Williams, during the San Francisco Consultation between ministers and Homophiles in August 1966, projected that the finest contribution any Minority had to make to its parent community was the fullest flowering of its own unique diversities. The true Homosexual's responsibility to his or her community to-day is to cultivate and extend his own revered and respected special instinct to the fullest reaches of his sexual personality. The true Homophile Minority's responsibility to Society is to contribute to *all* men and women the harvests we reaped of our long and lonely exile, our knowledge of transcendent sexual wholeness, our errors and lessons learned, our failures and our triumphs, in achieving the higher reaches of love between equals on a subject-to-subject basis. We are responsible to bring within the grasp of ordinary people everywhere, at *whatever* levels we find ourselves, the full integrity of our vision of man's evolved instinct for a responsible caring re-lationship . . . quite independent of the co-conscious concerns of reproduction and child-rearing . . . the conscious and fully sexual calling of one another into being . . . the caring responsibility for a particular other's fullest capacity for sexual and psychic growth, the instinctual call to affectionate bonding between equal com-rades on a subject-to-subject basis.

Originally published in *Concern* 6 (April 1967): 5–6.

"We, these elders, have become
the real enemies of unity"

I N THE FOLLOWING SELECTION, written two years before the
Stonewall riots, Hay offers a sharp critique of homophile leaders, arguing that a more activist posture is crucial to attracting a
new generation to the movement. He hoped to inspire a round of
self-criticism on the part of his peers, the homophile "elders," as
he terms them. He had become convinced that room had to be
made within the homophile movement for younger activists. In
Los Angeles, this meant challenging two organizations, which
had become locked into an ongoing rivalry—ONE, Inc., led by
W. Dorr Legg, and Tangents (later the Homosexual Information
Center), founded by Don Slater in 1965 after breaking with ONE
(and taking most of the organization's library with him). Following this episode, nearly every local Gay issue was subordinated to
the ongoing feud between ONE and HIC.[1]

Hay had become increasingly appalled by the bitter, sometimes
vicious infighting that characterized homophile organizations.
This fractiousness was fostered, in his view, by the reliance on parliamentary procedures and majoritarian voting. Although Hay
maintained open channels to both ONE and Tangents, remaining
a unifying figure in Los Angeles, he vowed never to join an organization that relied on voting, but to advocate instead for the kind
of consensus decision-making that the Mattachine founders had
successfully employed for three years.

Hay had little to lose by referring to his generation—including
Legg, Slater, and others—as "monsters" and "old aunties," terms

certain to strike home among middle-aged Gay men. By this time Hay's harsh judgment of homophile groups and their leaders was widely shared. For younger Lesbians and Gay men the accommodationist stance of the older homophiles made them seem irrelevant, even obstructionist. In 1968, the delegates to the North American Conference of Homophile Organizations in Chicago politely conducted their debates according to Robert's Rules of Order; two weeks later Chicago police were brutalizing young antiwar activists in the same city's streets.

Although the problems of what I term the three D's—dissension, disrespect, and denunciation—are a frequent topic of discussion today among those active in community organizations and political groups, I find it surprising that they are not more often addressed in public forums and the Lesbian/Gay media. I am sure many activists today would join me in wishing that the principles Hay advocates here would be adopted by the diverse elements of today's sexual minorities.

An Open Letter to All Homophile Organizations

Dear Friends:
Many fine men and women in positions of leadership in our numerous Homophile organizations and service groups have come increasingly to see the need to join their efforts by coalition in pursuit of their aims and goals along common fronts of similar but independent endeavors.

The increasing awareness, by an ill-prepared public, of homosexuality in its midst is already giving rise to those ominous oppositions that often crystallize in acts and legislation inimical to the well-being and healthy morale of our total society. Such blind oppositions ever threaten piece-meal destruction of non-unified minorities, making yet more urgent the call to Homosexual organizations to band together lest they be picked off one by one.

Yet in our movement toward one another as organizations, even though we have mounted with the most cautious optimism and with very few expectations, we are appalled by the depth and extent of fear and mistrust of one another that appears the moment we try to join forces. The young and idealistic among us are filled by this with angry despair, while we who have engaged ourselves in Homophile organizations over the years dissipate our energies in futile plays for power alternating with bouts of stagnant self-pity and apathy. Such behaviors ill befit those in whom the disasters and failure of so many bright-eyed endeavors ought to have ripened into wisdom and serenity, with clearer perception of our goals and hopes and a richer knowledge of how to bend means to purposes.

We elders have not yet perceived that we must release ourselves from servile adulation of the now shoddy and worn self-images on which we have lavished our energies over the years. The heart of our Movement's present difficulties is that we elders, old now, are but wickedly wise—merely once vital, are now grown monstrous, blind and destructive.

What deflects the reach for unity in the Homophile Movement is neither the passion and impatience of the young nor the seeming reluctance and lack of response of the middle groups. It is rather the persistence, unabated, in us—the elders—of those pathetic faults and fears that took root in our generation under the terror of the McCarthy, anti-homosexual inquisitions—the paranoia, the unreasonable suspicions of everyone and everything, and the inflation of the ego that mounted, in compensation, in those who dared in such times to move forth in opposition. We, these elders, who yet possessively grasp at positions of power and influence in our organizations, have become the real enemies of unity. The young of today are not as we were—they are far closer to one another; much more ready to extend the hand of fellowship. The middle groups meanwhile suffer in silence the anguish of our obscene struggles with one another, yearning for the day when they will break loose from our strangle-hold.

It is time we elders realize that we need not be such monsters. It is a very short step to one's mirror to see that we are in fact, only *old aunties*, wrinkles and bald pates and all. It is a very short step to get to where we truly are—moved on to the position of service— where not our old resentments, not our outworn concepts, our now shoddy idealisms, our timidities, which are in the main all we have had to show as the product of our experience but the *work*, the work's the thing. Truly, we elders have little else left but to offer all that we are, all that we know, in the service of others.

Yet, this alone is not enough. In utmost humility, we must make prodigious amends. This letter is being written to commend, for your most earnest considerations, the anonymously proposed document (accompanying) which is an open recital of ways of the spirit that should never have had to be stated, being as they are the inmost guides of men and women of true maturity and integrity, in whom they lie too deep for words.

But unless we elders will drink the bitter cup of contrition by making an open espousal of, and giving our deepest inner allegiance to, the principles set forth in the accompanying document,

we shall live to see our dreams, and the dreams of those far wor-
thier than are we, wrenched and defiled beyond belief by counter-
forces of bigotry and unreason.

171

A PROPOSED CODE FOR A COALITION
OF HOMOPHILE ORGANIZATIONS

Preamble:

This document is in two parts. It consists of a summary and reminder of the purposes of our several organizations as they might
relate to a proposed coalition of Homophile organizations. It pro-
poses, secondly, a set of ethical guidelines which we will need to
enable us to cooperatively work together.

Section I
PURPOSES OF ORGANIZATION
Educational Purposes:

1. For too long we have accepted the opinions, the poorly authenticated studies, and misdirected inquiries of psychiatrists and
   others who argue that we are sick and, by implication, weak or
   evil. Only a few people in the scientific fields have found more
   rational ground for discourse and they are too seldom heard. It
   shall be our purpose to encourage research in the creative and
   constructive aspects of homosexuality while at the same time
   endeavoring to enlighten our fellow Homosexuals who may be
   victimized by the idea of sickness.
2. To discover unequivocating words and phrases for ourselves by
   which to clearly articulate what we have always known about
   the meanings and values of homosexuality, and to teach one another potentials of homosexuality as a basis for a creative way
   of life.

3. To provide our non-Homosexual fellow men and women with a clear understanding of these meanings and values and to extend to them their right and responsibility to aid us in making this contributive aspect still more truly and widely recognized.

172

Social Purposes:
1. To enable Homosexuals to establish and maintain for themselves in our society space for living in which to work and play as free citizens.

Reform Purposes:
1. To join with our fellow citizens to reform the laws which harmfully restrict the civil rights of all men and women in the sexual realm.
2. To expose and correct the prevailing social mores which in the area of administrative and social codes harmfully restrict Homosexuals in their right to employment and advancement.

Purposes of Organizational Coalition:
While we rejoice in the wide range of diversity of character and purpose marking our organizations, and the individual persons they comprise, we nonetheless seek, through coalition of our organizations, to further those aspects of the diverse aims and purposes which we can recognize as common to us all. We define coalition as a friendly and trusting collaboration of our organizations with each other in specific projects of common-front or united action.

Section II
ETHICAL GUIDELINES IN OUR ACTION IN COALITION
Because we recognize that real and effective action in coalition is absolutely impossible without trust and confidence in one another,

we wholeheartedly pledge ourselves, both as persons and as organizations, to be guided in our work by the following principles:

1. Each to respect the integrity and the underlying purpose and aims of all the others, withholding neither constructive criticism nor well-earned praise for the acts of others taken in pursuit of those aims.

2. Never in the spoken word nor in any of our publications to attack the character or the motives of those with whom we disagree, but always to restrict our criticisms solely to the argument or action with which we disagree.

3. To freely grant the right of any group or organization to choose not to participate in a course of action adopted by the majority, when the right is claimed before the course of action is crystallized and the reasons for the claiming of the right to refrain are candidly stated.

4. To present at all times to the non-Homosexual community a true picture of ourselves as joined in a common front.

5. In working with one another to discover and implement a specific course of action in coalition, to strive wholeheartedly and speedily to reach a level of agreement in regard to the action at issue. In order to do this we renounce, as far as is humanly possible, the inevitable desire that it be our plan that is exclusively adopted and our ego that is thereby gratified.

6. That we pay particular attention to our various publications and seek in all instances to have them conform with the ethical standards of responsible journalism, both in the areas of reporting and editorializing.

7. In asserting our purposes in Education and Reform we accept that an open and frank confrontation of the general public by ourselves as acknowledged Homosexuals is essential to our goals, and we charge all to support fully those who, to the ends

174

of action in coalition, can and do accept the hazards of such exposure. But such a role is imposed on no one and toward the secret or partly secret groups and organizations among us the freedom not to participate in public action is freely granted.

Signed Henry Hay. Published in *Vector* 3(6) (May 1967): 21, 25–26.

Note

1. See Stuart Timmons, *The Trouble with Harry Hay: Founder of the Modern Gay Movement* (Boston: Alyson, 1990), pp. 215 ff.

"Our goal is *total liberation*"

I N 1969 HAY ONCE again contributed to the crafting of a charter document of the Gay movement—the statement of purpose of the Gay Liberation Front of Los Angeles, adopted that
December following a series of meetings organized by Leo Lawrence, Morris Kight, Hay and others. Hay served as the first
elected chair and proposed that the group reject majority voting
in favor of consensus—the younger activists eagerly embraced the
idea.[1]

In this declaration, Gay liberation is seen as part of sexual liberation, which involves transcending guilt, finding an "antidote" to
social alienation, and offsetting aggression. While Gay liberation
seeks to free all "sexual beings," the specificity and reality of being
homosexual is still affirmed—there is no call for universal bisexuality. Rather, the "natural" state of human sexuality is seen to be
varied and diverse, not homogenous or undifferentiated. Nor are
there speculations about what "causes" or "constructs" homosexuality—only an unqualified affirmation of homosexual presence. Today this would be termed "essentialism" and "identity
politics"—but these were ideals and politics that inspired an
entire generation to come out. Gay liberation, as this document
asserts, was first and foremost *self*-liberation, beginning in self-
acceptance and pride in being Gay. Education and "street actions"
follow from this. At the same time, Gay liberation is seen as one
element of a broad coalition of minorities and disadvantaged
groups seeking "full rights" and "total liberation."

We might ask, what has changed between this statement and
the one adopted by the Mattachine founders in 1951? In terms of

analysis of oppression and plan of action, almost nothing—both
call for identity politics as the basis for a mass movement of
homosexuals as a minority seeking its own freedom, and both
project this movement as part of a broader coalition for social
change. In terms of tone and self-esteem, however, *everything* has
changed. Gone is the fretting over "ethical and social principles"
and providing a "dignified standard" for "social deviants." In its
place is an in-your-face affirmation of homosexual naturalness
and rightness, an utter refusal to make apologies or even respond
to stereotypes—these are all "establishment hang-ups." Such an
attitude, which we take for granted today, was unimaginable,
even to the radicals who founded Mattachine, in the 1950s.

Statement of Purpose—
Gay Liberation Front,
Los Angeles, California

History: 1969 was the Year of the New Homosexual. During that
year new groups, projecting a militant, activist, and determined
viewpoint, began to spring up around the country: Committee for
Homosexual Freedom, San Francisco; Gay Liberation Front, New
York; Gay Liberation Front, Berkeley; Gay Liberation Front, Minneapolis—new ones every week, with the current count at twenty-
five. During December 1969, Gay Liberation Front, Los Angeles,
was founded.

Community of Interest: We are in total opposition to America's
white racism, to poverty, hunger, the systematic destruction of our
patrimony; we oppose the rich getting richer, the poor getting

poorer, and are in total opposition to wars of aggression and imperialism, whoever pursues them. We support the demands of Blacks, Chicanos, Orientals, Women, Youth, Senior Citizens, and others demanding their full rights as human beings. We join in their struggle, and shall actively seek coalition to pursue these goals.

General Methodology: Gay Liberation Front, Los Angeles, will be a one-human, one-vote, non-exclusionary organization, welcoming all concerned homosexuals and sexual liberationists into its association. Decision-making process is by consensus. There is no formal membership; participants are called "Associates." Meetings are weekly, on Sunday at 4:00 p.m. Until further notice we are meeting in the offices of the Homosexual Information Center, as their guests. A future project will be to establish a working center.

Philosophy: We say that homosexuality is a perfectly natural state, a fact, a way of life, and that we enjoy our sexuality, without feelings of inferiority or guilt. We seek and find love, and approach love, as a feeling of loving mutuality. We refuse to engage in discussion of causation, "Sickness" (A LIE!), degrees of sexuality, or any other such Establishment Hang-Ups. We accept ourselves with total self-respect, and respect our associates as they are, not what some social arbiter says they should be.

Self-liberation: One of our foremost goals is to bring all sexual beings into total acceptance of their sexuality. We believe that homosexuals can best serve themselves by accepting the total naturalness of their homosexuality. We believe that, as quickly as possible, homosexuals should find ways to inform their friends, families, employers, and associates of their homosexuality, that through this confrontation might come freedom from gossip, blackmail, guilt feelings, and self-destruction.

Education: We shall as quickly as possible inform one another of our knowledge of life, and then take that knowledge out into the community to educate the Philistines who have for so long made life in America a petrified, joyless Puritanism.

Action: We shall go immediately and militantly to the defense of one another and any homosexual deprived of his [*sic*] right to a joyful, useful, and personal life. Street actions are now being organized, more will come; we shall not waste our energies, however, on irrelevant issues. Our goal is—*total liberation—life is for the living! We are alive! We want all to be alive! Sex is a* sure *cure of boredom and an antidote to the violence that is so American—*

(((((((((((((Power to the People)))))))))))))

Gay Liberation Front, Los Angeles

Adopted December 1969.

Note

1. Hay recalls: "At our second meeting, which, as I remember, may have been in early November, I had been elected chairperson. Morris [Kight] attempted to put through a Robert's Rules of Order type constitution. I told the group about TILL [Committee for Traditional Indian Land and Life] and described 'consensus.' The group loved it. They adopted that whoever participated in the meeting was an 'Associate,' we'd pass the hat instead of dues—you put in what you could afford to share—each meeting would have a 'facilitator,' and decisions would be made by consensus. Morris tried every which way to get it back to parliamentary procedure and voting—to no avail then. (By 1975, through the rise of a new wave of assimilationism, he finally won out.)" Pers. comm.

Through the
Gay Window

1970–1980

HAY'S SPECULATIONS concerning the biological basis of homosexuality did not lead him to make sweeping pronouncements lumping together every instance of it in world history or explaining individual behaviors by reference to genes instead of social context. Rather, his new ideas concerning the origins of homosexuality actually freed him to approach Gay liberation in increasingly spiritual terms. With the stigma of an origin in deviation, accident, or moral failure removed, anchored in the conviction that homosexuality exists because it serves humanity, Hay began to explore the deepest levels of the meaning of being Gay, returning to the questions he first posed in Mattachine: who are we? where do we come from? what are we for?

This change in Hay's approach was apparent in the essay in the previous section, "The Homosexual's Responsibility to the Community" (pp. 162–66). It is even more pronounced in his 1970 address to the Western Homophile Conference, which follows. Hay declares that "we are a Minority of common Spirituality," and he draws specific parallels between Gay oppression and that of women and racial minorities. He also uses for the first time the concept of the "Gay window," later supplanted by "Gay consciousness." Clearly, Hay had absorbed the influences of the 1960s and made them his own—but instead of the Age of Aquarius, his call was for the Community of Free Spirits and Gay liberation was its avatar.

During the years he lived in New Mexico (1970–1979), Hay found himself increasingly dissatisfied with the language and concepts available for thinking about Gay people, and he continued to experiment with both. But phrases alone were no longer enough. At a deeper level, Hay found himself struggling with the basic tenets of his political philosophy—Hegelian-derived dialectics—and the assumption that all natural and social processes were based on the agonistic interaction of pairs of opposites. This went to the core of Marxism, since Marx and Engels had constructed their theory of political economy by applying dialectics.

182

Hay's re-evaluation of Marxism was triggered not only by the obvious failings of the Soviet experience and the homophobia of the American Left, but also by the cumulative effect of the scientific advances of the twentieth century—especially theories such as Einstein's principle of relativity, which undermined the suppositions of Cartesian objectivity, the separation of observing subject and observed object. As Hay put it, science had learned that "Nature *could not be fitted into the binary system.*" Indeed, by the 1960s, the very basis of the scientific claim to truth and authority was being questioned. In "The Hammond Report," Hay noted the trend that has "re-cast Scientific Theory as a 'mode of discourse,' in contrast to its earlier eminence as a series of given dogmatic systems of divinely revealed polarities and irreversible acceptances."[1]

By the 1970s, critiques of Western knowledge, including the way in which it promoted the objectification of others and of nature were common. Indeed, everyone seemed to be seeking a language to talk about the "worldview" of Western societies and what might be its successor. Feminists talked of patriarchal consciousness. Environmentalists and eco-feminists talked of the "disenchantment" of nature. Social and intellectual historians revealed the unscientific core assumptions of Western science by telling its history. Hay, characteristically, took these critiques one step further. If science contradicted the assumptions of dialectics, Marxism had to change if it was to retain its claim to being the

"scientific" theory of social change.[2] Further, if Marxism, in relying on dialectics, fostered the consciousness of objectification—
the common denominator of sexism, racism, homophobia, and   183
social and environmental exploitation—then it was a part of the
problem instead of a solution.

Indeed, the fundamental binary, the one from which all others
can be shown to derive—and the most insidious of all because of
its claim to being natural—is that of male and female. In any
binary system of sexuality and gender, homosexuality will invariably come off looking as derivative, a deviation or an accident of
heterosexual maleness and femaleness. This led Hay to conclude
that Gay oppression itself was rooted in binary ideology. Further,
dialectics project a world in which antagonism and competition
are the natural state of affairs, and Hay had become convinced
that competition was *un*natural for some people, including Gays.
There had to be room for the principles of sharing and cooperation. Hay had become convinced that such ideals were also a part
of "human nature" by his observations among the Pueblo Indians
of New Mexico, functioning examples of highly cooperative and
egalitarian communities.

The breakthrough for Hay occurred when he combined the critique of binarism with his emerging sense of Gay consciousness.
This occurred in April 1976, while writing a letter to a fellow
Leftist. In trying to explain the inner difference he felt as a Gay
child, he described how other boys seemed to consider girls
merely as sex objects, to be manipulated into "giving in," and the
girls, for that matter, seemed to think of the boys as objects, too.
"But HE whom I would *love* would be another ME—not an object
but another *subject*." At this point, as Hay likes to say, he "had a
rush of brains to the head," and the phrase "subject-SUBJECT"
came to mind as the essential characteristic of the kind of relationship he had always dreamed of, while "subject-OBJECT" described

the consciousness based on projecting Others—women, minorities, Gays, animals, nature, and so forth—as alien and non-
184   human, that is, as non-subjects, as objects. At this point,
Hay recalls, he pulled the letter from his typewriter and started
the essay included here, "Gay Liberation: Chapter Two"
(pp. 202–16).[3]

Hay derives subject-SUBJECT partly from the logic of same-sex
relationships. In a society founded on the inequality of genders,
relations *within* genders tend to be where ideals of equality are
developed and practiced. Hay also saw subject-SUBJECT as a
product of the particular experience of growing up Queer in a heterosexual society. Not oriented toward the opposite sex in the
ways our peers are, we sometimes escape indoctrination into the
habit of viewing others as objects, sexual or otherwise. In our
dreams, as Hay so evocatively relates, we imagine our lovers as
subjects, like ourselves, supplements who inspire us, not comple-
ments who supply our sense of inner lack.

The two most important influences on Hay's concept of
subject-SUBJECT were both Gay men—Walt Whitman and
Edward Carpenter. Whitman had made strong political, cultural,
and spiritual claims for love between equals: "I say democracy
infers such loving comradeship, as its most inevitable twin or
counterpart, without which it will be incomplete, in vain, and
incapable of perpetuating itself."[4] Whitman referred to this special kind of bonding as "adhesive love," and the images he used to
represent it were predominantly homoerotic.[5] Carpenter, too,
advocated the political and spiritual values of comradely love,
adding to the formulation his notion of Gay people as "intermediate types."[6]

The essay Hay wrote in 1976 also reveals the influence of a
book that had a seminal impact on the New Age movement—

Louis Pauwels and Jacques Bergier's *The Morning of the Magicians* (published in French in 1960 and in English in 1963). These authors weave together occult legends and recent science with a reinterpretation of the past suggesting that secret societies and esoteric knowledge have been the unseen hand in history. The book is perhaps best remembered for its exposition of the Nazi fascination with magic and the occult. Its more sensational assertions aside, the authors manage to marshal a wide range of evidence hinting at an impending watershed in human history. "It is not the first time in the history of humanity that human consciousness has had to switch to another level," they argue, using what would become one of Hay's favorite images. "In normal life we only use a tenth of our potential resources of attention, prospection, memory, intuition and co-ordination. We may well be on the point of discovering, or rediscovering, the keys that will enable us to open within ourselves doors behind which a mass of new knowledge is awaiting us."[7]

185

It was these authors' speculations on modes of consciousness that most impressed Hay. They wrote: "How does the brain normally work? It functions like an arithmetical machine—a binary machine: Yes, No, Agreed, Not agreed, True, False, I like, I don't like, Good, Bad. In the binary field our brain is unbeatable. . . . We believe that the human brain also can, in certain circumstances, function like an analogical machine. That is to say, it should be able: (a) to assemble everything possible that can be observed about a thing; (b) Draw up a list of constant relationships between the manifold aspects of an object; (c) Become, in a sense, the thing itself; assimilate its essence and discover everything about its future destiny."[8] In "Gay Liberation: Chapter Two," Hay links this notion of analog thinking to his earlier ideas on Gay consciousness and the "Gay window"—the result is

subject-SUBJECT. This concept represents Hay's answer to the
fourth criterion of the national minority formula—shared psychological make-up. However, subject-SUBJECT consciousness
involves much more than a sexual preference or a social identity.
It is a mode of perceiving the world, processing information about
it, thinking about oneself and others, and relating to others, as
well as an ethical orientation.

186

Having pinpointed the source of Marxism's shortcomings in its
binary, subject-OBJECT assumptions and methods, Hay believed
it could be redeemed by supplementing dialectics with the intu-
itive, empathic mode of subject-SUBJECT thinking. From Hay's
perspective, the result is not "post-Marxism"—the abandonment
of materialism, class analysis, or mass-based movements—but
rather the *enspiritment of Marxism*, the integration of human
individuation and politics. Marx and Engels saw humankind's
spiritual nature revealed in its struggle for survival defined as the
avoidance of starvation. For Hay, survival cannot be reduced to
the hunt for food alone but encompasses the religious, cultural,
symbolic, and aesthetic elements of the hunt—and the men and
women who specialize in these functions. There is a purposeful-
ness in natural selection and evolution, an implicit valuation of
the survival of the species, the collective good, over that of the
individual. For Hay, the transcendence of the individual, the discovery that one is part of an interconnected whole, is the truth of
life itself and the essence of spirituality, as well as the source of
political ideals.

In defining human nature in bio-spiritual terms and relating
identities (such as man, woman, Gay, etc.) to emergent properties
in humankind's inherited legacy of survival techniques, biological
and social, Hay provides a basis for recognizing other classes in
addition to the traditional "working class" as agents of social

change. The vision of society that emerges from this interconnection of spirituality and politics is multicultural, cooperative, and decentralized. Rather than objectifying diverse communities as "Other," subject-SUBJECT consciousness fosters the extension of common humanity to all. Affirming the other who affirms you does not require the erasure or denial of difference.

187

For Hay, Gay activism informed by spiritual values is the modern version of the community service traditionally performed by third-gender figures like the Native American Two-Spirit. But Hay stresses that his visions and ideals are a "call"—for those who hear the message in their hearts as well as their minds. A spirit quest can never be imposed, required, legislated, or prescribed, nor can matters of the spirit be reduced to political discourse. But, of course, taking ourselves seriously, inquiring into the nature of our sexuality and its deepest meaning, and loving ourselves and each other for being Gay remain crucial first steps toward liberation. Gay politics thus begins in the realm of the human spirit, and while politics can never take the place of spirituality they eventually lead us back to that realm, as we seek to find the language to express our visions of a better world.

Notes

1. Henry Hay, "The Hammond Report: A Deposition, with Subsequent Commentary on the Conspiracy of Silence anent Social Homophilia," *ONE Institute Quarterly* 6(1,2) (Winter–Spring 1963): 6–21, p. 10.

2. Of course, Hay has not been alone in seeking a mode of thought that transcends dialectics. The school of deconstructive philosophy linked to Jacques Derrida also seeks to deconstruct binaries, albeit in quite different ways.

3. Somewhat similar concepts and even terminology have been employed by other authors, before and after Hay. Martin Buber, for example,

wrote of "I-Thou" relationships in *I and Thou* (trans. Ronald G. Smith [Edinburgh: T. & T. Clark, 1937]), and Paulo Freire gave his ideas a radical political application in *Pedagogy of the Oppressed* (New York: Herder and Herder, 1970). Hay was not aware of other usages, however, when he coined "subject-SUBJECT," and he rightly insists on the unique meaning he gives it. Subject-SUBJECT is not, for example, a synonym for "empathy," which implies one person doing something to another who remains passive, or some other version of middle-class notions of being "nice." Subject-SUBJECT relating requires two active subjects voluntarily engaged in mutual and reciprocal communication. It cannot be exercised unilaterally.

4. Walt Whitman, *The Collected Writings of Walt Whitman*, vol. 9, *Prose Works, 1892*, vol. 2, ed. Floyd Stovall (New York: New York University Press, 1964), 414.

5. Robert K. Martin, *The Homosexual Tradition in American Poetry* (Austin: University of Texas Press, 1979); Michael Lynch, " 'Here Is Adhesiveness': From Friendship to Homosexuality," *Victorian Studies* 29(1) (Autumn 1985): 67–96.

6. Key works by Edward Carpenter include *Love's Coming of Age* (1896), *The Intermediate Sex* (1908), and *Intermediate Types Among Primitive Folk* (1914). In the 1970s, Hay was not alone in asserting that the particular features of relationships between individuals of the same gender could be the source of contributions to politics and/or spirituality. This claim is implicit in many of the contributions to such important Gay liberation collections as Karla Jay and Allen Young's *Out of the Closets* and Len Richmond and Gary Noguera's *The Gay Liberation Book*, and fully developed by Arthur Evans in *Witchcraft and the Gay Counterculture* and David Fernbach in *The Spiral Path*. More recently, Mark Blasius has argued that the "erotic reciprocity" of Lesbian and Gay sexuality, "in which the active partner is only competent to the extent that she or he gives pleasure and in which being the passive 'receiver' of pleasure is an active position" is the basis of a distinct Lesbian/Gay ethic (*Gay and Lesbian Politics: Sexuality and the Emergence of a New Ethic* [Philadelphia: Temple University Press, 1994], pp. 90–91).

7. Louis Pauwels and Jacques Bergier, *The Morning of the Magicians* (1960; London: Granada, 1963), pp. 23, 28.

8. Ibid., p. 239.

"A Spirit call to freedom"

THIS ESSAY, AN ADDRESS to one of the last of the homophile conferences, reflects the transformation in Hay's style and ideas that occurred in the 1960s. The counterculture had cast its spell on him. As Del Martin observed, "This was a different type of Harry Hay than we had seen before—one who was filled with the joy of life and love and spirituality. And one who could speak our language. He was a different character than we knew in the fifties."[1]

In these remarks, Hay uses terms like "Queer" and "Faerie," both of which would later gain popularity as political labels, and he develops an analysis linking sexism, racism, and homophobia—a project he would return to in the 1980s. Even more striking is his use of the phrase "Gay window" to refer to the perspective Lesbians and Gay men acquire as a result of being social and sexual outsiders. The "Gay window" involves not only unique perceptions of social reality and heterosexual ways, but distinct values as well. Hay argues that there is a "communion of spirit" in Gay relationships—that is, relationships between social and psychological equals—that heterosexual relations currently lack because of the social inequality and psychological differences that society fosters between women and men. Hay is not claiming Gay superiority, however. The "Gay window" is simply "a worldview neither better nor inferior—but *athwart*." As such, it has something to contribute to the community at large.

The sense of striving to communicate something so new and different that it escapes ordinary language is apparent not only in Hay's writing style but in his typography as well. In writing this essay, Hay gave full play to his penchant for capitalization and underlining.[2] Indeed, the shift from lower to upper case is a good metaphor for the leap from an old to a new level of consciousness that he calls for. It is his way of signaling new and transformational ideas and raising the discourse on homosexuality to a level heretofore denied it.

Western Homophile Conference Keynote Address

With all the members standing in a circle made suddenly transcendent through the fellowship-power of its crossed-hands couplings, the Moderator requests that they each repeat after him the following:

> Let us hereby resolve that no young person among us need ever take his first step out into the dark alone and afraid again!

Does that sound like some fragment of a Gay Liberation ritual? Well, it is! It is the concluding sentence of the New Member Welcoming Ritual of the *first* Gay Liberation Movement in the United States—the original Mattachine Society, 1950 to April of 1953.

That first Movement called Homosexuals to a brotherhood of love and trust; it called Homosexuals to rediscover their collective—as well as personal—self-respect and integrity. It raised into consciousness, for the first time, the concept of the Homosexual Minority complete with its own subculture, with its own Lifestyles. It struggled to perceive—however dimly and with little language to help it—that, in some measure, the Homosexual Minority actually looked out upon the world through a somewhat different window than did their Heterosexual brothers and sisters. The Homosexual worldview surely deviated in dimensional values from that of its parent society—a worldview neither better nor inferior—but *athwart*.

Rejecting the ultimately unexaminable assumptions of Heterosexual Psychiatry, mired as they were—and still are—in the obsolescent modes of Aristotelian thinking, the first movement called to its own fellowship to search themselves and their several cultures to find out at last "WHAT we are" and "WHO we are." It called to its membership to assemble these findings and then introduce to the Parent Society that widening dimension of spiritual consciousness our contributions would bring. And finally, upon the gift of such contributions, it postulated the integration of our Minority into the Parent Society *as a group*—*not* a "passing" assimilation by individuals but integration by the *total* group—for this was 1950–1953, and Montgomery and Birmingham and Selma still lay in the unpredictable future.

In the scant generation between that largely non-verbal *then* and now, a host of new scientific modes of discourse have flooded us with resources, language, and revelations, to firm up our early hesitant footings—Ethology, Etho-Ecology, Bio-Genetics, Cultural-Genetics, to name a few. Penetrating voices, speaking in these dimensions that presage new horizons of higher consciousness for the Spirit of Man, have caught the ear of the new generations who would be free—Konrad Lorenz, R. D. Laing, Herbert Marcuse. And within their contexts, *we are there*—if we will but seek at last to define and disclose ourselves.

In the long years between the miscalculations of, and the headlong flight of brothers from, that first dream of Liberation and its rebirth in the Spring of 1969, the many elements of the earlier Society—continually grouping and regrouping—devotedly attempted to retain such basic principles of the Mattachine Idea as were salvageable when the root thinking (the radicalism motivating and inspiring the original vision) had been precipitated out. Adjusting their sights to the more tried-and-true forms of the middle way, the new groups sought respectability rather than self-respect, parliamentary individualism rather than the collective trust of brotherhood, law reform and quiet assimilation rather than a community of rich diversity within the Family of Man. One might say that they sought to be exactly the same as the D.A.R. [Daughters of the American Revolution]—except in bed.

This is not to say that the long and futile struggle of the Homosexual Minority Movement to wear shoes that could never fit did not have its gallant and contributive aspects. For it did—and a number of the consequences are far-reaching. Occasionally these managed momentarily to deodorize spots in our putrefying society within which the organizations wheel-and-deal. Also, in the larger healthier growing edges of social consciousness, Homophile organizations have postulated several right questions—albeit for mostly the wrong reasons.

Yet—for all that—until now, the head count of the memberships throughout the United States was never able to equal the thousands who rallied, in California alone, to the original Mattachine Idea between 1950 and 1953.[3] Why do the shoes of middle-class respectability and conformity never seem to fit? Why do our essays at right questions time and again bear witness that we postulated wrong reasons? Why is it that Homosexuals presumably high-principled and disciplined enough to join and serve the Minority's Democratically-run Service Organizations comprise so small a percentage of the Minority? Why is it that non-organized Homosexuals—in their thousands over the years—opine smugly that

Homosexuals kid themselves when they think they can effectively organize at all—because they really have nothing in common but their sex drives? Why? Why? *WHY?*

Because . . . when the Queens of closet rank chose to seek respectability by turning their backs resolutely on their brothers and sisters of the Street, they shut out from their perspectives the first and primary task laid upon the Minority by the Original Mattachine Vision—the task of discovering "What *are* we?" and "*Who are* we?"

We Homosexuals know much about ourselves that we've never talked about—even *to* ourselves. History knows much about us that it doesn't know it knows—but *we* could recognize it if we would look. Myth and Legend, Tradition and Folk-ways know much about us that has been deliberately obscured by endless politically motivated Conspiracies of Silence—*which we can explode if we will.* As the Free Generation and the Third World have revealed beyond any possibility of longer denying it, our vain-hallowed culture is slowly sinking into a veritable kitchen midden of obscenely generated *unexamined assumptions*, learned by rote, inherited without question, and having not one shred of a basis for possible justification in the modern world. That the three largest oppressed Minorities in the United States today are victims of politically motivated unexamined false assumptions, sanctimoniously parading as religious *Revelations* of our Hallowed Western Civilization, should come as no surprise.

From the marriage of Hellenistic philosophy and Judaeo-Roman politics, projected to God-head and named Christianity, we proudly inherit through *Revelation* the unassailable proof that *Women are inferior.* From the Divine Revelations of Renaissance Humanism, and the Reformational Elect, we inherit the unassailable proof that *both Women and non-Whites are inferior.* From the

White Anglo-Saxon Protestant "Best of all Possible Worlds" we inherit the unassailable proof that *both non-whites and Queers are inferior.*

194

Second-class citizens *all*—it should not be surprising that as oppressed and harried Minorities *we three* learned lessons and share certain levels of consciousness in common. As with the largest oppressed Minority—Women—the Homosexual Minority knows the shape and substance of Male Chauvinism—we too have lived under its lash all our lives. As with the second largest oppressed Minority—the non-Whites—the Homosexual Minority knows the bitter harvest of being the Village Nigger!

Women know that no man has ever been able to describe or project what it means to be, and to feel like, a self-appreciating woman. Yet she does not need to be explained or defended. She is existential. She IS! Today Blacks are making it unmistakably clear that no *Whiteman* has ever been able to describe or project what it means, and feels like, to be a self-appreciating Black. Nor does he need to be explained or defended. He is existential. He IS! Homosexuals know that *no Heterosexual man* has ever been able to describe, or begin to project, what it means to be, and feel like, a self-appreciating Homosexual. To update Descartes, *cogito ET SENTIO ergo sum!* [I think *and* I feel, therefore I am!] And for each of our three Minorities, *to know this is to make us free within ourselves,* and requires us (whether we like it or not) to move to social consciousness, and foretells our several potentials as allies in the struggle for the new world a-coming.

What *is* it that we know of ourselves that no Heterosexual as yet has begun to perceive? It is that we Homosexuals have a psychic architecture in common, we have a Dream in common, man to man, woman to woman. For all of us, *and for each of us*, in the dream of Love's ecstasy—the God descends—the Goddess descends—and for each of us the transcendence of that apotheosis is mirrored *in the answering glances of the lover's eyes.* FOR WE SHARE THE SAME VISION—Like to Like. Heterosexuals do not partake of such a communion of spirit. Theirs is . . . other. And—in this mating of like to like—what is it we seek? Not the power and vanities of dynasty, not wealth or property, not social contract or security, not status, nor preferment, as does the Parent Society. We seek union, *each with his similar*—heart to mirroring heart—free spirit to free spirit!

We are a Minority of a common Spirituality, we are a Free People—and we have always been so—throughout the millennia, each in his generation! No allegiance, no sanctions, no taboos or prohibitions, no laws have ever been encompassing enough or powerful enough to stand between us and the pursuit of our Dream. It was no accident, no poetic stroke of whimsy, that translated our persons—in the King James Testament—as "Fools," nor translated our vision quests as "folly." Tradition knew us well—"Fools rush in where Angels fear to tread!" Throughout our millennia we were, and are now, in faithful service to the Great Mother—Earth—Nature, and in loyal service to her children—the people who preserved the Great Mother's ecological harmonies, both psychically and materially, in the ritual of their everyday lives. To those of the communities who granted us respect and acknowledged our integrity, we gave loyalty beyond ordinary measures of endurance—*Les Sociétés Joyeuses*, or Fool Societies, of Feudal and Monarchical France give ample testimony to that. *But*—to tyrants, and to alien usurping Gods, the clear unflagging flame of our Dream was, and remains still, heresy, treason, witchcraft—the unforgivable sin. Towards the expropriators of the Spirit of Man we Homosexuals are forever alien; in their eyes we are forever Anathema!

We Homosexuals are a Minority, who share each other's Dream whether we speak the same language or not, who share a common psychic vision whether we share the same cultural make-up or not, all the days of our years. Though we are born with all the aggressive fighting instincts of our common humanity, the psychic architecture—characteristic to our Minority natures—begins to reshape and redirect these vital energies with almost the first stirrings in us of spiritual consciousness. The aggressive competitiveness, taken for granted as an eternal verity by our Heterosexual Parent Society, in us *redirects*, under the guidance of the Blueprint of our Minority nature. In us, this genetic redirection transforms our perceptions of unconsciously inherited animal Maleness or Femaleness into appreciations of—nay even a life-long passion to call forth, to call into being—the grace and tenderness *behind* that competitive strength, the humility and compassion *behind* that territorial ruthlessness, in our fellow siblings of the Great Mother. For grace and tenderness, humility and compassion are revealed to *us* as being implicit in the *aspect*—the spirituality—of the Masculine Ideal, the Feminine Ideal. He who answers, she who answers, our call into being is our *like*, our *similar—the one who finds in our aspect the ideal we find in his*—that ideal which we can understand in him, in her, and cherish in ourselves, because we share its outlook in common. This shared commonality of outlook is a worldview totally unfamiliar to the accrued experience of our Parent Society. It is a view of the life experience *through a different window*.

The Free Generation, the young Millions now striving to perceive the dimensions of the Family of Man, also seek to achieve that redirection of the fists of territorial aggression into the compassionate hand-clasp of the Community of Spirit. That capacity for redirection has characterized our Minority from the beginning. We were its proving-grounds in the processes of natural selection. We carried—we carry—through the millennia of lived experiences, the promise that one day all mankind might be able to learn to make that redirection manifest.   197

For three hundred years, our useful contributive past in Western Culture has been pulverized and effaced by deliberate politically motivated Conspiracies of Silence. In this hell of Anomie, we of the Homosexual Minority have been reduced to semi-conscious rudderless wanderers, driven like sheep to conform to social patterns which atrophied our perceptions and shredded our souls, beset on every side by the bacilli of—to us—alien value-judgments which riddled the very sinews of our Dream. But now, even in this late hour, there is a light at the end of our long tunnel. There are voices on the wind giving dimensions to the freeing of the *Spirit* of Man. The time is *now* for our Minority to begin at last to comprehend what we have known for so long. The time is NOW for us to speak of, and to share, that which we have lived and preserved for so long. The reappearance of the "Gay Liberation Ideal" calls to each of us to stoke anew the passionate fires of our particular vision of the Community of Spirit. The breathtaking sweep of "Gay Liberation" challenges us to break loose from the lockstep expectations of Heterosexual life patterns so obliterating of our natures. Even the Free Generation, seeking a widened angle of worldview, challenges us to throw off the Dream-destroying shackles of alien thought that we may exhibit, at long last, the rich diversities of our deviant perceptions.

To liberate our Minority lifestyles, we first must explode once and for all the obscene unexamined assumptions by which *we bind ourselves* into the obsolescent social conformities—as for instance our concern with "Image." I conform to no Image; I define myself. *We define ourselves!* To a people who would be free images are irrelevancies. Again, we assume that to govern ourselves we must

198

enact forcible restraints upon each other, and that the cumulative detriment will be negligible so long as these restraints are patently disguised as "Democratic" procedures. In this field, the great unexamined assumption is that Robert's Rules of Order achieve a maximum of free expression within a minimum of collective restraints. To the competitive, to the territorialists, to the ego-ridden, to the status-seekers of our decaying Society the parliamentary coercions of "majority" votings—of special interest lobbyings, of cloak-room obligations cunningly connived, of filibusterings and steam-rollerings—do appear to provide a set of minimal repressions whereby the random aggressions of delegates may be controlled. The sad truth is that, because of the failure of the Spirit of Man to surface into collective consciousness in our Western Society, these procedures serve only to assure the continued *domination of the pecking order*.

All this is *not* of us! These are the shoes that *never* have fitted us; these are the shackles of alien thought that—brainwashing us to accept a worldview through the *wrong* window—hold us to our bondage. Our Homosexual Liberation Movement *must* consist of far-ranging Communities of Free Spirits.[4] What have Free Peoples to do with politely masked repressions of one another? With coercions or with laying claims upon one another? What have Free Peoples to do with the voting principles that divide people from one another, or with the pretentious mounting of resolutions? Each of these restrictions seeks to shame and cajole the many to conform to the ego-mania or the wishful-thinking of the few. Have we permitted our perceptions to become so atrophied that we can allow fellow Homosexuals, or ourselves for that matter, to be *vulnerable* to being shamed and cajoled by brainwashed sell-outs in our midst? Being shamed and cajoled by pressures inimical to our natures has been the ever-present bane of our Homosexual

life-experience; we are past masters in the arts of dissembling and/
or vanishing under an invisible cloak whenever such pressures
threaten.

The Community of Free Spirits is not just a fantasy in the minds
of wool-gatherers such as I. It has a history of long-lasting and ex-
ceedingly viable Societies outside of Western Europe (and even of
smaller contained communities within Western Europe) to recommend it. Anthropologists, who in recent years have learned to
perceive societal systems as things-in-themselves wholly within the
context of their own self-developed referents, confess that individual lifestyles within such systems are more free than lifestyles conceived in Western Civilization. Our Homosexual Liberation Ideal
mandates such a community of Free Spirits. Not for us the constructions of political parties, of leaders who presume to speak for
us, of experts who conspire to think for us, of alliances that obli-
gate us to act in the name of others or that permit others to expro-
priate the use of ours. We come together in a voluntary sharing of a
spiritual outlook. We touch hearts. Together we grow in consciousness to generate issues, *and actions upon these issues*, which make
manifest the fleshing out of our shared world-vision.

We consense, we affirm and re-affirm the Free Community of
Spirit, we acknowledge a spokesman to voice our thinking when
such voicings seem called for. Sometimes we may do a thing together and so we will act in the name of the Community. Other
times we are, each or several, off on our own thing and here we act
in the name of the self-liberated (or in the name of the group, de-
pending entirely upon the specific group's feelings in the matter).
BUT—within this Community—let the Spirit be betrayed, let coercion or opportunism attempt to bind any of us against our will
—and PRESTO, like the Faeries of Folk-lore, suddenly we are no
longer there. Shame me, call me names, resolve me to a position I

do not share, couple me to an opinion I do not hold, vote my presence to an action against my grain—and I'm *long* gone. "Once bitten, twice shy!"

200

Our Faerie characteristic is our Homosexual Minority's central weakness—and paradoxically also the keystone of our enduring strength. For whether we are self-liberated or still self-imprisoned within the territorial conformities of our oppressors, we Homosexuals are moved to answer *only* when the call is to the special characteristics of our psychic natures. We Homosexuals are moved to act *only* when the call—as heard in our hearts—is a Spirit call to freedom.

> Signed Henry (Harry) Hay. Delivered at the Western Homophile Conference, Los Angeles, February 13–14, 1970. Published in *The Ladder* 14(9–10) (June–July 1970): 13–17.

Notes

1. Stuart Timmons, *The Trouble with Harry Hay: Founder of the Modern Gay Movement* (Boston: Alyson, 1990), pp. 224–25.

2. Hay explains that he would have used italicization if it had been available; much of his capitalization here has been rendered in italics.

3. See Marvin Cutler, ed., *Homosexuals Today: A Handbook of Organizations and Publications, 1956* (Los Angeles: ONE, Inc., 1956), p. 31.

4. Hay had in mind the medieval communist heresy, Brethren of the Free Spirit, which preached sexual freedom and other radical doctrines (Norman Cohn, *The Pursuit of the Millennium: Revolutionary Millenarians and Mystical Anarchists of the Middle Ages*, rev. ed. [New York: Oxford University Press, 1970], chap. 8).

"Subject-to-SUBJECT,

equal to equal, sharer to sharer"

I N MAY 1970, a few months after delivering the previous selection, Hay and Burnside moved to New Mexico. The couple was soon immersed in the local political scene, networking with Chicano activists, Native American traditionalists, nearby Lesbian collectives, and Gay students from Albuquerque. Inwardly, however, these were years of intense intellectual turmoil for Hay. In Los Angeles, he had been swept up by the excitement of the counterculture and its ideas, from its coalition politics reminiscent of the Popular Front to its visionary, even millenarian rhetoric of a dawning New Age. He had begun using terms like "Gay window" and, in 1972, "Gay consciousness" more or less intuitively. But what, exactly, did they refer to? What were the contents of a Gay consciousness? Now Hay sought to seriously reconcile these new ideas with his long-held Marxist convictions.

The more he thought about it the more he felt the need for a comprehensive synthesis of his ideas. Eventually this led him to question many assumptions of Marxist theory that he had previously taken for granted. In the following essay, Hay argues that the shortcomings of Marxism are due in part to its reliance on dialectics, which is a form of binary thinking based on the Cartesian separation of observer and observed, subject and object. The next evolution in human consciousness, he concludes, will be based on "analog thinking," in which this separation is no longer presumed. In trying to find words to describe this mode of thought Hay coined the phrase "subject-SUBJECT" (not remembering that he had used a very similar phrase, "subject-to-subject," nine years earlier). The concept of subject-SUBJECT consciousness provided the synthesis Hay had been seeking, encapsulating in a single, talismanic phrase what he had been trying to convey about the worldview and the values fostered by an emotional orientation to bond with one's own gender.

202

Gay Liberation: Chapter Two
Serving Social/Political Change
through our Gay Window

A POSITION PAPER

It is important to say, at the outset, that the following is written from the Gay Masculine point of view. We fully respect the comprehension that Feminine Consciousness is quite different from Masculine Consciousness—and that Gay Feminine Consciousness may be very different *indeed* from Gay Masculine Consciousness. Insofar as it is known to the writer, the Gay Women have not addressed themselves to the matters about to be discussed. Until they do so, it would be hubristic for any Masculine writer to presume either their assent to, or their inclusion in, propositions such as the ones here being thrashed out. If our Sisters would choose to come to such Conferences as the writer hopes these remarks may engender and thrash out these new insights and intuitions with us, the outreachings and outpourings of our love shall surmount all obstacles.

In 1878, when Engels was writing his *Landmarks of Scientific Socialism*, the Grand Science of Aristotelian classifications and categories, of Cartesian analysis, of Newtonian Formulae, was at last

firmly ensconced within the long-sought upward-sweeping spiral unlocking the last secrets of the Universe. Objective Analysis, wholly in the control of the Experimenter as detached observer—also referred to as the Dialectic or Binary perspective—in ascendance triumphantly leveled the last barriers in Physics and Chemistry to irreducibles. Great Thinkers on the Human Condition could declare with certainty that "all things in Nature will soon be knowable to Man." Within a decade the great French Chemist, Berthelot, would be able to write "from now on there is no mystery about the Universe."[1] It was regarded as established beyond all doubt that the Sun was composed of incandescent coal. Light waves were transmitted in Space through Ether. Time, Matter, and Energy were all absolutes. All events throughout the Universe occurred simultaneously. Matter consisted of a fixed number of elements, none of which could be turned into another, nor could matter be transformed into Energy.

It was a time of swelling triumph, the pre-Dawn already savoring and anticipating the inaugural of the Intellectual and Scientific Millennium. Cartesian analysis had laid everything bare. Physics thus was a subject totally exhausted—no more mysteries there. Biology, too, had revealed all its secrets. And then, suddenly, giddily, with the advent of the year 1887—sweeping, *overwhelming* DISASTER! (Great Authorities in many branches of Science would, *and even today still do*, go down to their graves in absolute despair—never being able to comprehend *what* had gone wrong.) The Michelson-Morley experiment of that year made continued belief in the Ether impossible and in so doing also demolished forever the logical basis upon which nineteenth-century science had been built, the dependence upon models derived by "common sense," i.e., ordinary life-experience. Freud had already demonstrated that the *intentioned* objectivity in the social sciences of that cornerstone of nineteenth-century Absolutism, "the detached observer," was an impossibility. With the establishing of the Heisenberg "uncertainty principle," these rigid articles of the Scientific Faith—"the Detached Observer" and "Absolute Objectivity"—were driven out of the last stronghold, Physics.[2] The Curies, in 1898, negated the contentions of Berthelot by demonstrating that elements *do* indeed transmute themselves into other elements. Dr. Marie Curie had isolated, and thus in effect had discovered, Polonium (to be followed later by Ionium and Radium) from the element Uranium—eventually demonstrating that Radium itself breaks down into the elements Helium and Lead. Worse—for the continued relevance of the concept of the Unity of Opposites—the Curies' work consolidated Roentgen's discovery of the X-ray in 1895, and verified A. H. Becquerel's discovery of Radioactivity in Uranium in 1896. The principles involved in X-rays and in Radioactivity blasted the rock-solid certainty of the heretofore proven principles of the Conservation of Mass and the Conservation of Energy—by demonstrating *the equivalence* of Mass and Energy, by demonstrating the one could be transformed into the other at will.

With the Einsteinian negation of the simultaneity of Time, Newtonian Mechanics was wholly dethroned. The logics of Reason and of "Common Sense" were finally recognized as no longer valid as tools in the comprehension of Nature. In the new Physics, propositions could be *both* true and false: an entity could be at once continuous and discontinuous, since Light, for instance, must be accepted *as both* a discontinuous particle *and* a continuous wave. Though our brains function in, and our languages are limited to,

Binary (at best Dialectical) dimensions—by 1900 it had been once-and-for-all demonstrated that Nature *could not be fitted into the Binary system which governs the workings of our brain in its nor-*

mal state. Good-bye to the nineteenth-century dream that Man would one day CONQUER Nature, that Man could *objectify* Nature (or anything else, for that matter)—in effect territorially seize her, bend one or more of her powers to his will out of the context in which it had been developed, manipulate her, control her. The new Physics had, in actuality, dethroned the Hetero Chauvinist Sexist Arrogant *Man-god himself!*

To comprehend the new data, Science has had to move from the Aristotelian-Cartesian logics of Binary-analytical-classifying objective thought to "analog" thought, from formula-type thinking in categories to modular thinking, from two-dimensional inter-processes of *Dialectical* thinking to three-dimensional or *triangulational* thinking. Whereas the BINARY, or digital, computer studying a given problem functions in terms of opposites—in terms of Go/No-Go, true or false, yes or no, add or subtract, A or B, man *or* woman, with nothing in between according to the Aristotelian "Law of the Excluded Middle"—the ANALOG computer, in studying a given problem, essays to *become the problem,* by becoming a three-dimensional map or model of the problem. To further illustrate the profound difference between the two computers, whereas, in the Binary thinking process inherited from Aristotle via the Renaissance, the Researcher (under the false assumption that he could be a detached observer) *objectifies* the problem, finding ways and means to fit the components of the problem (bending them a little occasionally) to his manipulatable formulae of irreducible opposites, in the ANALOG thinking process the Researcher attempts to study the problem *subjectively*—he attempts, as the saying goes, to get inside it, to appreciate what it has to share, to respect it. The old obsolete approach was the way of arrogance, with the certainty of conquest taken for granted. The new approach is one of humility with a willingness to live in doubt.

Science, with the aid of its newly developed ANALOG-type technology, can and has moved forward in step with these enormous breakthroughs in perceptions of the Natural World. But the Social Sciences—Anthropology, Sociology, Psychology, Philosophy, History, Political Science—are all still caught up in the straitjackets of Cartesian-limited nineteenth-century thought. Every single one of these disciplines *still* presupposes the false illusion of the "detached observer." Every single one of these disciplines still presupposes that it can objectify its sphere of study. Every single one of these disciplines is still shackled with the limitations of traditionally inherited Binary thinking—arithmetical propositions such as plus or minus, add or subtract (electric calculators all multiply and divide as super-functions of adding or subtracting), Yes or No (mechanisms of the Binary Democratic process), Go or No-Go (if you're not a man you're a substitute woman—what else is there?)—and analysis by classifications and categories examined by arithmetical logic and the results *abstracted* and then *even further reduced* in order to be fitted into measurable formulae (in Sociology people are reduced to formulae of behavior, and behavior in turn is further reduced by being fitted to "roles")—the *exact opposite* of the ANALOG thinking process of map-making, of model-making, where you keep *putting in* as much data as possible—*not taking it out*. Thus, even propositions examined dialectically in terms of fundamental opposites in processes of interrelationships—however the imagination leaps and thrusts at the barriers of consciousness to find new organic processes by which to encompass in the Humanities a parallel to the Scientific breakthroughs—*are still functions of the Binary Mind*.

In the above regard it must be perceived that Marx and Engels, writing and pondering considerably *prior* to Science's point-of-no-return confrontations of 1887–1906, and its historic qualitative leap forward from the obsolete logics of reason and "common sense," nevertheless were themselves anticipating such a leap. The tools they derived from their own "breakthrough" Theory of Historical Materialism, and their praxis of applying its hypothetical components, such as the principles of the Unity of Opposites and of the Negation of the Negation, to the political struggles of their times were then and are now *precisely those exercises by which the Human Mind acquires the skills and dexterities to make the qualitative leap from Binary to Analog thinking.* The one perception they were unable to experience, because they both were dead before the Heisenberg "uncertainty principle" had been arrived at, was the need to re-orient the focus of their concern from objective to subjective dimensions. So exemplary had been their integrity in testing their theories against the best scientific thinking available in their day, they would have been in the forefront of those negating the proven-to-be-obsolete competitive territoriality of deforming Nature to Man's willful control (which Lysenko, attempting to objectify Genetics to fit his Binary illusions, *would attempt in their name* in the 1950s—the after-effects of which the Soviet food-production efforts are still suffering from).[3] They would have had no difficulty in relating to the subjective respect which EMPATHY requires of all those who seek to learn how to fit into someone else's shoes—for, in illustration after illustration, this is exactly what both of them, independently, did in developing the magnificent models from which they derived the principles of Historical Materialism. And here, the process of model-making is identical, alike for the researcher in History or Ethology: one steeps one's self in all the observations that one's Binary functions can deliver. Then

208

one invokes Inspiration to flash upon a model that can organize, correlate, and combine into a usable concept the chaotic mass of information gathered. This preliminary having been accomplished, one learns, through the crutch of the model and the exercise of Empathy, *to become the problem* (subjectively) and to feel in the very tissues of one's intuitions the generative processes that will birth the problem's resolution. Surely Engels's essay "The Mark" was the product of just such a resolution,[4] while Lewis Henry Morgan's unfortunate theory of "progressive evolution" (eventually to be utterly negated by both Biology and Ethology) *was not*!

The way out of our comprehensional stalemate, the quagmire into which the Binary inheritances of our brain-training and our cultural superstructure have hurled us, would appear to be to find ways to activate the seven-eighths of our minds which up to now have not been made responsive to consciousness. Humanity must expand its experience from persons (subjects) thinking objectively, thinking competitively—in a nutshell, thinking *opportunistically* and nearly always in terms of self-advantage—to thinking subject-to-SUBJECT, equal to equal, sharer to sharer, to thinking in terms of loving-sharing. Humanity must expand its experience to thinking of another, that other, *not as object*—to be used, to be manipulated, to be mastered, to be *consumed—but as subject*, as another like him/her self, another self to be respected, to be appreciated, to be cherished.

But might Humanity, this late in the evolutionary process, find the inspiration to so drastically alter the course of its social development? And, if so, where might guides and mentors be located? Interestingly enough, in this regard, we have an unexpected resource in the (even now not too well understood) findings of Charles Darwin. Natural Selection, early on in human evolution, set into the evolving whirl a small percentage of beings who appeared to counterbalance a number of prevalent characteristics of the emerging Human conformity. Humanity, thus, would be wise to finally give consideration to these deviants in their ranks—the Gays—to begin to grant them the peace and the growing space they will need to display and to further develop in communicable words and in models of activity the "gift," *the singular mutation* we Gays have been carrying so unfalteringly and preserving so passionately even over the centuries of despair and persecution since the Great Mother Nature breathed the first incandescent spark into our primevals. For the Gift, of course, is that ANALOG VISION through our Gay Window *by which we perceive the world in Gay Consciousness* IF WE WILL BUT GRASP IT, FLESH IT OUT, EXERCISE IT AFFIRMATIVELY!

Operating with ANALOG VISION is where our Gay Potential has been all along. Each of us has exercised this function over and over, *never necessarily knowing that we did so*, even as our Gay Brothers have perceived magnificent overviews of their parent world from their Gay windows over the millennia (Plato's vision of his "Republic" is a case in point) never guessing that their Hetero *Binary*-fitted siblings couldn't even conceive of the *three*-dimensional models *we Gays thought everybody saw*. Each of us has exercised this function over and over in order to preserve the beautiful Dream in his heart while managing to move and function *somewhat* unnoticed and unremarked through the mazes of Hetero conformities that comprise the environs of our parent societies:

- Non-competitively inclined since earliest memories, non-aggressive, kicked out of the nest too young because we smelled wrong to Papa's and/or siblings' unconscious compulsions toward bio-cultural inheritances *to which we do not incline*, we worked hard in our heads to make models of their unconsciously inherited unexamined assumptions so that we could learn *consciously* the behavior role-plays they so easily and so simply took-for-granted;

· Seeking our alter-egos, our loves, our Golden Dreams—not as objects to be bent to our will but as subjects, as equals— equals to be respected and cherished.

The Hetero monogamous relationship is one in which the participants, through bio-cultural inheritance, traditionally perceive each other as OBJECT. To the Hetero male, woman is primarily perceived as sex-*object* and then, only with increasing sophistication, as person-*object*. The Gay monogamous relationship is one in which the participants, through non-competitive instinctual inclinations *and contrary to cultural inheritances*, perceive each other as Equals and learn, usually through deeply painful trials-and-errors, to experience each other, to continuously grow, and to develop *with* each other, *empathically*—as SUBJECT. The Gay Lover's relationship is actually hindered by his cultural inheritance. The pleiotropisms[5] of his non-competitive instinctual inclinations permit him, at the beginning at least, to *perceive* his vision, his dream of the lover *empathically as Equal and as Subject* (the supreme example of ANALOG VISION—even if we don't know that we know it, and don't understand that we exercise it; learning after all is more often than not merely finding out about what we already know). But so continually are we bombarded by the Madison Avenue techniques of our social environment (the inescapable Church/Family in the olden days) that the moment we embark upon a relationship we find ourselves unconsciously *objectifying* one another, attempting in one way or another to dominate, to get our way, to gain or abstract sympathy—rather than to give empathy *or indeed to become empathic*. To dominate the beloved *is to*

destroy the Equal! How piercingly our Gay Brother Oscar Wilde
said it in "The Ballad of Reading Gaol," "Yet each man kills the
thing he loves/By each let this be heard!" Learning to live with, *and*
to grow with, one's Equal is a long and wracking process concerning which there exists neither arcane lore nor contemporary recorded experience to guide or advise. To call another into being, to
continuously challenge one's self *and that beloved other*, into
being and becoming the total exponents of that soaring growth
and development each is capable of—the Love-Dream and ANA-
LOG VISION of Equals—is what the Gay monogamous relationship is all about!

211

Our Gay Window on the World affords us ANALOG VISION, a
most revealing triangulational "fix" on the Hetero world folks and
their tragically destructive objective relationships with each other,
if we will but grasp it:

· Thinking about *thinking about* being Gay and learning, as
  Gays, to apply Gay Consciousness *to thinking* is the actual
  model by which we teach ourselves to function with ANALOG
  Consciousness. This can be one of the ways by which we
  prepare ourselves to bring the gift of our "mutation" to the
  service of our Hetero brothers and sisters—no, rather to the
  eleventh-hour last-ditch redemption of us all. And, most
  significantly, as we closely examine this process we shall find
  ourselves learning to become proficient in the exercise of the
  "Unity of Opposites" and the "Negation of the Negation,"
  and the quantifying of meta-(beyond)-Binary experiences as
  preparation *preliminary* to the qualitative leap to the new
  levels of perceptual dimensions now required if Society is to
  remain viable.
· Thinking about applying Gay Consciousness to the very

212

nature of our power-potential to triangulate through our Gay Window the Heteros' traditionally objective or Binary experience has much to teach us about ANALOG model-making and, in time, about how to transmit that knowledge to interested Heteros. Above, we talked about how the Scientist and the Historical Materialist prepare themselves to conceive the particular model needed in a given relationship—but this was a highly disciplined *Binary* approach. What we invoke here is the subjectively *felt* experience common to the background of most Gays. Thinking about how we thought about that mysterious tingling something-golden-someday-promise (what was going to turn out to be Gay Consciousness later) suddenly reveals to us that we each made (had to make) in our heads not a two- but a THREE-dimensional model of how Hetero boys and girls seemed to relate to each other in mysterious taken-for-granted ways, in order to teach ourselves how to do likewise, so as not to be unduly victimized for our differences. To the extent that we were able to trigger the girls into responding to us in the same way as they responded to the Hetero boys, we succeeded—learning in the process more about how the Hetero Genders react to themselves and to each other *than they are likely to know about themselves and about each other*. (We hardly could be expected to know that such performances as ours were perfect illustrations of the world-famous Stanislavsky techniques commercialized and degraded in America by Lee Strasberg as "Method Acting.")

It is this Gift—this mutational potential, implicit in most Gays, of initiating and developing Modular comprehensions and then, through empathy, being able to become the modular Daemon of

that comprehension in subject-to-subject relationships of equals—
that Gays have to contribute to those groups who seek social
change through radical alternatives. It is this triangulational vi-   213
sion, this seeing-around-corners of mostly unconscious Hetero
community gender-role interplays that we can offer through the
gently mocking healing laughter-magicks of "Camp." Our use of
self-mocking but self-loving laughter, as a corrective for error, and
as a healer, may help our Hetero brothers and sisters learn the art
of penetrating criticism and self-criticism as a way to help the loving-sharing society function more truly. With this Gift of being
Gay, this Gift of an ANALOG, modular, triangulating vision of
the world through our Gay Window when exercising Gay Consciousness with high integrity, Gay Radicals should find themselves called upon to constitute an *independent*, collectively self-
motivated, self-disciplined caucus in every radical organization or
group. The Gay Radical Caucus must be dedicated, as our Gay
Brother Socrates so characterized himself long ago, as the Gay
Conscious Gad-flies of the radical movement. As such Gay Conscious Gad-flies, they would constantly challenge assumptions,
constantly confront motivations from the standpoint of analog-
type, or *three-dimensional* value judgments, and constantly pro-
voke re-appraisals, if not outright constant re-examinations, of
basic propositions with the aim of training their Hetero fellow-
travelers to make the qualitative leap to ANALOG perspectives.

  With the aid of the modular insights our Gay Windows afford
us, we must—by our contributions—aid our Hetero neighborhood communities to learn to respect us *precisely for* our behavioral and perceptual differences from them. Once the Hetero Community groups begin to appreciate the truly greater depths of
perception our triangulation, or ANALOG, vision affords them,
laws and customs favoring us with Space and Freedom—within

which to grow ever more expansively in Gay Consciousness and to flourish as only our true Fairy persons would have it—will take care of themselves.

214

A CALL TO ACTION

Long have we carried this promise for Humanity as a secret hoard, a something-somewhere-ache-in-the-genes that the total parliament of our instincts uninterruptedly thrashed about with—seeking unconsciously (as does the Weaver Bird with the twig before the accidental twining of one twig with another has triggered *cognition*) the ache's fulfillment. Now that we are becoming aware of our particular Gay Window upon the World and the contributive vistas our Gay Consciousness, used with integrity, affords us through that window, *it is time for Gay Liberation to re-awaken*!

Now that we are beginning to have a glimmering of how to earn for ourselves Space in which to contemplate affirmatively *our particular dimensions of self-realization*, IT IS TIME FOR GAY LIBERATION FAIRIES TO RECONSTITUTE THE AGE-OLD AND AGE-LESS RINGS OF THEIR FOLK RESPONSIBILITIES!

Now that we are beginning to find words and images to think about being Gay and thinking about the self-realizations we've always known about ourselves that we didn't know we knew, about that modular way we have always used to think about the Straight World that we didn't know until now was the new Scientific Way *the Heteros must learn if they are to remain viable*, IT IS TIME GAY LIBERATION REGENERATES ITSELF INTO THE GAY FAIRY FAMILY OF LOVING-SHARING EQUALS, each choosing of his own volition to be responsible for himself, each choosing of his own volition to be responsible to each of the others of his chosen fairy ring!

Now that we may be able to find a way to aid Hetero Alternative and Hetero Left Groups to restore the Historical-Materialist outlook for Marxism to its lead position as the Vanguard of Community-revolutionizing dynamics by liberating its ongoing historical-political insights from the dead hand of the nineteenth century's obsolete scientific outlook, IT IS TIME FOR GAY LIBERATION TO GATHER FOR COLLECTIVE REBIRTH AND RENEWAL!

Now that we are beginning to perceive how great a treasure of commonalty we share collectively at the spiritual levels of our bio-cultural inheritance, just *below* the levels of that inadequate obsolete Binary Hetero makeshift of a language we Fairies are earth-bound by, IT IS TIME WE FIND NEW WAYS AND MEANS TO CONFER AND CONVOKE THE FORGING OF THE NEW LANGUAGE WE WILL NEED TO COMMUNICATE THE GLORIES OF OUR TREASURE, OUR "GIFT TO BE GAY."

P.S. We should not expect the Hetero radical masses, taken as a whole, *to like us.* We shall probably make them uncomfortable more often than not. We should learn how *not* to trigger their deeply ingrained Homophobias, which may be seen as part of *their* inheritance by Natural Selection, until such times as we have breathing space in which to discover suitable neutralizers. For the moment, however, we should ask only that the Hetero radicals *respect* the ANALOG dimensions of our Gay Conscious Integrity; we should ask only that they appreciate, and make full utilization of, our Gay Conscious contributions.

> Signed "Harry and John," April 20, 1976, Circle of Loving Companions, San Juan Pueblo, New Mexico.

Notes

1. Quoted in Louis Pauwels and Jacques Bergier, *The Morning of the Magicians* (1960; London: Granada, 1963), pp. 10, 13.
2. Heisenberg's uncertainty or indeterminacy principle states that it is

impossible to determine with complete accuracy both the position and momentum of a subatomic particle, thus converting the laws of physics into statements about relative probabilities.

3. On the Lysenko controversy, see Julian Huxley, *Soviet Genetics and World Science: Lysenko and the Meaning of Heredity* (London: Chatto and Windus, 1949).

4. Friedrich Engels, "The Mark," in *Socialism Utopian and Scientific*, trans. Edward Aveling (New York: International Publishers, 1935), pp. 77–93.

5. "Many, though not quite all, genetic differences produce what are known as pleiotropic, or manifold, effects; they alter two, or several, traits that do not have any obvious developmental interdependence. . . . If you are puzzled why natural selection has established as species characters, and even as characters of higher categories, some apparently useless morphological traits, remember that the useless traits may be parts of pleiotropic syndromes that also include less conspicuous but more vitally important components" (Theodosius Dobzhansky, "On Types, Genotypes, and the Genetic Diversity in Populations," in *Genetic Diversity and Human Behavior*, ed. J. N. Spuhler [Chicago: Aldine Publishing, 1967], pp. 1–18, esp. p. 14).

"The Hidden Ones"

A SERIES OF ARTICLES by Arthur Evans in *Out* and *Fag Rag* magazines in 1973 and 1974, later published as *Witchcraft and the Gay Counterculture*, inspired Hay to return to his historical research.[1] Evans had zeroed in on much of the same evidence Hay had found in the 1950s concerning the survival of pre-Christian goddess-worship and roles for Gay people in ancient Europe. At the same time, Hay felt Evans had missed a crucial episode in this history, one he relates in the following essay.

Hay reconstructs the origin of the priesthoods that were a prominent feature of ancient city-states in the Near East and Mediterranean from tribal roles like those of the shaman and the Native American Two-Spirit. Many of these priesthoods, especially those of goddesses like Inanna, Ishtar, and Cybele, involved gender-variant, homosexual men. Hay goes on to argue that these priesthoods played a fateful role in the process of goddess religions and women-centered customs and institutions being replaced or compromised by male-dominated social practices. "Berdache priesthoods," whose functions included administration of the temples that served as important economic institutions, were compromised, manipulated, and infiltrated by male usurpers, the result being what Hay terms an "androcratic takeover." It was not a revolution, since the means of production were not transformed, but an appropriation in which basic institutions were taken over and administered so as to redirect the social surplus to the new rulers. This leads Hay to make a distinction between "State Berdache," those priesthoods controlled by the androcratic ruling groups, and "Folk Berdache," the popular, folk-level practices rooted in tribal Two-Spirit traditions that often existed side-by-side with state institutions. Memories of all this, Hay argues, are reflected in the ancient Hebrew traditions surrounding the figure of Adam, whom Hay argues is the *original* closet case.

By the 1970s, Hay was not alone in seeking to reconstruct pre-patriarchal culture and history (although he certainly was in the 1940s). This was the central project of authors like Gimbutas, Reiner, and Starhawk. But surprisingly the historical narratives of cultural feminism almost never make allowance for the presence of homosexuals, male or female. All too often they reproduce heterosexist assumptions—that there are only two sexes and one sexuality (namely, the attraction between opposites). The following essay offers an important corrective to reconstructions of ancient history in which Lesbians and Gay men have been missing.[2]

Christianity's First Closet Case
A Study in the Application of
Gay Consciousness

An interesting case through which to begin further studies of Gay Consciousness, in its application to historical disciplines, is one that Arthur Evans, in his pell-mell fury to write *the* Universal Gay History and publish it in *Fag Rag*, missed! We are thinking of the Story of Adam, of the Adam-and-Eve garland of moral tales and anecdotes which, through the political opportunism of the *Pax Romana*, first sculpted and then governed the guilts of Western Europeans for the better part of the last two thousand years.

But Brother Art is in good company. The Classical Scholar who really should have tumbled onto this "misreading of icons" (his own favorite phrase about other Scholars' mistakes)—but instead let his slightly myopic Homophobia blow dust in his eyes when writing his otherwise excellent *Hebrew Myths* (which I shall be quoting as a source for stuff further along)—is Robert Graves.[3]

219

To lay the groundwork, we shall have to fog off into the misty dims . . . say 45,000 B.C. give or take a millennium. The cave-paintings and drawings of the mid-Aurignacian period (circa 30,000–20,000 B.C.; Herbert Kuhn, *The Rock Pictures of Europe* [London: Sidgwick and Jackson, 1966], pp. 3–52) demonstrate an already articulated religious cognition, together with a body of so-cial experience to accompany it. Thus we can safely assume that *sapient* Humanity, in the prior millennia moving toward the Au-rignacian culture-concentration, were in the process of gathering and accumulating the component predispositions, including all the obstinate fixations of territorial aggressions, which will char-acterize their peculiarly *Hetero* post-Mesolithic leap to "Civiliza-tion" in the most recent five thousand years of their Natural Evo-lution. In all fairness to the Heteros, it must be said that Biologists recognize that species Human hasn't always been territorially and competitively *lethal*. For all of the first and perhaps also a large part of the second of their hypothetical two-million-year career as Hominids, Humans practiced what the Biologists, in technol-ogese, call "close social cohesion" (Gottfried Kurth in *Genetic Di-versity and Human Behavior*, ed. J. N. Spuhler, pp. 199–216 [Chi-cago: Aldine Publishing, 1967], pp. 204, 214).[4] It was only by this primeval form of the loving-sharing tribal family that this spindly little creature, who had neither speed nor fang nor claw, who had not yet developed the opposed thumb nor the freely expanding brain, nor certainly what Robin Fox calls cortical control leading

220

toward consciousness (in Bernard Campbell, ed., *Sexual Selection and the Descent of Man* [Chicago: Aldine, 1972], pp. 285–93), could possibly have survived, let alone have multiplied.

To come back to 45,000 B.C. (still some 37,000 years earlier than the English Marxist Gordon Childe's Neolithic Revolution, with its kitchen-garden-based village economies supplemented by hunting and herding), the still somewhat socially cohesive tribal hunting-gathering people undoubtedly by now practiced fairly extended and elaborate *rites of passage*, including that of initiation from youth to adulthood. Their drawings somewhat later will evoke a long tradition of such concepts.[5]

It seems to be (and to have been) the case with most hunting-gathering tribal peoples, alike for people with semi-permanent living areas as for Nomads, that sending their young people on vision-quest ordeals into the Hostile Unknown—as the *whole outside* beyond the Tribe's sphere of familiarity would have been known—was a spiritual testing, to find those most worthy to be received as adult members into the Tribal Community and most highly regarded. And by this time, most tribes had experienced the small percentage of young men who received the *wrong vision* or who were befriended by the *wrong totem*—the Moon, for instance, as a beautiful mature Goddess, a luminous wind-painted penumbra, one's self, the Astral Alter-Ego, robed in the Goddess's flowing garments—or, fearfully, the Trickster who changes sex and personhood at whim and can never be depended upon.[6] At first, in all tribal families, as myth and legend and long-preserved ritual seem to indicate, these receivers of *wrong visions* were never permitted to return home from their quest ordeals, were considered to have failed the Tribal Family's requirements for Hetero adulthood. Then, as now in any number of situations, such persons were to be regarded, for all intents and purposes, as having died in their travail. For many generations—and in quite a number of tribal situations *forever*—these Deviant Experiencers were driven away from the very perimeters of the tribal areas of experience to wander the dreadful wastes of hunger and thirst and the fearful realms of Earth's frightful Supernatural Forces, where shortly they would undoubtedly perish (as did most Hetero travelers [to those regions] in the Tribe's normal experience) at the hands of the dreadful nightmare world of Spirits.

In time, however, a number of Tribes in varying parts of the ecological niches of the inhabited world began to notice that a significant albeit small number of these Deviant Experiencers—these "Contraries"[7]—did *not* perish, but rather seemed to have come to terms with the powerful Spirit Forces that shrieked and thundered just outside the given village's mud or brush walls. Of course, it was quite correct that these small percentages of Deviants should be sent to wander the wastelands upon receiving their wrong visions, and it was quite correct that their bereaved families should ritually renounce them as having died. All tribes with whom they had any commerce were totally in agreement with such procedures. Still—now that these queasy creatures (who seemed to prefer each other rather than persons of genders opposite to their own) appeared to have developed excellent working relations with the Powers of the Universe, perhaps they should be invited back to live *just outside* the tribal camp area, in an "off-limits-except-on-special-consecrated-occasions-place"—the *temenos*, the proto-Greeks would call it later, from their archaic word *temnos*, "cut off."[8] From this proscribed place these Contraries, appareled as the Living-dead to warn off the curious and with their hair dressed like the Women's—because *certainly* these poor creatures were not *men* as the Village normally knew these things (and the children mustn't be misled, it might be catching)—could intercede with the Spirits for their new benefactors. Then, on special days and by special ceremonials of song and mime, they could communicate to their former mates and siblings how the Village persons had offended the Powers of Nature or had actually manifested *wrong action*. Perhaps these Sacred Ones (for since the Deviant Ones were now dead to their families and their Village, they should now be regarded as semi-spirits themselves) would carry messages *from* the Spirit World, perhaps even blessings, perhaps even miracles. Perhaps and perhaps and perhaps! (A. C. Bouquet, *Comparative Religion: A Short Outline*, 4th rev. ed. [London: Penguin Books, 1953], p. 56).⁹

The Gay Primevals whose portraits adorn the walls of the Caves of Les Trois Frères, of Les Combarelles, Le Font-de-Gaume, Tuc d'Audoubert, Lascaux, and the Megalithic burial at Champaigne are interesting stories to be explored another time.¹⁰ For now, our focus is on the ecological niche of Hither Asia [the Near East], the upland plains of Susa between the Zagros Mountains and the Diyala River in what is now southwestern Iran, and upon the smaller niche surrounding the first level of what is now the ancient City of Jericho. Here, around 6500 B.C. the social cohesion into permanent agricultural villages takes place. Humans, as Childe explains, ceased to be parasitic and began deliberately cooperating with Nature (Gordon Childe, *The Prehistory of European Society* [Harmondsworth, England: Penguin Books, 1958], p. 34). The recognition of Earth as a Great Mother who generates and brings forth (and razes and re-absorbs) blossoms in Human Consciousness. Villages form around Women's skills and knowledges with vegetation for palatable foods, fibers, and drugs. (One of the earliest ways of taking fresh-water fish seems to have been by stupefying them with macerated plants discovered by the Women, according to Carl Sauer [in S. L. Washburn, ed., *Social Life of Early Man* (Chicago: Aldine, 1961), p. 266].)

Villages also formed around a central granary, and the Matrons of families—to be later projected as Priestesses and still later the Priestesses projected as Goddesses—see to the equitable distributions of the harvests. This Neolithic practice was common to all of Hither Asian agricultural societies, to Helladic Greece and the Minoan Aegean. Lewis Henry Morgan studied this practice in depth in the agricultural society of the Native American Iroquois Confederacy in 1865–1875. And the sixteenth-century Franciscan Historian Father Bernardino de Sahagún, reported of Toltec-Aztec Teotihuacán that the civil administrator (who supervised all food distributions in the City-State) was the Cihuacoatl, a life-long celibate Priest whose title translated as "Snake-Woman."[11]

Peasant Societies, then as now, seem always to have represented the most conservative of social organizations. Ceremonials and rituals, recreating the bountiful harvests of a given Society's "Golden Age," the mythic memory characteristic of all Agricultural Societies without exception, were adhered to jot and tittle in order that, in the new season coming up, the Great Mother once again would be bountiful. If the harvest was *less* than expected, then obviously somewhere along the schedule a "jot" or perhaps a "tittle" had been overlooked, had been slighted, had been slurred! Obviously the Great Mother had *not* been properly acknowledged, or thanked, or propitiated.

The development of the Neolithic Village seems to have stimulated not only a considerable increase in population but an increase in longevity. Villages begin to display not only a considerable diversity in food-stuffs but a number of semi-specialists begin to appear, as well, such as milling households, smithing households, and crafting households. It is possible that the Bardic or Rhapsode households and miming households also begin to appear in this time (Childe, op. cit., pp. 78–82). Such households, to judge from similar semi-specialist communities to be observed in Malta and perhaps Sardinia in Megalithic times, and in the Aegean in Minoan times, were most often separated from the mainstream of the Village, in off-bounds or, more probably, in the *temenos* or "sacred" precincts, the compound *just outside* the Village walls. In the later times they were composed solely of men or solely of women and were renewed periodically by co-option, less often by adoption (George Thomson, *Studies in Ancient Greek Society: The Prehistoric Ægean*, rev. ed. [London: Lawrence and Wishart, 1954], pp. 332–33). Surrounding these semi-specialties—those of milling, smithing, the arts of the Rhapsode, and the arts of the Mime—was the powerful social sense that these activities were "other," were agilities and talents that more properly belonged to the supernatural, to the World of Spirits, and should be properly abjured by the world of Humans except during special ceremonially consecrated periods.[12] Even then people approached these places only after being ritually purified and blessed for protection against the unforeseen powers of "sacra."

Sometime between 7000 and 5000 B.C., as the Neolithic Villages prospered and multiplied into Towns, the cozy annual refertilizing of the fields through the ceremonial copulations between the male Steward and/or Heads of families with an unrelated Matron of a given Village, were removed from the fields themselves to the more controlled and stageable areas of the *temenos*, or the sacred temple compound (H. and H. A. Frankfort, John A. Wilson, and Thorkild Jacobsen, *Before Philosophy: The Intellectual Adventure of Ancient Man* [Harmondsworth, England: Penguin Books, 1949], pp. 214–15; Samuel N. Kramer,

History Begins at Sumer: Thirty-nine Firsts in Man's Recorded History, 3d rev. ed. [Philadelphia: University of Pennsylvania Press, 1981], chap. 33).[13] And sometime, shortly thereafter, a demographic crisis begins to become evident. Through a millennium of fifty generations of inter-marriages there were more and more families no longer able to participate in the annual fertility renewal ceremonials because of the universal customs of Exogamy, the latter seemingly devised almost in species universalis to guard kinship systems against violations of the dread incest taboos. The traditional Matrons, now Priestesses, representing the eternal continuum of the "first families" of the village-town-community, were fast becoming hopelessly inter-related by blood to all available kinship clans in the area. The harvests were falling off, even in the face of ever more little mouths to feed; droughts were becoming ever more periodic.

In the pre-dynastic alluvial ecological niches of both the Nile and the Tigris-Euphrates Valleys of this historical evolution (to be repeated slightly later in daughter colonies on rivers traversing the coastal plains of what are now Lebanon and Syria), the set-up of farm-village households seemed to consist of a large, almost self-sufficient compound known as the Women's quarters and of a different set of rooms, such as armories and dormitories, arranged around a common eating hall known as the Men's quarters—the separate Women's and Men's Tents of the long-lasting Megalithic-period camps now made permanent by burnt mud brick construction. The two areas were connected by a corridor from the Men's Hall to a bed-chamber occasionally inhabited by the husband and wife of the given establishment. This chamber was as far into the woman's quarters as the husband *ever* penetrated.

As attested to by the now well-researched records of the Matrilineal Minoan Aegean and its faint echoes in Homer, in Antedilu-

vian (circa 3300 B.C.) Sumerian Temple accounts of the City Goddesses, and in the Canaanite myths of Hither Asia, all of the above
being patterns followed by most early pre-Indo-European Mediterranean cultures where the Women were responsible for the worship of a central Goddess, from Mycenaean Pylos in the southwestern Peloponnesus to the Macedonian highlands of King Philip's
day—in the Women's quarters of the Farm the entire business of
the household crafts was planned, organized, and administered,
from the preparation of flax and wool for spinning, weaving, and
clothes-making for the entire household, to the gardens, orchards,
apiaries, byres, and barns. Children were born and reared, edu-
cated and dressed in Women's ways until it was time for the boys to
be initiated into the ways of the Men. However, stories, myths, and
legends in all of these cultures tell of *occasional boys who did not
leave the Women's Quarters*. Oft-times such persons were referred
to as "Hidden Ones" or "Favorite Ones." In Homer, Achilles is
such a one, hiding in Woman's dress in the Women's Court to evade
Agamemnon's press-gang which has come to claim draftees for the
Trojan War. (Within these Women's households, it should be mentioned, there were feminine companions of the Mistress and her
sisters who might seldom if ever have any relationship with men.
Scholarship knows little about these women as yet except that
often they were musicians and/or teachers, and that they were
equally sources of comfort and of strength in times of danger and
stress when the household men were away on their innumerable
and endless forays and wars.)

Sir Flinders Petrie (*Religious Life in Ancient Egypt* [London:
Constable, 1924], pp. 45–46), deducing the origins of the Ancient
Egyptian Priesthood from the most primitive titles, notes that the
Royal Heiress (Pharaoh was ruler by reason of his being married to
the Heiress of the given generation) was herself, in addition, the liv-

ing representative of the Great Goddess. In the pre-dynastic Delta, she would be most often the Goddess Hat-Hor. In "Women's Town" (an ancient city reputedly near the Lower Delta's capital city Heliopolis, in the eighth Nome of the Lower Delta region) the living Goddess was known as the "Commander" and her priest as the "Hidden One"; elsewhere she was called "Divine Mother" and her priest the "Favorite Child." The boys who remained dressed in Women's styles in the Women's Quarters were known, in Mycenean Crete, as the *skotioi*—the Children of Darkness, the Hidden Ones, precisely because the Women's household was an area totally forbidden to the men, a place of mystery in which sacred mysteries were practiced and, thus, to the Male Hetero mind, a place of darkness.[14]

The pre-dynastic priests, in service to the Great Mother Goddess Hat-Hor, wore the garments of her service, and in ceremonies carried the wands and ornaments of her office and wore the headdresses and masks of her authority. The English Marxist Scholar George Thomson, describing contemporary findings in the Minoan Palace of Hagia Triada, says, "The procession on the Hagia Triada sarcophagus includes a young male lyre-player—a budding Apollo. We know his sex by the colouring of his skin. Otherwise we should certainly have taken him for a woman, because he is dressed in a long robe reaching to the ankles with a bodice open at the breast, exactly like the girl in front of him. *He is dressed as a woman because he is performing a woman's task*" (italics—HH), and, "The traditional costume was sacred, charged with magic, and therefore indispensable" (op. cit., pp. 488, 486). It would have been the sacred traditional costume which magically transformed him—*not into the goddess's representative*, but into *the goddess herself*.

But where and how did such practices arise? For the answer, we

228

need to go back to the Neolithic Villages of the Susa Plain, two thousand years *before* these interesting enactments, where the Matron Priestesses were no longer able to perform the ritual Spring Fertility Renewals, or Sacred Marriages as they would later be called, because they were now inter-related by blood-ties to the male heads of the Village families. We project that at a given though currently unknown moment one of the Sacred Forbidden Ones of the off-limits *temenos* just outside the Village had a vision: Were he and his comrades, who knew they were capable of welcoming the active sexual services of the Village Family Stewards, to don the robes and headdresses of the Fertility Goddess, they could then perform the ceremonial pantomime of fertility as surrogates for the Matrons *without invoking the incest ban*—because the very fact of their having been cast out of the mainstream of village life when they failed their vision-quest ordeal meant that, in terms of their former personhood, they were now counted as dead.

Whether this most significant religious contribution by our Gay Ancestors, culminating in the exploding growth into towns and cities out of the Exogamically functioning and thus ritually frustrated Neolithic Villages, occurred as a flash of genius in one town of the Tigris-Euphrates Watershed and spread like a welcome fiery miracle across the whole Near East into all the Mediterranean countries—or whether the Gordian knot (into which most of these independent ecological niches had ritually snarled themselves by the practice of Exogamy) was cut in a number of places simultaneously albeit independently, we do not know. Suffice it to say that by 3500 B.C. this welcome ceremonial employment of the "Holy Ones," the *qedeshim*, was widespread from the Ubaid cultures of the Mesopotamian Plain to the Nile Delta of Lower Egypt to the Islands of the Aegean to the Pelasgian Aborigines of the Attic mainland. In Attica's many valleys, from Mt. Athos to the western shores of the Peloponnesus, the Indo-Europeans—the Achaeans and the Peoples of the Sea—will encounter the Surrogate Priests and their religious discoveries a thousand years later and will themselves become subscribers.

Qedeshim was the Canaanite term for those special Priests who, long before their official consecration to the administration of the Goddess's Temple responsibilities, had served as Mediators between the Village-folk and the dread Spirits of the "Hostile Outside," had served as intercessors between the spiritual needs of the people and the Gods who made their moods manifest in lightning and thunder. Now the Sacred Ones *had merely assumed yet another mediation*, another task of intercession—that of being surrogate for Great Mother Nature in her aspect of "the womb of the living" who received "he who quickens the young." Though we know them primarily in their Hebraicized expropriated form of Temple Servants, such as singers or as servitor priests, *qedeshim* in the original Canaanite meant "those Holy Ones who are bored or pierced" in the name of the Great Mother. They were, of course, the Temple Prostitutes against whom the Hebrew Prophets so long inveighed.[15]

Against this background, let us then consider the interesting story of Eve, the Canaanite "Mother of All Living," a title also of the Love-Goddess Aruru (who was Enkidu's Matron in the Gilgamesh tale) and of Ishtar.[16] Eve also was known severally as Khebat, Khiba, Hebat, or Heba (in Asian Greek, Hebe, Heracles's Goddess-wife). It has been noted by the many Scholars of the several basic documents that make up the ancient sources of the Hebrew Legends underlying the thrice-told tale of Creation in our Bible's Book of Genesis that Jehovah clearly did *not* figure in the original myth. As Robert Graves puts it, "It is the Mother of all Liv-

ing, . . . who casts Adam out of her fertile riverine dominions because he has usurped some prerogative of hers" (*The White God-*
230   *dess: A Historical Grammar of Poetic Myth*, rev. ed. [1948; New
York: Farrar, Straus and Giroux, 1966], p. 257).

Let us now depart from the many interesting speculations that
the scholarly experts of the "J," "S," and "E" Documents have
made.[17] Let us consider instead the evidence presented in this paper—from the point of view of Gay Consciousness. However, we
must add one more ingredient that the J, S, and E Document Scholars know, namely that Adam's name means "Red Man," i.e., the
"Man made of Red Clay," and there are many glosses and Mid-
rashes concerning the fact that Adam was made of the red clay of
Hebron and many times is called "He of Hebron"—presumably,
even, his grave is one of the several *oracular shrines* attributed to
ancient Hebron. Elsewhere, in Canaanite and in Hebraic culture-
history, Red Clay is "infertile Clay"—the clay used for pots and
burnt for bricks. How, then, could Adam, the man made of *infer-*
tile clay, *possibly* be "He who Quickens" the Mother of All Living,
as the Genesis Legend would have us believe? Yet Heba is equally
known to have been the one who cast Adam out *because he had*
usurped a prerogative of hers.[18]

Who, then, *was* Adam *really*? We feel with certainty, putting all
the pieces together, we finally must perceive that Adam was the
qedeshoth Priest to the Matron representative of the Mother Goddess of Hebron, the "infertile" vessel who could thus *receive* in ceremonial mime the fertile semen of the heads of families, in Her
name and in Her place, back in the dim Neolithic Canaanite mists
of approximately 3000 B.C., in order that the land be quickened to
flow as always with milk and honey.[19] With the arrival in Hebron
of the Sumerian Herders [i.e., the people represented by Abraham—WR] shortly after the time of Hammurabi—rough and pu-

ritanical as only denizens of the desert's empty places can be—*the Adam* (the Title of the *qedeshoth* Priest of Hebron) is persuaded, bribed, cajoled, flattered into turning Opportunist. Throwing in with the invading Patriarch-minded Expropriators, the "Adam" forsakes his gay nature *and his sacred dedication AND THE POWERFUL MAGIC OF HIS SANCTIFIED LIFE-LONG VOWS.* He asserts the double sexual nature of which he may have been physically capable, and—in performing the ritual marriage of fertility with his former Matron—reduces her from the Great Goddess to merely the Royal Heiress. This is, of course, the Scholars' long-sought-after "usurpation." But, more importantly, it is this dreadful betrayal of sacred oaths, this anathema, this turn-coating on the Great Mother and attempting to "use" her, *which is the real original sin*!

This knowledge may not have been even particularly hidden in the millennium between the Songs of the Patriarchs and the Songs of Deborah, the Judge—one of several of Israel's Judges before the arrival of Joshua. This knowledge's obliteration didn't become important until David had done the same thing in his socially opportunist climb to the Kingship. The setting down in writing of the earlier sagas such as the Songs of Deborah [c. 1130 B.C.], the recited stories and legends in the several "Documents" that Scholars now generally assume preceded the preparation of the Hebraic Septuagint, seems not to have begun much before the death of Solomon, David's son. It may even have been undertaken *ostensibly* to rinse away all evidences of the Matrilinear nature of the world of Abraham and his brothers, but in actuality the "documenting" was an effort to obscure forever the Hebraic beginnings in betrayal and Anathema, the paralleling of which would also shame the memory of David the King. Had the land been Canaan or Caphtor (the Hebraic name for Mycenean Crete), Jonathan, Saul's heir to

232

the throne, and his beloved David, in Gladys Schmitt's words, "might have ruled hand in hand upon a double throne, and worn twin diadems, and gone down at last into the same grave" (*David the King* [New York: Dial Press, 1946], p. 106). Instead, David also asserts a double-nature—he marries Michal, Saul's only daughter, flees away to the enemy (Philistia), and with them raises an army against Saul. With Saul and Jonathan safely dead, his earlier marriage to the Royal Heiress paves his way to Israel's throne.

It is an interesting sidelight on the possible techniques of ancient manipulations of data that in the Talmud, which presumably contained all the highlighting tales for the "historical materialism" contained in the Septuagint, there is no mention *whatsoever* of the sexual sins of Sodom and Gomorrah (although the sexual goings-on of others go on and on till they come out your ears) *and no reference whatsoever to the love relationship between David and Jonathan!*[20] There is, however, in the "Nashim" section of Mishnah, the Oral Law of the Talmud, an extensive discussion on the conditions which prescribe the behavior of those of "doubtful sex" (characterized in the text by the Greek functional definition *androgynos*) and the total *proscriptions* against those of "double sex" (characterized in the text by the Asiatic Greek functional definition *hermaphroditos*). Those of double sex would never be permitted even to go near the Temple or have to do with any part of its many community-supplemented sacred enemies, would never be permitted to marry, and were generally to shun the company of the elect. Those of doubtful sex, to the extent that they demonstrated satisfactorily that they loved the Lord God and respected the Law, could marry *a man*, and could share inheritances equally with other *heiresses*.[21]

In light of the interesting acceptance of the *androgynoi* it does not take much speculation to perceive that the ancient transgression of "the Adam," like that of David the King's, is perhaps the earliest recorded instance of Homophobic triggers, wherein, from the typical unconscious Macho point of view, the Penetrated—and thus inferior—One turns-coat, requiring as his price for betrayal *that he be seen the socio-political Equal* of his former Penetrators. Heaven only knows what further deeply begrudged advantage he will claim next! It is, however, attested fact that, as Indo-European Androcratic Invaders and Expropriators (truly Patriarchal *only* in Judea) wrested the lands bordering the Mediterranean and their bounties from the Matrilineal Aborigines, Priest Surrogates of Great Mother Goddesses, in City-State after City-State, turn-coated from Priest-prostitutes to Priest-KINGS. These are shameful pages of the Chronicle of WHO we are, and WHERE we have been.

The permissive attitude of Jewish Law-making (from the time of Solomon to the Diaspora) toward the Androgynoi, however, is pleasantly instructive. It tells us that the ego-less devoted service of the priest-Mediators, the priest-intercessors, the priest-councilors and comforters, the sometimes-when-called-for-Surrogate—in modern terms, "He of loving compassionate Gay Consciousness"—was respected and appreciated. It was, and is, only he who is merely self-centeredly homo*sexual* who was, and is, to be mistrusted and abhorred.

> Signed Henry Hay, Circle of Loving Companions, San Juan
> Pueblo, 1976.

Notes

1. Arthur Evans, *Witchcraft and the Gay Counterculture: A Radical View of Western Civilization and Some of the People It Had Tried to Destroy* (Boston: Fag Rag Books, 1978).
2. Hay's own citations appear in the text. I have updated them using recent editions.

3. Robert Graves and Raphael Patai, *Hebrew Myths: The Book of Genesis* (Garden City, N.Y.: Doubleday, 1964).

234

4. Kurth wrote: "Hominid survival was guaranteed in spite of the lack of special defense mechanisms such as large canines by a particularly close intragroup cooperation. . . . Additionally, life in such small units represented the only existing social environment for human hominids for nearly two million years."

5. See, for example, Peter J. Ucko and André Rosenfeld, *Palaeolithic Cave Art* (New York: McGraw-Hill, 1967), pp. 160–61, 177–78, 225.

6. Hay's notion of the vision quest is based primarily on Plains Indian patterns, where visions and dreams were the basis for life transitions and personal identity. Several tribes specifically attributed to the moon the power to transform individuals into Two-Spirits. The Lakota credited the goddess Double Woman with this power. In compiling tales and myths for *Queer Spirits*, I found the moon a recurrent symbol associated with Gay themes and characters, and often explicitly contrasted to the sun, the symbol of paternity, fatherhood, and godhead.

7. The Contraries were a Cheyenne warrior society for men who had dreams of Thunder spirits and thereupon took vows to do everything backwards. The *heyoka* were their counterparts among the Sioux.

8. Hay had received a powerful confirmation of this thesis in 1960 when his Pueblo friend Enki showed him a separate area of habitation at the ruins of Tsankawi, above the Rio Grande valley, and told him, "This is where *your* people lived."

9. Bouquet wrote, "But these abnormal personalities, however awkward as members of a community, are sometimes useful—like 'the beeboy who is not quite right in his head' but has second sight, like his mother, and 'can do anything with bees.' So although they may get expelled into solitude, or wander away, they are still consulted—and feared, as being peculiar, and drodsome [*sic*], and possibly in touch with the Sacred." The Bee Boy is a character in Rudyard Kipling's *Puck of Pook's Hill*.

10. Hay has in mind the cave images of shamanistic figures; for examples, the famous "sorcerer" of Les Trois Frères, a deer-like figure who dances on his hind legs with a human penis protruding backwards from between his legs and the lone male figure with distinctly unerect penis standing among a troupe of matrons and girls at Cogul, Spain.

11. George C. Vaillant, *Aztecs of Mexico: Origin, Rise and Fall of the*

Aztec Nation, rev. ed. (Garden City, N.Y.: Doubleday, 1962), p. 95; J. Eric Thompson, *Mexico Before Cortez: An Account of the Daily Life, Religion, and Ritual of the Aztecs and Kindred Peoples* (New York: Charles Scribner's Sons, 1933), p. 111.

12. See also Mircea Eliade, *The Forge and the Crucible: The Origins and Structures of Alchemy*, 2d ed. (Chicago: University of Chicago Press, 1978).

13. Hay follows many scholars of the Frazerian school in projecting the so-called sacred marriage ceremony known from Sumerian records as a near universal practice in ancient societies. Most of the actual evidence for this ceremony is literary and comes from the Sumerian Third Dynasty of Ur (2100–2050 B.C.E.) and the Isin Period (2050–1800 B.C.E.). It is not clear if the "marriage" was purely symbolic or if actual intercourse was involved. Many artifacts, some dating back to the Early Dynastic Period (3100–2390 B.C.E.), have been interpreted as referring to or depicting this rite. Beyond the "sacred marriage," sexuality seems to have been thoroughly incorporated into Mesopotamian religious life, especially through so-called "temple prostitution." See Samuel N. Kramer, *The Sacred Marriage Rite: Aspects of Faith, Myth, and Ritual in Ancient Sumer* (Bloomington: Indiana University Press, 1969) and Jeremy Black and Anthony Green, *Gods, Demons and Symbols of Ancient Mesopotamia: An Illustrated Dictionary* (Austin: University of Texas Press, 1992), pp. 150–52, 157–58. On an ancient Hebrew version of the sacred marriage, see Samuel N. Kramer, *History Begins at Sumer: Thirty-nine Firsts in Man's Recorded History*, 3d rev. ed. (Philadelphia: University of Pennsylvania Press, 1981), pp. 315–20.

14. See Robert Graves, *The White Goddess: A Historical Grammar of Poetic Myth*, rev. ed. (1948; New York: Farrar, Straus and Giroux, 1966), p. 213, and *The Greek Myths* (New York: George Braziller, 1959), 1:107.

15. Hay relates the term קדר (qdr), "to cut, bore, drill," to קדש (qdsh), "to be holy, sacred," from which the term *qedesh* is formed, referring to a class of male temple functionaries. *Qedeshîm* (pl.) are mentioned in Deuteronomy 23:17; 1 Kings 14:24, 15:12, 22:46; 2 Kings 23:7; Job 36:14 and in texts found at Canaanite Ugarit. They apparently lived in the temple precincts, kept busy with sacrifices, cared for sacred objects, and, if we are to believe the Hebrew rhetoric, engaged in some form of religious sexual acts (see William F. Albright, *Archaeology and the Religion of Israel*,

4th ed. [Baltimore: Johns Hopkins University Press, 1956], pp. 158 ff.; D. Winton Thomas, "*Kelebh* 'Dog': Its Origin and Some Usages of It in the Old Testament," *Vetus Testamentum* 10 [1960]: 410–27; David F. Greenberg, *The Construction of Homosexuality* [Chicago: University of Chicago Press, 1988], pp. 94–96; and Beatrice A. Brooks, "Fertility Cult Functionaries in the Old Testament," *Journal of Biblical Literature* 60 [1941]: 227–53).

16. See Graves and Patai, *Hebrew Myths*, pp. 65, 69, 79, and Graves, *Greek Myths*, 1:35 and 2:206; Joseph Campbell, *The Masks of God: Occidental Mythology* (New York: Viking, 1964), pp. 9–30. Aruru was one of the names applied to the goddess Ninhursaga, also known as Nintur, Ninmah, and by other names. Ishtar was the Akkadian name for the Sumerian Inanna.

17. These are the reconstructed original documents on which the books of the Pentateuch are believed to have been based (see Robert H. Pfeiffer, *Introduction to the Old Testament* [New York: Harper and Brothers, 1948]).

18. See Graves and Patai, *Hebrew Myths*, pp. 60, 63, 80, and Graves, *Greek Myths*, 1:181 and 2:211.

19. There are interesting parallels to Hay's reconstruction of the function of the *qedeshim* as "vessels" from India and ancient Mesopotamia. A *hijra*, one of the third-gender followers of the goddess Bahucharā Mātā, told an observer in the late nineteenth century, "We are broken vessels." The underlying image is that of transmission—but rather than semen, it is the power of the goddess, or *shakti*, that the *hijra* transmits. Similarly, an Old Babylonian omen advises that, on the occasion of the breaking of a pot, one should "look upon a *kurgarrû*"—the gender-variant priests of Ishtar. Presumably the *kurgarrû*, being *like* a broken pot, could draw away the bad luck (see Will Roscoe, "Priests of the Goddess: Gender Transgression in Ancient Religion," *History of Religions* 35[3] [1996]: 295–330).

20. Hay discusses Sodom and Gomorrah in "The Moral Climate of Canaan at the Time of Judges," *One Institute Quarterly* 1(1,2) (Spring–Summer 1958) 8–16, 50–59.

21. Such, at least, seems to be implied by *some* passages of the Mishnah. For example, according to a commentary in Bikkurim 4.5: "An *androgynos* is a creature by itself, and the Sages could not decide about it

whether it was man or woman. But it is not so with one of doubtful sex, since such a one is at times a man and at times a woman" (Herbert Danby, *The Mishnah* [London: Oxford University Press, 1933], p. 98). See also Baba Bathra 9.2 (Danby, *The Mishnah*, p. 378). Other references to "doubtful" and "double-sexed," however, do not appear to make a distinction between them. Hay may have had in mind Isaiah 56:4–5: "For thus saith the Lord unto the eunuchs that keep my sabbaths, and choose the things that please me, and take hold of my covenant; Even unto them will I give in mine house and within my walls a place and a name better than of sons and of daughters: I will give them an everlasting name, that shall not be cut off." He might also have cited the passage from the apocryphal *Wisdom of Solomon* 3:13–14, "And blessed is the eunuch, who with his hands hath wrought no iniquity, nor planned wicked things against the Lord; for unto him shall be given a special gift of faith, and a more desirable inheritance in the temple of the Lord" (in *The Apocrypha of the Old Testament*, ed. Edwin C. Bissell [New York: Charles Scribner's Sons, 1880]).

237

"A Call to Gay Brothers"

H AY'S "CALLS" AND ESSAYS in the 1970s slowly found a responsive audience. Gay men began making the pilgrimage to New Mexico to seek out the legendary founder of Gay liberation. Two of these visitors, Don Kilhefner, who helped found the Los Angeles Lesbian/Gay Community Services Center, and Mitch Walker, a Jungian-oriented therapist, formed especially synergistic relationships with Hay. In 1978, Hay, Kilhefner, Walker, and Burnside put out a call for a "Spiritual Conference for Radical Fairies" to be held on Labor Day weekend. (Hay and others began using the older spelling, "faerie," after 1979).

Since the organizers were based in New Mexico, Los Angeles, and Berkeley, respectively, while the gathering itself was held in southern Arizona, consensus required endless phone calls and long letters in which the goals and procedures of the conference along with myriad practical details, from meal preparation to sanitary facilities, were worked out. In the spring of 1979, when Don Kilhefner drafted the text for the flyer announcing the conference, he drew from these conversations and his correspondence with Hay. The result, which appears below, drew over two hundred Gay men from throughout the United States and Canada.

Spiritual Conference
for Radical Fairies:
A Call to Gay Brothers

It's in the air. Heard everywhere. At the World Symposium on Humanity the talk is about "New Age Politics"—beyond Left and Right—a synthesis of the political and spiritual movements of the past two decades. Sitting in the Kiva at Lama, high in the Sangre de Cristo Mountains of northern New Mexico, Ram Dass talks about the need for "conscious beings" assuming responsibilities for social and political change—a radical Circle of Dharma. In the holy halls of academia, the temple prostitutes are whispering about a "paradigm shift"—something new is happening in our society with more and more people living and perceiving their lives differently—and they haven't figured out yet how to contain it. Deep in Oregon's lush Umpqua forest, at the annual fairy-like gathering of the Rainbow Family Tribe, late into the night people talk about the merging of political consciousness and spiritual consciousness— an interest in healing society rather than championing exclusive claims to "rightness."

> New Age politics is a politics in which we learn to assume
> personal and collective responsibility for the ways we treat
> one another, and nature, and ourselves. A politics in which
> we assume this responsibility not out of a sense of grim duty,
> but out of a sense of real, virtually untapped possibility.
> Mark Satin

Does all of this political/spiritual ferment have any relevance to gay men? Is there a gay vision of New Age society? Is a "paradigm shift" in gay consciousness also manifesting itself? The answer to all these questions is: YES!

240   And many gay brothers are feeling the need to come together . . .

> To share new insights about ourselves;
>
> To dance in the moonlight;
>
> To renew our oaths against patriarchy/corporations/racism;
>
> To hold, protect, nurture and caress one another;
>
> To talk about the politics of gay espiritment/the enspiritment of gay politics;
>
> To find the healing place inside our hearts;
>
> To become Inspirer/Listener as we share new breakthroughs in how we perceive gay consciousness;
>
> To soar like an eagle;
>
> To re-discover/re-invent our myths;
>
> To talk about gay living/loving alternatives;
>
> To experience the groundedness of the calamus root;
>
> To share our gay visions;
>
> To sing, sing, sing;
>
> TO EVOKE A GREAT FAIRY CIRCLE

The Call goes out to gay brothers everywhere—poet, Sufi, musician, revolutionary, shaman, heretic, community organizer, farmer, artist, healer, city dweller, Buddhist, dancer, magician, political activist, yogi—whoever you have become since the last time we came together.

The Call goes out to all who know that there is more to us than hetero-imitation. To all who are ready to move on. To all who have broken through and are ready to share those breakthroughs with your fairy brothers.

"A Call to Gay Brothers"

The term "spiritual" represents the accumulation of all experiential consciousness from the division of the first cells in
the primeval slime, down through all biological-political-
social evolution to your and to my latest insights through
Gay Consciousness just a moment ago. What else can we
call this overwhelmingly magnificent inheritance—other
than spiritual?   Harry Hay

The gathering is to be called, among other names, "A Spiritual
Conference for Radical Fairies." It will be held over the Labor Day
weekend, August 31–September 1 & 2, 1979.

The conference site is a comfortable ashram located in the beautiful Sonora desert of southern Arizona—Don Juan country—near
Tucson.

There will be a conference fee of $50 to cover the cost of vegetar-
ian meals, lodging, and other incidental expenses involved in putting on the gathering. No one will be denied participation in the
conference because of inability to pay. . . .

> Come forth, o children,
>   under the stars,
> And take your fill of love!
> I am above you and in you.
>   My ecstasy is in yours.
>   My joy is to see your joy.
>   A. Crowley

Written Spring 1979.

Radical Faerie

1980–1995

I CAN STILL REMEMBER the thrill of seeing the words *radical* and *spiritual* used together for the first time in the call put out in 1979 for the first faerie gathering. It was the realization, as I heard a Gay man recently put it, that there was something more that I could do with my sexuality besides simply "accept it." By the late 1970s, the commercialization and depersonalization of the urban Gay scene had alienated great numbers of Gay men, while those of us with progressive politics found ourselves constantly thwarted by middle-class assimilationists who had taken over leadership positions in the movement. Most discouraging of all was the declining level of mutual respect and support within the community, whether manifest in political factionalism, division between Lesbians and Gay men, or the competition of the bar and cruising scene. Our political progress was being held back by a lack of equal progress in Lesbian/Gay identity development, spiritual growth, and community-building. Somehow—it seemed to me and many others who came to faerie gatherings—we needed to start practicing *now* the values and culture we were seeking to achieve politically.

Faerie gatherings multiplied and spread. The basic idea was simply to get out in nature, away from prying and judging heterosexual eyes, and be with other Gay men. Out of this has come an international network of Gay men involved in spirituality and the inspiration for myriad political and culture projects—from the Sisters of Perpetual Indulgence and Nomenus, the faerie sanctuary in Oregon, to Gay theater projects, alternative health-care networks, safe-sex education efforts, books, films, and more.

Once again, Hay was there at the beginning.[1] What emerged from the faerie gatherings, however, was not a "movement," as Hay likes to explain, but a "development": "Radical faerie isn't a group or a movement—it's a process for self-development, growth and change, a way of 'being and becoming.' "[2] When the faeries hit the streets, Hay saw his dream of a modern society of Fools being realized. If, for me, the faerie "development" has remained too focused on the gatherings as an end in themselves (as delightful as it can be to spend a few days in nature with loving Gay brothers), it is undeniable that they have touched the lives of thousands of Gay men.

The 1980s and 1990s have been Hay's most productive years since the founding of Mattachine. Following the first gathering in 1979, Hay and Burnside moved back to Los Angeles. The Lesbian/Gay movement "rediscovered" its founder and Hay began to receive requests to speak at and participate in events throughout the country. Meeting these commitments and keeping up with the growing number of faerie gatherings keep Hay and Burnside on the road a good deal of the year.

Hay sought new applications for his concept of subject-SUBJECT consciousness, and he continued to advocate the cultural minority model. In 1983, he wrote that Lesbians and Gay men were "a separate people," a kind of tribe whose unifying trait was a unique way of perceiving the world. In calling on fellow Gays to stop imitating heterosexuals, he argued, "Some of us may be a combination of both hetero masculine and hetero feminine, but mostly we are a *combination of neither*." He often used the phrase "Gay not-men" to emphasize their distinction from heterosexual men (and to counter those who claim that Gay men's behavior is based in masculine socialization).

Hay also continued to emphasize the notion of an imminent

and necessary transformation in human consciousness. In essays from the mid-1980s on, he argues that human social patterns and institutions that evolved during the millennia-long epoch characterized by a scarcity of goods are no longer relevant in today's economy of abundance and its bounty of disposable goods. In fact, the social patterns and institutions of the mind-set of an economy of scarcity are now dysfunctional. This includes the extensive social apparatus that serves to enforce compulsory heterosexuality and procreation. Hay charges the Left with failing to realize that "the first act of the qualitative leap in consciousness must be to loosen and discard the bonds of absolute conformity to the cultural-emotional-spiritual mindset of the Economy of Scarcity—*which can no longer guarantee our survival.*"[3]

In the early 1990s, influenced by new research on the Two-Spirit tradition, Hay began to suggest that contemporary Gay men (and possibly Lesbians, too, although Hay hesitates to speak for them) were also a third gender. Here, his use of the term "gender" is the same as that of feminists—he means socially acquired roles and identities, not biological sex. The "third gender" formulation seems to have struck a chord. The possibility of a realm beyond male and female, beyond binaries, beyond even androgyny, is intriguing to many. It circumvents the stereotypes of Gay men as "womanish" and Lesbians as "mannish," but highlights the distinct *gender* difference that many of us feel.

One theme appears continuously in Hay's recent writings: the need for Lesbians and Gays to explain to the larger community who and what we are, to develop a "*legitimacy* for our Minority as a socio-political *contributive* entity on the American political scene." Throughout the 1980s and 1990s, Hay has criticized the Gay movement for failing (indeed, refusing) to provide society with an explanation of the nature of homosexuality. It remains to most Americans a nasty, dirty practice, on a completely separate plane from heterosexual love and its ideals. The image-conscious, professional lobbying approach of the movement's largely self-appointed leadership, Hay argues, has been ineffective in combating homophobia.

One of the interesting extensions of the concept of subject-SUBJECT that Hay has made is in the area of sexuality. Although Hay has been critical of the so-called sex radicals for relying on basically bourgeois conceptions of privacy and sexual libertinism (and failing to relate their program to broader goals), he has hardly been among the ranks of the sex-negative Gay men and feminists who would battle pornography. Hay refers to Gay men's sexuality as "our gateway to spirit," our insistent sexual drive as a "question" demanding an answer. For Hay, even our occasional, instantaneous connections with strangers can involve almost telepathic communication and the exchange of intense and affirmative erotic energies.

The more exotic practices of S/M sexuality hold little appeal for Hay, but when asked whether subject-SUBJECT ideals mean that Gay sex has to be "vanilla," Hay replied that the principle of subject-SUBJECT was "enjoying each other's enjoyment." If a "top" enjoys the pleasure he gives the "bottom," and vice versa, then the partners are in a subject-SUBJECT relationship: "If you allow me to tune in, nonjudgmentally, on your enjoyment, whatever that might happen to be in your consciousness as we approach each other, as I hope you will, in similar fashion, tune into my enjoyment—it could follow that it wouldn't matter whether you were large or small, or fat or thin, or old or young, *or soft or hard*: We would be intimately tuned in to sharing each other's enjoyments as subjects, each to the other, and each to himself as well."[4]

In fact, Hay has long been intrigued with what he considers to be the untapped potentials of Gay sexual responsiveness. Why is sex so important for Gay men? For Hay, the answer relates to a "vision I've held since I was a boy: that the overwhelming urge to sexuality I've felt since perhaps the age of eight or nine (and which I had always recognized was far more powerful in me than in Hetero boys my age) had been always urging me that we are supposed to discover something about our sexuality *collectively—something it is supposed to accomplish* when we invoke it as one voice collectively."[5] One thing sexuality does for us, Hay believes, is heal. Beginning in 1991, he has held yearly "sex magic" workshops to explore these potentials with other Gay men committed to subject-SUBJECT relating.

Having lived through the McCarthy era, Hay has remained alert to new and unexpected sources of repression. Of all the measures associated with the so-called "Reagan revolution" of the 1980s, Hay was most alarmed by the Family Protection Act. Provisions of this act would have allowed the government to deny a wide range of benefits not only to homosexuals but also to anyone who *advocated* the Gay lifestyle.[6] Hay was the only commentator I am aware of who pointed out the "thought control" elements of these provisions. As he argued in 1953 at the first Mattachine convention, proving that you're *not* homosexual can be much more difficult than it might seem. Hay still fears that Gays and political radicals might have to resort to the protection of the Fifth Amendment, as he was prepared to do when he appeared before the House UnAmerican Activities Committee in 1955.

Although Hay is sometimes characterized as the quintessential Gay separatist, he has been continuously involved in non-Gay progressive causes since the 1960s. In the early 1980s, he participated in draft-resistance networks. When Jesse Jackson ran for President in 1984 and 1988, Hay helped organize the Lavender Caucus of the Rainbow Coalition. He has, for several years, been a contributing editor for the progressive journal *Crossroads*. In the early 1990s, he helped form the Progressive Unity Council in Los Angeles, a coalition of labor and community groups. In all these groups and networks, Hay participated as an out-of-the-closet, in-your-face radical faerie, constantly challenging (and often irritating) his heterosexual colleagues. To these audiences, Hay consistently stressed the multidimensionality of Gay identity and challenged the narrow, often condescending ways in which Leftists viewed Lesbian and Gay issues. His political goal has always been the creation of multicultural, consensus-based coalitions of grassroots organizations and groups moving toward broad social change—a new Popular Front, but one informed as equally by conscious, spiritual values as by political goals and a materialist analysis.

This hardly exhausts the subjects and issues Hay has commented on in the past two decades. As Stuart Timmons notes, "On sheer principle, and with a strong reminder that he was not yet through kicking, he took on the most feared and despised issues within the community, issues no one else would touch."[7] One of these was the controversy surrounding the North American Man-Boy Love Association, or NAMBLA. Hay's position on this subject is represented here by his article, "Our Beloved Gay/Lesbian Movement at a Crossroads." No less controversial has been Hay's criticism of assimilationist tendencies among Lesbians, especially those women who refuse to explore their Lesbian differences, claiming that "all women are sisters." At the same time, Hay acknowledges the differences between Lesbians and Gay men. He has frequently called on both to explore these differences and re-articulate the basis of their alliance—and to stop pushing each other's emotional "buttons."

Hay has also challenged Bisexuals. From the perspective of a

politics based solely on a sexual definition of Gay people, the
inclusion of Bisexuals is completely consistent. From the perspective of a Gay *cultural* politics, however, it is problematic.
In distinguishing themselves from Gays, Bisexuals, perhaps
unwittingly, have reasserted the primacy of sexual categories,
aligning themselves with the assimilationist position that "we're
no different except for what we do in bed." For Hay, such an
understanding of Gay identity is reductionist and antithetical to
the community-building of a grassroots movement. Being Gay is a
cultural affiliation that does not necessarily preclude bisexuality,
because it is not strictly defined in terms of sexual behavior. Hay
asks of Bisexuals: Is yours a cultural identity, too?[8]

Today, the forces for progressive social change hardly seem to
register on the radar screen of American politics. But a time of
broad-based social movements will come again, and the principles Hay has articulated all his life will move back to the center of
politics, Gay and non-Gay. In the end, it's hard to imagine a Gay/
Lesbian movement, now or in the future, *without* the basic elements of Hay's political vision—the affirmation of Gay identity,
the cultural minority model, and the politics of community-
building and coalition.

Notes

1. Of course, Hay does not claim to be *the* founder of the radical faeries
any more than he claims to have single-handedly started the Gay movement, although his role in each was pivotal. In the case of the faeries, there
were other independent manifestations of Gay men's spirituality, such as
the San Francisco fairy circle organized by Arthur Evans in 1975–1976.

2. HH to Homosexual Information Center, March 19, 1991.

3. Harry Hay, "Understanding Gay Roots," unpublished ms., 1988.

4. In Mark Thompson, *Gay Spirit: Myth and Meaning* (New York: St.
Martin's, 1987), p. 288.

5. Harry Hay, "Where Have We Been? and Where Are We Now?" in *Visions of Gay Spirit: Keynote Addresses from the First Annual Celebrating Gay Spirit Visions Conference, November 2–4, 1990*, pp. 3–11 (Atlanta: Stepping Stone Publications, 1991), p. 10.

6. In 1981 both the House (Hansen Bill HR #311) and Senate (Laxalt-Jepsom Bill #1378) versions of the bill were voted out of committee.

7. Stuart Timmons, *The Trouble with Harry Hay: Founder of the Modern Gay Movement* (Boston: Alyson, 1990), pp. 295–96.

8. What Hay would like to see is a completion of the formula "homosexuality:Gay identity::bisexuality:X identity," where X stands for the cultural identity that might be based on bisexuality.

252

"This new planet
of Fairy-vision"

WRITTEN IN THE MONTHS after the first Gay men's faerie gathering, this essay reveals the catalytic effect that event had on Hay. Here he continues to explore the concept of subject-SUBJECT consciousness as the successor to dialectics and as the particular worldview Lesbians and Gay men learn through their life experiences and relationships. He also refines a technique he uses more and more in writing and speaking—retelling experiences from his own life to illustrate a key point. I think one of Hay's special gifts is this ennobling vision, the ability to see a deeper meaning in the everyday lives of Gay people. His tales of archetypal childhood experiences—what it's like to be excluded by others for being "sissies" or "tomboys," or to exclude ourselves when we discover we don't share other children's interests—reveal layers of ethical, social, and political meaning in our lives that we all too often overlook.

Hay's cultural politics were never more sharply defined than in the period following the first faerie gatherings. In 1980, he began calling on Gay men to "maximize the differences" between themselves and heterosexuals as a means of highlighting and enhancing their Gay traits. I still remember the riveting effect this had on me the first time I heard it—it went to the root of my lingering attachment to heterosexual approval. As we grope to understand who we are, there is a point where it becomes beneficial to detach oneself emotionally, intellectually, and socially from the oppressor and his symbols as a kind of spiritual exercise. (Hay is not a separatist, however. For him, the whole point of identifying the gifts we have and/or acquire as Lesbians and Gay men is to be able to *share* them with the larger community.)

254   Hay ends by calling on Gay men to form "Families of Conscious Choice." At the time, Hay had in mind the kind of "radical faerie circle collective" he was then trying to form in Los Angeles. In fact, Gay men in large numbers would form "families of conscious choice" in the 1980s—we called them "support networks"—in response to the AIDS crisis. As Hay points out, there could be no better example of subject-SUBJECT than the way in which Gay men have cared for themselves and each other in the face of this calamity, and no better example of subject-OBJECT than the way in which society at large has reacted to those afflicted with HIV disease.

Toward the New Frontiers of Fairy Vision . . . subject-SUBJECT Consciousness

This last Summer [1979] that wonderful Gay brother Don Kilhefner, together with John Burnside, Mitch Walker, and I, evoked a Spiritual Conference for Radical Fairies to be held in the Arizona Desert over the Labor Day weekend. At the opening of that Gathering, we called upon Gay Brothers to tear off the ugly green frog-skin of Hetero-male imitation in which we had wrapped ourselves in order to get through school with a full set of teeth to reveal the beautiful Fairy Prince hidden beneath.

Perhaps—before I go any further—I should explain what I mean by Fairy Spirituality. To me the term "spiritual" represents the accumulation of all experiential consciousness from the division of the first cells in the primeval slime, down through all biological-political-social evolution to your and to my latest insights through Gay Consciousness just a moment ago. What else can we call this overwhelmingly magnificent inheritance—other than spiritual?

The pathways we explored, during our Desert Retreat, to transform ourselves from Hetero-imitating Gays into Radical Fairies were many. Because the old ways of fairy transformation were obliterated during the nightmarish centuries of Judeo-Christian oppression, we felt ourselves free to invent new ones. So . . . to begin with . . .

- We reached out to reunite ourselves with the cornered, frightened, rejected little Sissy-kids we all once were;
- We reached out to recapture and restore in full honors that magick of "being a different species perceiving a different reality" (so beautifully projected almost a century ago by J. M. Barrie's *Peter Pan*) which may have encapsulated our boyhood and adolescence;
- We told that *different* boy that he was remembered . . . loved . . . and deeply respected;
- We told him we now recognized that he, in true paradox, had always been the real source of our Dream, of our strength to resist, of our stubborn endurance—a strength, again in true paradox, that few Hetero Males can even begin to approach, let alone match;
- We told that beloved little Sissy that we had experienced a full paradigm shift and that he could now come home at last to be himself in full appreciation.

Carl Jung, in this respect, proved to be absolutely right. When the Fairies reached out to make reunion with that long-ago-cast-out shadow-self so long suppressed and denied, the explosive energies released by the jubilations of those reunions were ecstatic beyond belief. When we caught up that lonely little Sissy-boy in an

ecstatic hug of reuniting, we were recapturing also the suddenly remembered sense of awe and wonder of Marvelous Mother Nature
who in those years so powerfully surrounded him. We were—
yes—even recapturing the glowing innocence of that Sissy-boy's
Dream. And in that Dream, the glowing non-verbal dream of
young Gayhood, may lie the key to the enormous and particular
contribution that Gay people may have to make to our beloved
Humankind—a key known as *subject-SUBJECT Consciousness.*

How to infect other Fairies with the same excitement we bubbled with in the Desert, and have soared and circled with ever
since? One way would be to share the steps by which *we* made the
breakthroughs to riveting perceptions hereinafter to be known as
subject-SUBJECT Consciousness. And then, beyond that, to share
some of the gleaming insights these new dimensions to the Gay Vision lend to problems that heretofore have locked us in.

To begin: How old were you when you first began to be aware
that you held a sense of beauty, an excitement, within you that
was different from what other boys felt? I must have been about
four when one night I inadvertently beheld my father's genitals. I
thought they were the most beautiful things I'd ever seen. And—
equally—in that flashing instant I knew I could never tell this *to
anybody*! I was nine when my Father attempted to *unmake* the
Sissy in me by teaching me to use a pair of boxing gloves—and I
simply *couldn't* understand why he wanted me to hit somebody
else (sixty years later I can still feel the stifling paralysis of that be-
wilderment). I didn't want to hurt the other boys, I wanted to be
tender to them in the same way I wanted them to be tender to me—
even as I also knew, in that very same moment, that here again I
couldn't share such heresies WITH ANYONE. All this time I would
pretend that I had a friend who felt the same way as I did, *and who
understood everything*. But of course I knew there was really no

such person. I knew that I was the only one like this in the whole world!

And then came that wonderful day—that shattering day, full of glitter and glisten and fireworks in my head and tumult of thunder and trumpets in my blood—when I discovered *a word*, a name, even though it was not yet in ordinary dictionaries, for me—FOR US! I wasn't the *only* one after all. I wasn't a wicked genie. I wasn't possessed by Evil or, maybe, crazy. There had been *others*—maybe even now others—maybe even one whom someday I could meet. Another—*just like me*—who would understand *everything*. And he would reach for my hand and we would run to the top of the hill to see the sunrise . . . and we'd never be lonely again! My source, of course, was a book by Edward Carpenter, in the locked glass cabinet behind the Lady Librarian's desk. There was another book in the case—about grass—by a man named Whitman, which I would discover on another day when the Librarian had to step out on an errand.

I suppose I was about eleven when I began first thinking about, and then fantasizing about, *him*! And, of course, I perceived him *as subject*. I knew that all the other kids around me thought of girls as SEX-OBJECTS to be manipulated, to be lied to in order to get them to "give in," and to be otherwise (when the boys were together without them) treated with contempt. And strangely, the girls seemed to think of the boys as objects, too. But HE whom I would *love* would be another ME. We wouldn't manipulate each other—*we would share*—and we'd always understand each other completely *and forever*!

Then came that second shattering day in my life, when I first met that other. And suddenly, between us, that socially invisible Arc flashed out and zapped into both our eagerly ready bodies *total systems of knowledge*; perhaps one of those inheritable consciousnesses which Dr. Ralph Sperry of Cal Tech has recently been rewarded for discovering—a system of knowledge which our flesh and brains had always been capable of but never, until that moment of imprinting, had actually contained. Like two new-hatched chicks whose incubator-attendant has now sharply tapped on their tray so that their feet, registering the vibrations, suddenly trigger body-mechanisms by which the chicks can know to peck at the ground around their feet thereby triggering further, in turn, how to feed and drink—so we two young Fairies knew, through that flashing Arc of Love, the tumult of Gay Consciousness in our vibrant young bodies in ways that we, in the moments before, never could have imagined and now would never again forget for as long as we lived. And this, *in ourselves and, simultaneously, in each other*, we also knew—subject-to-SUBJECT!

We must not suppose that we share subject-SUBJECT vision *only* in the spheres of Love and personal relations. Actually, almost at once, we also begin to become aware that we have been accumulating bits and pieces of subject-SUBJECT perceptions and insights all our lives—talking to trees and birds and rocks and Teddy Bears, and remembering what all we had shared by putting it down in poetry, storing it all up for that wonderful day when we finally would flash on to what it all meant. The personal collecting and storing up of these secret treasures, these beautiful beckoning not-as-yet comprehensible secret sacra, is part of the hidden misery-cum-exaltation of growing up Gay. For the world we inherit, the total Hetero-Male-oriented-and-dominated world of Tradition and of daily environment, the *summum bonum* of our history, our philosophy, our psychology, our culture, and very languages of communication—*all* are totally subject-OBJECT in concept, in definition, in evolution, in self-serving orientation. Men and Women are—sexually, emotionally, and spiritually—*objects* to one another.

Under the "fair-play-without-which-there-ain't-no-game" rules
of Hetero-Male aggressive territoriality, even the Hetero-Males—
precisely because they conceive of themselves as in lifelong competition each with the others—engage themselves endlessly in
tug-of-war games of Domination and Submission. The most lofty
system of governance the Hetero-Male has devised—Democracy
—must be seen as a domination of Minorities by a Majority,
a tyranny of the Majority if you will. Domination-submission,
subject-OBJECT. Fair play, the Golden Rule, Equality, Political
Persuasion, give-and-take—all of these are conditions of subject-
OBJECT thinking. In each case, a given person is the *object* of another person's perceptions, to be influenced, persuaded, cajoled,
jaw-boned, manipulated and therefore, in the last analysis, *controlled*. In the parliaments of government, the game of administration is to persuade Minorities to make of themselves *objects of approval* instead of objects of *dis*approval—but *objects* nonetheless.

To all of this we fairies should be, essentially, alien. Because
those *others* with whom we seek to link, to engage, to slip into, to
merge with are others *like me*, are SUBJECTS . . . like *ME*! I say "we
fairies *should be* alien" to as many aspects of our Hetero-Male-
dominated surroundings as we can be sensitive to, because we also
know, all too glumly, just how easily and how often we fall prey
to self-invited oppressions. How often do we allow ourselves,
through fuzzy thinking, to accept or to identify with Hetero-
originating definitions or misinterpretations of ourselves? The
Hetero-male, incapable of conceiving that there could possibly be
a window on the world other than his own, is equally incapable of
perceiving that we Gay People might not fit in *either* of his Man/
Woman categories, that we might turn out to belong to quite other
classifications. He might not be able to handle perceiving that the
notion of all persons being only varying combinations of male and

female is simply a Hetero-male-derived notion suitable only to Heteros and *holding nothing of validity insofar as Gay people are concerned.*

260

Yet we fairies allow Bully-boy to persuade us to search out the "feminine" in ourselves—didn't good ole Bully-boy used to tell us we threw balls like a girl? Wow, that surely is pretty sexist thinking we've internalized right there. Did you ever ask the girls back then if they thought you threw a ball like them? *They'd* have straightened you out in nothing flat! *They'd* have told you that you didn't throw a ball like a girl, but like something *other*. You were *not* a feminine boy, like the boys said, you were OTHER!

What *other*? Let us enter this brave new world of subject-SUBJECT consciousness, this new planet of Fairy-vision, and find out. All kinds of our friends would like to hear what we see. For instance, the Women of Women's Liberation would give their eye-teeth to know how to develop some measure of subject-to-SUBJECT relations with their men. And we who have known the jubilation of subject-to-SUBJECT visions and visitations *all our lives* have neither shared nor even spoken!

Of course, we haven't as yet spoken because we haven't as yet learned how to communicate subject-SUBJECT realities. Subject-SUBJECT is a multidimensional consciousness which may never be readily conveyable in the Hetero-male-evolved two-dimensional, or Binary, language to which we are presently confined. And we need more than mere words and phrases. We need what Scientists invent out of whole cloth when they attempt to describe and communicate new concepts. We need working models, a whole new mathematics, perhaps a new poetry—allegories—metaphors —a music—a new way of dancing. *We must re-examine every system of thought heretofore developed*, every Hetero-male-evolved subject-OBJECT philosophy, science, religion, mythology, politi-

cal system, language—divesting them every one of their binary subject-OBJECT base and re-inserting a subject-SUBJECT relation. Confronted with the loving-sharing Consensus of subject-
SUBJECT relationships *all Authoritarianism must vanish*. The Fairy Family Circle, co-joined in the shared vision of *non-possessive love*—which is the granting to any other and all others that total space wherein each may grow and soar to his own freely selected, full potential—reaching out to one another subject-to-SUBJECT, *becomes for the first time in history the true working model of a Sharing Consensus*!

To even begin to prepare ourselves for a fuller participation in our Gay subject-SUBJECT inheritance, we must, both daily and hourly, practice throwing off all those Hetero-imitating habits, compulsions, and ways of misperceiving which we constantly breathe in from our environmental surround. For this practice we need the constant company of our Fairy Families. We need the spiritual and emotional support of that non-verbal empathy which Sociologists assure us comprises almost seven-eighths of communication in any culture, that empathy we now refer to as Body Language. We need the marvelous input of each other's minute-by-minute new discoveries, as each of us begins to explore this vast new universe, this subject-SUBJECT frontier of human consciousness. As ours are the first deliberate feet upon this pristine shore, there are no guide-posts as yet erected, nor maps to be found in bottles, nor even the prospectuses of ancient visionary seers.

Well . . . not *quite* right. Sufi, for instance, is a philosophical discipline capable of bringing its students to subject-SUBJECT ways of relating and perceiving the landscapes of earth and heaven around them. It was invented and developed by Gay Persian mystic poets and kindred Islamic scholars, such as the great philosopher-poet Omar Khayyám, during the eleventh and twelfth centuries A.D.[1] It has long been generally recognized that Sufi vision was a capacity open only to a few—though the theory never went on to say *why*. For those capable of cultivating subject-to-SUBJECT vision, explanations were not necessary. For the Heteros, who were incapable of subject-to-SUBJECT perceptions, explanations could only have been incomprehensible.

In the last decade, Hetero Flower Children have revived some of Sufi's trance-inducing rituals *without*, however, comprehending the spiritual prerequisite that the participants be capable of relating *to each other*, as well as to the landscape and skyscape around, subject-to-SUBJECT, physically as well as emotionally and intellectually. Now it is time for Fairies to reclaim these penetrating exercises and restore to Sufi its liberating and transcendent capacities for subject-to-SUBJECT thought and perception.

Re-working all previously developed systems of Hetero thought will mean, of course, that all the data we previously have gathered concerning Shamanism and Magick must also be *re*-examined, *re*-worked, and *re*-organized along subject-SUBJECT evaluations— which is just as well because, for instance, failing to perceive the *lethal* subject-OBJECT character of most traditionally evolved Berdache ritualism and priestcraft, Gay scholars have tragically *misled* brothers and sisters of vulnerable minorities and thereby, in consequence, toxified themselves at precisely those moments when we desperately needed their crystalline clarifications.[2]

It is time, therefore, that we Fairies faced the reality that *no* Hetero-dominated culture, geared as each of them is to subject-OBJECT conformities, is ever about to discover acceptable Gay-Consciousness-tolerances with themselves if left to their own devices. *Only* when we Fairies begin to validate the contributions Gay Consciousness is capable of developing and delivering are the Heteros going to begin to sit up and take notice. Only when we be-

gin to manifest the new dimensions of subject-SUBJECT relationships superimposed over the now-obsolete Hetero subject-OBJECT
traditions—*and the Heteros begin to perceive the value of that su-*
perimposition—will they begin to see a value in altering their pri-
orities. Only when they begin to become aware of their need for
our contributions to their world-visions (and when they equally
discover *that their laws are in our way*, impeding our further out-
put in their favor) will they find themselves sufficiently challenged
to restructure their perceptions of essential human variations.

In the meantime, Fairies everywhere must begin to stand tall
and beautiful in the sun. Fairies must begin to throw off the filthy
green frog-skin of Hetero-imitation and discover the lovely Gay-
Conscious not-MAN (*anandros*, as the discerning early Greeks
called us) shining underneath. Fairies must begin creating their
new world through fashioning for themselves supportive Families
of Conscious Choice within which they can explore, in the loving
security of shared consensus, the endless depths and diversities
of the newly revealed subject-SUBJECT inheritances of the Gay
Vision!

Let us gather therefore—
    in secure and consecrated places . . .
To re-invoke from ancient ashes our Fairy Circle . . .
To dance . . .
To meditate—not in the singular isolation of Hetero subject-
    OBJECT praxis, but rather in Fairy Circles reaching out to
    one another in subject-SUBJECT evocation . . .
To find new ways to cherish one another . . .
To invent new rhyme and reason and ritual
    replacing those obliterated in the long nightmare of our
    Oppression—*and so*, in fact, *re-invent* ourselves . . .

To break through to ever more spiritually encompassing and
emotionally resurrective Gay Families and Fairy Family

264   Collectives, who by the very mutuality of their subject-
SUBJECT sharing are strengthened to reach out
contributively *to the Hetero community around them* . . .
And so finally—
To penetrate ever more comprehensively the essential nature
of covenants needed to lay the groundwork of a new
worldwide subject-SUBJECT consciousness SHARABLE BY
ALL!

Signed Harry (Henry) Hay, Los Angeles, July 5, 1980. Versions
published in *RFD* 24 (Summer 1980): 29–34 and *New Men, New*
Minds: Breaking Male Tradition, ed. Franklin Abbott (Freedom,
Calif.: Crossing Press, 1987), pp. 196–202.

Notes

1. Jalāl al-Dīn-Rūmī (1207–1273 C.E.) is another Sufi whose poetry
exudes homoerotic sentiment. See Will Roscoe, *Queer Spirits: A Gay*
Men's Myth Book (Boston: Beacon, 1995), pp. 202–7.

2. Hay means that Berdaches were involved in the spiritual belief systems of their tribes, which reflected a predominantly heterosexual orientation. Blind imitation of Two-Spirit roles or romantic idealization of their
social status misses a crucial distinction. Only in recent history have those
individuals who now identify as Gay had the opportunity to form genuinely subject-SUBJECT relationships and to develop a self-conscious "Gay
window."

"Essential to the orderly pursuit of happiness"

THROUGHOUT THE 1980s, Hay sought to apply a radical faerie perspective to issues facing the Lesbian/Gay community. A major setback in these years was the 1986 U.S. Supreme Court ruling on *Bowers v. Hardwick*, which upheld the Georgia sodomy law. In this essay, Hay analyzes this ruling and argues that it is an indictment of the ineffectiveness of Lesbian/Gay leadership since the 1970s and the political strategy he terms assimilationism. Hay asks, "What, after ten years, has assimilationism gotten us?" To judge by the *Bowers v. Hardwick* ruling, not much. In fact, information published since this essay was written reveals that Hay's analysis was on target. The ruling reflected the judges' own debased view of homosexuality—a view identical to the one held by the public at large, according to opinion polls that Hay cites.[1] Our behavior is still consistently equated—morally, legally, and symbolically—with prostitution, drug abuse, sexual coercion, perversion, and so forth.

Radical Faerie Proposals to the "March on Washington" Organizing Meeting

It would be a Radical Faerie perception that—given the current American reality in the wake of the Supreme Court's Georgia Sodomy Decision—a Gay Community March *on* Washington *making demands* would not be appropriate. Rather, we think, the Gay Community might stage a "Coming-Out March" *in* Washington, D.C., so that at last our Gay Minority could be heard and seen *as it wishes to be seen and heard*! Our reasoning is laid out in the following position paper.

The U.S. Supreme Court was quite aware that their decision was buttressed by a solid foundation of public support. According to the *Los Angeles Times*, an opinion poll taken in 1973 revealed that in the matter of whether the public felt that Homosexuality was right or wrong, 76 percent of those surveyed thought that Homosexuality was *wrong*. Over ten years later, in 1985, the *Los Angeles Times* poll asked respondents the same question and found that now the percentage of those thinking it was *wrong* had dropped, from 76 percent to 73 percent—*3 percent change in ten years*—after all the TV programs and the proliferation of respectable Gay Journals and carefully honed non-controversial Gay Pride Parades! At the same time, on the matter of whether Gay men and Lesbians should be hired without discrimination, 50 percent said yes. (Aside: This is one of the lovely paradoxes of grassroots Americanism—whether they like you or approve of you *or not*—they will usually agree that you are entitled to the basic decencies of civil rights). This nationwide opinion poll was published in December 1985.[2] The Georgia Sodomy Decision was handed down in the first week of July 1986, with Justice White's opinion speaking to and for that 73 percent.

Seventy-three percent of the American Public considers it *wrong* to be Homosexual? Seventy-three percent of the People think it's wrong to have blue eyes? *After all, we have about the same control over either.* Brothers and Sisters, this isn't homophobia. This is just plain ignorance! This is no different from Los Angeles County Supervisor Mike Antonovitch suggesting in the second week of November 1985, vis-à-vis the controversy over whether to close the baths, that "Gays should turn *straight again* for their own best interests as well as for the best interests of public health!"

When, back in 1948, I was beginning the thinking about how to get a Gay Group started, Homosexuality didn't concern *persons*— it concerned ACTS. Homosexuals were simply willfully perverted Heteros performing nasty unnatural acts. And now, in 1986, thirty-eight years and two movements later, for 73 percent of the American Public we still are, in their minds, only a perverse sexual variation of *them*. And, because we don't *choose* to do what they do *we are wrong*! Brothers and Sisters, isn't it about time we started to tell our parent Society who we really are? Isn't it about time we helped them to understand that rather than being merely a sexual variation of *them*, in all other senses exactly the same as they, we are a Separate People with, in several measurable respects, a rather different window on the world, a different consciousness, which may be triggered into being by our lovely sexuality?

But before we can do that, before we can start to tell them who we are, we shall have to begin telling *each other*. Up to now it's been easier to march in the streets and scream and holler than it has been to sit in a circle and examine and evaluate. It's been easier to pretend we're really *almost* the same as everyone else, although we don't fool the Heteros for a minute, than it is to dig and dig into the bicameral subterranean channels of collective memory—a cataloging and a collecting we've been avoiding like the plague. In typical 1970s Gay Liberation praxis, inherited from the counterculture rebellion (not revolution, as first assayed, but merely rebellion), we simply announced, "We are the children of all Minorities *and we got rights*!" The Georgia Sodomy Decision seems to have blown that certainty back into the company of a number of other deeply *unexamined* assumptions.

268

Here, perhaps, Pioneers like myself are the ones at fault. From the very beginnings of our Movement, along with the other Social and Political Radicals and Outlaws from whom I had learned the outlines and dimensions of class struggle, we all had also assumed that as citizens of these United States we had, among other blessings, the Fundamental if not God-given Right to privacy, once we would be able to obtain it for ourselves. Of course, in the 1920s, the majority of city people, the historical working class, and the recent comers newly off farms either lived in small houses where children and adults shared bedrooms, three to four people to a room at least, or they lived in rooming or boarding houses, where, again, people slept at least two to a room and sometimes, even, two to a bed. Privacy for most was still a Dream of Liberation—and in the meantime, the city outskirts, the hills, the sand dunes at the beach, or the shadows under the pier served for quickie-spots in the daytime, and the vacant lots or the temporarily empty bushes in the park served as substitutes for the "Children of Twilight."

Privacy for most, Hetero and Gay alike, would remain a *Fundamental right* (or privilege) rather than a reality until after the Second World War. But that *it was a Fundamental right* none of us ever had any doubts. *So it comes as a shock* to our Gay Community to discover that our supposed *Fundamental right to privacy* (the working-class equivalent to "a man's castle" ideal) does not enter Constitutional jurisprudence "even as an expansive reading of the due process clause of the Fourteenth Amendment"—*an expansive reading*, meaning the Court's recognition of the presence of certain Fundamental rights "enumerated nowhere in the document itself" (*Socialist Review*, September 1986, "The Abortion Debate")— until the plurality opinion in *Connecticut v. Griswold*, written by Justice William O. Douglas in 1965. And the Majority recognition by the court of every citizen's Fundamental "right to Privacy" does not come until the landmark Abortion Decision, *Roe v. Wade* in 1973. In Justice Blackmun's Majority-accepted Opinion, he found a "right of personal privacy" implicit in the concept of "ordered liberty," which included "activities relating to marriage, procreation, contraception, family relationships, and child-rearing education." (Aside: It may be important to note that *within* Blackmun's judicial recognition of the individual's Fundamental right to personal privacy lay a right of the government to regulate where the government's interests are compelling—one of these compelling interests being the government's responsibility *for the preservation of human life*. Eventually we Gay People may be able to make a claim here.) Justice Blackmun's "ordered liberty" phrase refers to the great Supreme Court Justices Oliver Wendell Holmes and John Marshall Harlan who, in two cases concerning educational policy, jointly wrote, "Liberty denotes not merely freedom from bodily restraint but also the right of the individual to contract, *to engage in any of the common occupations of life, to acquire useful knowledge*, to marry, *to establish a home and bring up children, to worship according to the dictates of his own conscience*, and *generally to enjoy those privileges long recognized at common law as essential to the orderly pursuit of happiness by free men.*"

Now, in contrast to all these formerly held hopes and dreams, it would appear in this new and sobering social climate confronting the Lesbian and Gay Community—as the shock waves of the Georgia Sodomy Decision begin to subside—that perhaps Justice Byron White, writing the Court's majority opinion, is speaking for the *Los Angeles Times* poll's 73 percent when he says, "Plainly enough, otherwise illegal conduct is not always immunized whenever it occurs in the home. Victimless crimes, such as the possession and use of illegal drugs, do not escape the law where they are

269

committed at home." It would appear that the 73 percent do indeed seem to perceive us still—just as they did in 1950 when our Movement began—as merely a willful and perverse sexual variation of *themselves* who, in refusing to conform, *are wrong.*

Hell's bells and tarnation! Our lovely and talented Gay Community with an enormous 100,000-year history of discovery and largely selfless contribution, our Minority of Ducks-in-whatever-henhouse-of-Chickens-they-were-inadvertently-born-into knows that we as a Separate People comprise a total deviation of consciousness that is not to be reduced and debased by the nasty sexual drooling of dirty legalistic inferior minds. How on earth did we Lesbian and Gay Folk in the latter half of the twentieth century land in such a pickle? I suggest it might be the fault of another "unexamined assumption"—the assumption that our Gay Liberationist Pooh-bahs knew not only the history but the theory and practice of the American Class Struggle when, in fact, by their very actions, they proved that they didn't. When, in the heady jubilees of Gay Liberation, we hit the bricks behind our exuberant Gay Zappers hollering, "We're a Minority, too—and we want our GAY Rights!" we had forgotten to check ourselves out against the shape and substance of the Minorities who had demanded and gotten rights in the decades and centuries before us. All such Minorities, including the Founding Fathers, who came to participate in the American Dream brought things in common which, upon being recognized, served to recommend in turn each new arrival to those others already ensconced. The things brought in common were that each group comprised, itself, an aggregate of God-fearing People disposed to presenting themselves as Law-abiding Nuclear Families bringing their labor-power to sell, and their artisan crafts and intellectual expertises to share. And, in exchange for the Labor Power which the exploding American Industrial Frontier so

270

ravenously needed, America grudgingly granted them *first-class citizenship*.

So, when the Gay and Lesbian Minority suddenly burst upon the scene in the post-Industrial 1970s, who *were* we really? And what did WE bring to share? Aye—there's the rub. Have we ever *really* told them who we are and what we bring? The Traditional Yankee is famous in song and story for knowing how to nose out a shrewd buy. "You don't buy a pig in a poke," they said—which translates out for us urban-types into, "We don't buy what we can't see." Well, many of us Gay Liberationist-types spent the 1970s in one consciousness-raising rap or another *telling ourselves* who we were and that we were okay, and even discovering that the very different ways by which we Gay People perceive *were not sick or distorted* but might even be contributive and inspirational. But did we bother to correlate these many discoveries into abstracts that the Hetero Community could recognize and apply? *No, we didn't.* In the patois of our traditional grassroots Yankee, we didn't let him see the pig in the poke. And this, I would propose, was where we went wrong. Where did we get the notion that we as a Separate Minority were entitled to rights without demonstrating ourselves as useful folks with gifts to share—as had all the other Minorities before us? It's no use crying over spilled milk—we didn't do this and we haven't—but in this Washington March organizing year we still can.

And I for one think we have brought, and continue to bring, immense capacities and gifts to share. I for one think we have been contributing down through the millennia all kinds of capacities and talents and idiosyncratic differences from *them*, which we now must begin to look at and recognize as our own *and appreciate and respect*. Like—f'rinstance—our capacities as Mediators through History—in cultures around the world as diverse as the

271

ancient Sumerians in the valleys of the Tigris and Euphrates, the
Neolithic as well as the Barbarian Celts of the Danube and Rhine
Valleys, the Achaeans of Macedonia, the Dyaks of Borneo, the Ar-
abs of nineteenth- and twentieth-century Morocco, and the Navaho of yesterday's and today's Arizona . . .

> . . . MEDIATORS *between the seen and the unseen*—as
> Berdache Priests and Shaman Seers, as artists and architects,
> as Scientists, as Teachers, and as Designers of the possible;

> . . . MEDIATORS *between the make-believe and the real*—
> through Theatre and Music and Dance and Poetry;

> . . . MEDIATORS *between the Spirit and the flesh*—as
> Teachers and Healers and Counselors and Therapists.

And in twentieth-century America—how do we differ?—and how
do we remain the same?

We must organize these talents and capacities into legal abstracts
which might fit the Constitutional prerequisites of Justices Holmes
and Harlan's findings for *privacy* and *ordered liberty*. In today's
community, where so many stable households are "live-in sanc-
tioned" rather than "marriage-sanctioned," surely an expansive
reading of Justice Holmes's right "to marry" and/or "establish a
home" will be extendible to "to couple" and/or "to establish a
home based on a stable relationship." Surely the analytical and organizing brains of our Gay Community can abstract the talents
and capacities above-cited to qualify under Justice Holmes's rights
"to contract" and "to engage in any of the common occupations of
life." Justice Blackmun, in his eloquent and moving dissent from
the Majority Opinion in *Bowers v. Hardwick* says, "The fact that
individuals define themselves in a significant way through their in-

timate sexual relationships with others suggests, in a Nation as diverse as ours, that there may be many 'right' ways of conducting those relationships, and that much of the richness of a relationship will come from the freedom an individual has to *choose* the form and nature of these intensely personal bonds." Such a respectful concept of the, indeed, many lovely and deeply rewarding relationships that are known to exist in our Community could easily be found to subsume Justice Holmes's right "to enjoy those privileges long recognized at common law as essential to the orderly pursuit of happiness by free men." When we Lesbian and Gay Sisters and Brothers begin to supply Justice Blackmun and others of like mind with the above-proposed materials on who *we really are* and *what we bring*, we may find ourselves being aided by many in developing materials for State and Federal legislation that will truly secure our "privacies" and "ordered liberties."

We Radical Faeries, then, propose that our March on Washington become instead a real "Coming-Out" March IN Washington, revealing at last for all to see who we really are and what we bring to share—a Separate People who seek to live collectively private lives of their own within their own communities but who have much to share, in great respect and affection, with the American community surrounding us . . . when we are invited to do so . . . and/or when occasions warrant it.

> Signed "For the Radical Faeries, Harry Hay," Los Angeles, October 10, 1986.

Notes

1. According to David J. Garrow, Justice Lewis Powell, who had employed numerous Gay assistants in his office, was heard to say that he had never met a homosexual and to refer to homosexuality as "an affliction."

John Stevens privately stated that he hated "homos" but took the stand that "we have to live with it" (*Liberty and Sexuality: The Right to Privacy and the Making of* Roe v. Wade [New York: MacMillan, 1994], pp. 659–60). The approach adopted by the attorneys who argued on behalf of Hardwick is a good example of an assimilationist strategy. Their brief made almost no reference to homosexuality—leaving unchallenged whatever misinformation, bias, and bigotry the justices themselves held—emphasizing instead "values of intimate association, and of sanctity of the home" (ibid., p. 658).

2. John Balzar, "American Views of Gays: Disapproval, Sympathy," *Los Angeles Times*, December 20, 1985. Cf. Garrow, *Liberty and Sexuality*, p. 622.

274

"Sacred persons"

W HEN HAY UNDERTOOK his research on the North American Berdache or Two-Spirit role in the 1940s—an alternative gender status for males and females who combined the
work and social roles of both sexes along with traits unique to
their role—homosexuality was still a tabooed topic in anthropology. Lesbians, Gays, and Bisexuals in the discipline, like Ruth
Benedict, Margaret Mead, and Clyde Kluckhohn, lived carefully
closeted double lives. Published in 1986, *The Spirit and the Flesh*
by Gay anthropologist Walter Williams was the first book-length
study on the subject of Two-Spirits.[1] In the following selection,
Hay reviews Williams's study, drawing on his own research and
years of contact with Native people. He raises important questions about Williams's interpretation of the Berdache role and
offers valuable corrections to some of his data.

In his 1963 article "The Hammond Report," Hay had reprinted
a long-forgotten account of the Two-Spirit role of Acoma Pueblo,
and demonstrated how ethnohistorical data could be distilled out
of otherwise homophobic sources. According to Hammond, an
Army medical doctor assigned to the Pueblo area in the 1850s, the
mujerado (a New Mexican Spanish term meaning "woman-ed"
or "made a woman") was an arbitrarily selected man who was
rendered "impotent" through excessive masturbation and horse-
riding.[2] This fantastic rationalization reminded Hay of the practical jokes he had seen his Pueblo Indian friends, who would never
confide to outsiders the real meaning or actions of their ceremonies, play on gullible tourists. In "The Hammond Report," he

sought to reconstruct the actual rituals and beliefs that might have lain behind the distorted information Hammond recorded.

276   In the late 1980s, Hay returned to the subject of the Pueblo Two-Spirit role. Drawing on Alfonso Ortiz's studies of Pueblo ceremonial life, he argued that Hammond must have been describing one of the means by which an individual became a member of a Pueblo medicine society—what Ortiz terms "trapping"—in which a society needing members actively recruited them, sometimes through trickery.[3] The account of the artificial creation of *mujerado* at Acoma that Hammond reported may have been an example of such a procedure, by a society otherwise faced with extinction. In this case, the medicine society would have been comprised of Two-Spirits. Hay's suggestion is provocative. The presence of a Two-Spirit medicine society, while plausible, has never been reported for the Pueblos. In fact, the Tewa Two-Spirit role was considered by the Tewa traditionals Hay knew to be a *ceremonial* status, not merely a social role or a personal inclination. Hay's argument with Williams is based on Williams's failure to appreciate the ritual and ceremonial nature of Two-Spirit roles, conflating them instead with modern conceptions of "Gay" and "homosexual." It is an important point that all anthropologists and scholars studying this dimension of Native American cultures would do well to heed.

Review of *The Spirit and the Flesh* by Walter Williams

The Spirit and the Flesh is a valiant first step in attempting to corral between a single pair of bookbindings the burden of what we know about the Berdache. Who were Berdaches? They were

Native American males who, as Explorers and Missionaries from the sixteenth to the nineteenth centuries protested, degraded their sex by stooping to such menial dress and behaviors as are suitable only to women. Yeccchhh! That these people, these Berdaches, would actually be collectively devoted persons role-playing fairly sophisticated sacred rituals in the daily life-processes of their given villages would be concepts totally beyond the limited love-starved consciousness of the Judeo-Christian God-ridden European Barbarian Invaders and their American Barbarian descendants—including this reviewer's Great-Grandfathers, Great-Uncles, and assorted cousins.

Having lived for a month in the summer of 1982 with an active and practicing *winkte*, the sacred or ceremonial term for the Native American Lakota half-man/half-woman, Dr. Williams manages, through extensive interviews, to convey a surprising miscellany of cultural detail. Yet, the pressure of time limits also seems to have at moments prevented him (and so us) from seeing the forest for the trees. We are told, sometimes quite engagingly but certainly with monotonous persistence, by both Dr. Williams and his several informants, that *winkte* (among the Lakota) or *bote* (among the Crow) or *nádleehé* (among the Navaho) are sacred persons trained to carry out ritual and ceremonial responsibilities vital to the continual well-being of their respective communities. But we are never presented with at least an overview of one of the sacred webs by which the given societies attempt, as Hamilton Tyler puts it in his *Pueblo Animals and Myths*, "to order its world and to establish Man's place in it," and thereby equally reveal the sanctity of the contributed thread-patterns or weaves for which the *winkte* or the *bote* or the *nádleehé* were venerated by their respective Cultures.[4]

And here we Gay Researchers and Scholars should be committing ourselves to serving *two* prime loyalties instead of the Hetero's usual *one*. We Gay Scholars—researchers and critics alike—must be bringing the particular fresh insights we perceive through our Gay Window, as they further illuminate the specifics of our particular Study, to the attention of the Hetero-oriented Academe to be sure. But we, equally, must marshal all our powers of insight to restore to the often-alienated Gay Indian Brothers and Sisters *what could be their own perceptions of Tradition* into which Gay values, possibly quite distinct from and even foreign to our usual Whiteman expectations, are interwoven.

It is in this area that I feel Dr. Williams's study from time to time loses track of what has to be its perspective—his appreciation of how the Berdache ceremonial institutions, as various Native American Communities conceived and shaped them, were granted space to develop their natural bent as Mediators between the seen and the unseen, between the heartspaces of persons and the Collective's best interests. It is a given universal that cultural communication, not only from one ethnic group to another but, equally, from one generation to the next even within a given group, is one-eighth verbal *and seven-eighths nonverbal*. Dr. Williams, by sharing spiritual as well as physical space for a summer month with a Lakota *winkte* acquaintance, certainly tells the sensitive reader how to put himself into an almost one-to-one contact with the *wakan*, the sanctity, that the *winkte* feels about himself. But in assuring us also that, during this single month, he also—Dr. Williams, Whiteman—was prepared by his *winkte* friend to engage in a *yuwipi* Ceremony, a Sun Dance, and a Vision Quest (which then became so private an experience that in consequence he can't share further)—the contextual nonverbal seven-eighths of the communication is suddenly snatched out of our reach. It's a little bit like someone's telling us that we needn't bother to read any of the well-known expositions on what Catholicism is all about or how an inquiring layman should perceive Catholicism in relation to himself, because you—our friend and correspondent—last summer lived with a Catholic teenager who was preparing for Confirmation "and so was able to get the whole scoop!" One might become suspicious that the seven-eighths of even Lakota spiritual communication turned out, for Dr. Williams, to be equally out of reach.

A major error of Dr. Williams's study is more basically a failure to comprehend himself how much he needed to thoroughly master the seven-eighths nonverbal values of the day-in-day-out life of Spirit that characterizes Native American Village and Pueblo life-processes, an appreciation that usually takes most students several years of intimate day-by-day confrontation to internalize. Totally ignoring the candid opinions of the Native American people he quotes on pages 217–18—and, indeed, in myriad other places in his text such snippets as (in talking about a Gay-identified person in the Village) "No, he's not *winkte*, because he's not *spiritual*"—Dr. Williams seems not to have ever appreciated that it was the ritual life-processes being observed and evaluated by the sixteenth-seventeenth-eighteenth-nineteenth-century God-driven Explorers that gave rise to the categorical epithets of *sodomite, hermaphrodite,* and *Berdache* in the first place. When Coronado came to Zuni in 1540, his Franciscans didn't see Gay men, they saw *lhaman-ona* (i.e., "the one who *is being lhaman*"), which was translated in the 1950s as "is being like a woman." Since "woman" in Zuni is *okya,* we'd give a pretty penny to know what the respondent really said. There is no possibility of a word in Zuni for "transvestite" and obviously *lhama* or *lhaman* has to do with something *quite other* than "woman," or even "woman-like." Similarly, La Salle and Marquette weren't seeing Gay men when they observed *ikoueta* among the Illinois or *aya'kwa* among the Fox.[5] They saw Ceremonial persons, whom they categorized as Berdache, performing the life-process invocations of ritually lived days—ceremonials and ritual processes, which, largely driven underground in the twentieth century by U.S. Government Agents and Missionaries, are now beginning to return. Yet Dr. Williams wants to call every Gay Indian he meets, whether in the Dance Plaza or in the pages of Edmund White's *States of Desire*, either a "Berdache" or by the particular name of this Ceremonial function sacred to a given tribe. In Native American values this is not permissible.

The regaining Queen Mother of the extant Gays at Hupa-Weitchpek in 1983 was Frank Colegrove, who had returned from being a Hollywood hairdresser in 1974. Known at Hupa as Fada, he had revived the Traditional Brush and Kick Dances, and was serving also as Tribal War Chief. But neither he nor Jerry Baldy, referred to several times as "Berdache" by Dr. Williams, had been *trained* as ceremonial Hupa Berdaches. Jerry Baldy, like Fada, was a Hollywood hairdresser. However, we were told when we visited Hupa in 1976, when "the Messenger" was then living there,[6] that after a lapse of many years, a young man *was* being ceremonially trained as a Berdache.

My great friend among the Tewa people, whom Edmund White, in his *States of Desire*, identified as "Arnie," and who was my source for the Tewa ceremonial terms *kwih-doh* (literally, "old woman/man"), may very well have been one of the most well-versed persons when it came to ceremonial minutiae of his particular Pueblo.[7] He would *never* have used *kwih-doh* (his tribe's ceremonial term for "Berdache") as describing himself because, indeed, he had never been so trained. His Pueblo has always been known as one of the stiff-necked ones, and training young Gay boys in the *kwih-doh* tradition might very well have been discontinued in the 1920s when the Federal Government circulated the infamous Secret Dance File, with its scurrilous accusations of sexual misconduct, to drum up anti-Indian sentiment, and clapped the entire tribal council of Taos Pueblo into prison to force them to abandon traditional religion—from there on any such trainings were simply allowed to drop away.[8]

Like so many other Native American cultures, as Claude Lévi-Strauss has observed, the Tewa Society is divided into two classifications (see Alfonso Ortiz, *The Tewa World*)—the "Dry Food People," or common Tewa, and the "Made People," or *patowa*, who have been ceremonially trained to life-long spiritual responsibilities. There is another class of spiritually responsible people among the Tewa, the *towa é*, who are appointed from the ranks of the Dry Food People for a year by the life-long Caciques of the Summer and Winter Moieties. "Arnie" had often served as *towa é*.

The rest of the Edmund White story, quoted unfortunately by Dr. Williams several times for its separate elements, is equally garbled. The young Anglo Professor whom White used as his source-contact was introduced to "Arnie" by me at Christmas 1975. I don't think the Professor ever actually saw a Harvest Dance—I think he only mis-heard about it from "Arnie" and me. "Arnie" would never have performed the mock-marriages. Only "Made People" like the K'ossa (the Winter Clowns) could do that. And I didn't know of any K'ossa among the Tewa or K'oshare among the Keres who were even Gay let alone *kwih-doh* (who, therefore, would also have been "Made People"). Dr. Williams also quotes me as having said that, at one point in the 1970s, three of the Pueblo Governors were Berdache (which, in Tewa, would be *kwih-doh*) and therefore "Made People" or *patowa*. But political officers must come from the "Dry Food People." There were (and still are) many Tewa *towa é* who were Gay, but insofar as I know only two of the Tewa Pueblos had resumed *kwih-doh* training by 1980. Errors like these can easily dismay, confuse, and even defeat Gay Indian Brothers and Sisters longing, and yet terrified, to go home.

All that being said, the book is also a vast compendium of gaily related information, chock-a-block full of new anthropological notions to explore, old academic confusions to clean up, and all of it very readable. The book contains unexpected gems as well. Plates 9 and 10 are photographs of the Zuni *lhaman-ona*, We'wha, located in the National Archives in Washington, D.C. by Will Roscoe. Plate 10 was labeled merely as "Children with their teacher in front of the school at Zuni." Will immediately realized that the adult standing in the middle was We'wha. Why the teacher—clearly standing by the doorway at the right of the picture—is cropped out here is not explained. It is certainly *not* a "group of Zuni Indians, females on the left, males on the right," as Williams has it.

The Spirit and the Flesh is, for all its faults, clearly a giant step in the direction of enabling, perhaps even empowering, Heteros to see Gay People as we wish to be seen and hearing Gay People as we wish to be heard. It is without doubt a book no serious library can in future ever be without.

> Signed Harry Hay, Los Angeles, January 25, 1987. A version
> appeared in the *Homosexual Information Center Newsletter*.

Notes

1. Walter Williams, *The Spirit and the Flesh* (Boston: Beacon Press, 1986).

2. Henry Hay, "The Hammond Report: A Deposition, with Subsequent Commentary on the Conspiracy of Silence anent Social Homophilia," *ONE Institute Quarterly* 6(1, 2) (Winter–Spring 1963): 6–21.

For background on the Acoma Berdache, see Will Roscoe, ed., *Living the Spirit: A Gay American Indian Anthology* (New York: St. Martin's, 1988), pp. 57–59, and *The Zuni Man-Woman* (Albuquerque: University of New Mexico Press, 1991), pp. 25, 26, 175, 251.

3. Alfonso Ortiz, *The Tewa World: Space, Time, Being and Becoming in a Pueblo Society* (Chicago: University of Chicago Press, 1969), p. 87.

4. Hamilton A. Tyler, *Pueblo Animals and Myths* (Norman: University of Oklahoma Press, 1975), p. ix.

5. For these terms, see Will Roscoe, "A Bibliography of Berdache and Alternative Gender Roles among North American Indians," *Journal of Homosexuality* 14 (1987): 81–171, p. 139, and La Salle in Louis Hennepin, *A Description of Louisiana*, trans. John G. Shea (New York: John G. Shea, 1880), p. 368.

6. Hay has never identified "the Messenger" in writing, although Peter Matthiessen names him in *Indian Country*. He played an instrumental role in Native American revivalism through the 1960s, and developed a genuine affection for Hay, whom he calls "Chief Longhair."

7. Edmund White, *States of Desire: Travels in Gay America* (New York: E. P. Dutton, 1980), pp. 99–101. Hay chose not to disclose "Arnie's" real name at the time he wrote this but has since identified him as Antonio Garcia, the well-known cultural expert of San Juan Pueblo, who served more than one term as that village's governor. I met Tony in 1983, a few months before his death.

8. On the infamous Secret Dance File, see Roscoe, *Zuni Man-Woman*, chap. 7.

"What we Two-Eyed Ones
have to share"

IN THE FOLLOWING TALK, presented to a community audience in San Francisco in 1991, Hay attempts to show that the experience of modern Lesbians and Gay men in reclaiming their self-esteem in the face of overwhelming homophobia has given them valuable gifts and insights they can share with other communities.

It should not be surprising that a lifelong Leftist would challenge the Left stereotype of homosexuals as bourgeois degenerates, by showing how, in fact, they contribute to social change by virtue of their sexual difference. In the discussion following the talk, however, some in the audience interpreted Hay as claiming that Gays were better than others, or that they were more oppressed, or that they were a vanguard. In fact, the dialogue never got past these points to a consideration of the validity of Hay's description of Lesbian/Gay social experience. This seemed to me partly based on a lack of awareness of Hay's long-term commitment to coalition politics, and partly on the continuing reluctance of many Lesbians and Gay men to seriously assess their personalities and lives. No one bristles when we speak of the great contribution Black spirituals have made to music; or of the contributions of Jewish artists and intellectuals to modern culture; or of the unique experiences women gain through motherhood. And yet the suggestion that growing up Queer gives us pertinent skills and outlooks, or that our experience in overcoming oppression might inspire others, unleashes such furious objections that the conversation soon comes to a halt.

Hay's intentions were quite the opposite of the criticisms made that evening. He believes that the social integration of Lesbian and Gays *as Queers*—not sanitized homosexuals who keep their sex life out of sight and public discourse—depends precisely on their ability to claim that homosexuality is good for something. This is not elitism but pragmatic politics. If homosexuality has nothing to contribute, if the social experience of Gay people offers nothing that might enrich American social life, then what makes us think that non-Gays would be willing to extend to us civil privileges that they believe they have earned precisely because of the sacrifices they make in conforming to the norms we seem to flaunt?

What Gay Consciousness Brings, and Has Brought, to the Hetero Left!

My years as a radical Community Organizer in California, and more specifically in Los Angeles, prepared me to figure out how to set up a group in which Gay Brothers and Sisters would feel *safe and secure* from the witch-hunts and publicized entrapments that threatened our lives and livelihoods daily in the 1930s, 1940s, and 1950s. They taught me also how to safeguard our thoughts and actions from the probings and ferretings out of the local Vice Squad who, like their Federal counterpart, the RED Squad, prowled our back-alleys, pressured our neighbors to tell tales, listened in on our phone conversations, and even steamed open our mail.

During the first Mattachine Society years of 1951 to 1953, I projected the concept, drawn from my years as a Marxist teacher, that we Gays and Lesbians constituted a "Cultural Minority." To the majority of the new members who flocked in from October of 1953 on, the "Cultural Minority" concept was anathema! To this second wave of Homosexual Middle-Class Respectables, "We were absolutely the same as everybody else except for a minor sexual variation," and "Homosexuals had absolutely nothing in common with each other except for their sexual inclinations." Yet, by 1969—when a positive Gay Identity had been firmly established, Mattachine's most significant achievement, in contrast to the negative self-deprecating, self-demeaning, bitchy, back-biting Hetero-gone-wrong or Hetero-turned-pervert that we all had been socialized into perceiving ourselves as being since time immemorial—the concept of ourselves as a "Cultural Minority" was almost universally regarded as one that had been central to our Homophile Community's thinking since the year One!

The Stonewall Rebellion of 1969 transformed our *positive Gay identity* from the single person to the Collective. And with that came the beginning of Gay and Lesbian groups expanding their functions to include political activity on an ongoing basis. Of course, there had been dozens of political actions between 1951 and 1969: entrapment cases openly fought in the courts and won; a U.S. Supreme Court case won; a motorcade in L.A.; openly advertised professional conferences in mainline hotels; protest demonstrations in L.A. and San Francisco; open forums on Berkeley's Telegraph Avenue; open dialogues on radio and TV; and polite picket lines in Philadelphia. But while such sporadic actions necessarily cleared the ground for future actions, they didn't touch to life the Gay Consciousness of the huge majority of the Homophiles still hiding away, still buried alive under the ancient negativity.

However, Stonewall's inevitable consequence was the simultaneous lighting off of the dozens of powder-trains by now previ-

ously laid by the twenty years of such sporadic efforts, and in dozens of cities suddenly groups of us Gays and Lesbians no longer had difficulty conceiving of ourselves as Political Cultural Minorities   287
with basic civil rights, presumably guaranteed by the U.S. Constitution, that were being denied us. The Mattachine Society experience, with its several dimensions of touching to life this *positive Gay Identity* and launching the concept of ourselves as a Cultural Minority, plus Stonewall illuminating politically the material dimensions of the Cultural Minority Collective, transformed the shape and substance of Gay Consciousness.

In April 1976, I flashed on a contextual vision incorporating the essence of the non-possessive love Gay men have the capacity for developing and sharing with one another—a dream I had been lugging along miserably, because I couldn't find words to share it, since its inspiration as a Gay transposition of the Wobbly ideal of Brotherhood that I'd received fifty years before. When I think of myself, I think of me as *subject*. When I think of that glowing OTHER who illuminates my life, I don't think of him as an object—an object to be manipulated or cozened, cajoled or persuaded, in every intent possible, to be controlled—I think of him as SUBJECT also, as I do myself, sharing with me as I with him, a double sharing to be celebrated. I don't think of his masking his weakness with my supposed strengths, or buttressing my weaknesses with his strengths—the Hetero man-woman pattern composing the complementary whole so admired by Modern Sociology—I seek a supplementary relationship. I don't seek a clinging vine, I seek another Faerie who is as independent, as resilient, as self-reliant as I am, who will stand shoulder-to-shoulder with me looking down the same road ahead with similarly shining inquisitive eyes. In short, the love I seek to complete my life is 180 degrees different from the ideal sought by Heteros. And this 180-degree-different-way-of-perceiving has been my window on the world for most of my life. I call this subject-SUBJECT Consciousness—and I, and the Radical Faerie Brothers, have been suggesting, since 1979, that our development of this subject-SUBJECT Consciousness (which we Radical Faeries don't all yet necessarily practice *but of which we are all quite capable*) may be the reason our NON-reproductive Minority keeps appearing millennia after millennia after millennia.

It is a truism of natural selection that no negative trait (and as you recall, a negative trait is one that does not reproduce itself) ever appears in a given species millennia after millennia after millennia *unless* it in some way serves the survival of that species. I suggest that what we, a Cultural Minority, a separate Sub-species whose time has come, bring to share with any Hetero Community who will welcome us is this subject-SUBJECT Consciousness, which is, as we can demonstrate, the basis of the loving-sharing consensus. To the many Hetero Societies in which subject-OBJECT Consciousness has been evolving and developing since at least the third glacial interstitial epoch, with enormous success and surpassing achievements, up to its twentieth-century apotheosis as Democratic "being and becoming," and is now hardening before their very eyes into a hodge-podge of ungovernable systems between which the inevitable confrontations can only be *lethal*—to such Societies I suggest that this new subject-SUBJECT Consciousness we Queers bring may be critical.

The Hausa people of West Africa say that the men and women of the village who relate to each other have, each one, an eye in their soul by which they perceive themselves, however dimly, on the right path in the dark and perilous realm of *SPIRIT*. But the souls of those men among them who relate to other men, and women who relate to other women, have *two* eyes![1] This Two-Eyes feature, different from the way Eurocentric Imperialisms might misinterpret it, bestows *neither* special powers nor privileges—instead it lays upon the Two-Eyed ones a sacred responsibility. For Two-Eyed ones have the capacity of vision to penetrate the dread gloom of the SPIRIT world to discern the path that their Group, their Community should follow to discover the next resting place, where they all will be temporarily safe and nurtured, on the SPIRIT journey all must take.

289

Frederick Douglass, speaking of the three-hundred-year struggle of the Afro-American slaves to win back the Freedom they had been so viciously robbed of, said the longest, the most frightening, the most terrifying distance on the road to Freedom that each Slave had to travel—alone and with only his or her soul as guide—was the immeasurable distance from his knees to his feet! And, oh, my dear Two-Eyed Brothers and Sisters, we Queers also know about that dreadful and terrifying distance, from closet-crouching in denial or self-loathing, to that almost unendurable wrenching rise to our feet, in the moment of "coming out," with only the dream in our hearts to guide us.

But—differently from the Slaves who thought they needed only to discover and forge the political route to Freedom across the Mason-Dixon line—we Gays and Lesbians, we Queer folk, having as the Hausa say the Two-Eyed capacity, have an additional responsibility to the larger Community of which we are a part. As the Hausa very clearly teach us, there are *two roads* to Freedom *and they both must be traversed*! We Queers have had to discover it through the agony and heart break of twice patterning our Gay and Lesbian Movement on Hetero-imitative behaviors that do not bespeak us. After Stonewall, *Gay liberation* was indeed a rebellion against the Hetero-male-oriented systems of Laws—but the Rebellion itself developed in terms of Hetero-male-oriented cultural values. Within five years the dominant Gay Assimilationist Culture had gutted it just as they had gutted the Homophile Movement twenty years before.

290   In 1979, I called the Radical Faeries to recognize that since we are *not* Heteros, we Gays had no business imitating them. I called upon my Faerie Brothers to tear off the Hetero-imitative conformities with which they've been spiritually crippling themselves by adopting them or adapting *to* them. At Faerie Gatherings and Faerie Workshops we've begun to recover our own *not*-man values, our beautiful *un*-Hetero ways of perceiving—so long obscured when not indeed temporarily obliterated by Police or State torture, and by Church-sponsored public burnings and autos-da-fé of both Medieval and Modern Holy Inquisitions. Little by little we have begun to redeem and redevelop our own NOT-MAN values of self-love, self-esteem, and self-affirmation. *We are re-discovering our own faerie way to rise from our knees to our feet!* And—this year—the younger generations of Queer Nation are joining with us.

What we Queers have learned through Terror and Tears, what we Two-Eyed Ones have to share, is very clear. The Hetero-male Imperialist Dominators, Anglo-European and Israeli alike, clearly hold their Colonialized Minority Communities in the thrall of Slavery still—*spiritual slavery*! Their shackles, which we today call racism, continue to deny those Communities held in bondage the necessary access to the SPIRIT redemptions, grounded in their own ethnic symbols and values, that those communities must have to finally be enabled to rise to their feet in *spiritual freedom*!

Among the really first-class facilities the Imperialist Dominators lovingly maintain for keeping Spiritual shackles in place—for instance—are the three State-approved organized Religions: Judaism and its offshoots, Islam and Christianity. Christianity, particularly, and Judaism both have served willingly as shackles, by each requiring that the particular Colonialized Folk's universal need to *"live in the spirit* of Community Love and Compassion" be expressed solely in the symbols and values, as well as language, of the Dominator's own system—even to the total denial, even obliteration, of the Folk's own traditional core of heart and soul. Between these three—Islam, Judaism, and Christianity—the re-sprouting, re-budding, and re-blooming of new shoots of self-love, self-esteem, and self-affirmation are kept firmly subdued.

We Queers can tell you Black or Chicano or Asian Hetero Brothers and Sisters precisely what this shackling of the spirit and of the heart is like *because you folks continue to do the same to us*! Even as Gay Spirit could hardly have been expected to launch and fly on Hetero-centric wings, so also any given Afrocentrism, or whatever combination of NON-Anglo-Ethnic-centrism speaks for you—that "being and becoming" SPIRIT that moves to redeem traditional cores of self-love, self-esteem, and self-affirmation—cannot be expected to launch and soar successfully on *Eurocentric* pinions. If, by our example of how we Radical Faeries and Queer Nations have reclaimed our own very UN-Hetero values of self-love, self-esteem, and self-affirmation, we can inspire the Spiritually STILL-indentured Colonialized Minority Communities to invent similar ways to rise from their White-imitative servitude to stand once more in joyously reclaimed centric self-affirmation—no longer in the values and symbols of the *dominators*, but in terms of what they, as Separate Cultures, have to contribute to the betterment of everybody—what a triumph of the Human Spirit that could be!

We suggest that the Colonialized Racial and Sexual Minorities can rise from their knees to their feet in reclaiming their own appreciation of self-love because we Queers, against every combination of tyranny the Hetero Oppressors could devise, have done it. Among the several contributions we bring to you, the first is our example . . . *and our courage*!

292

To the Marxist Left, we Queers have to say "thanks"—for the Spiritual tools and concepts you furnished, which got us launched on our long walk, with particular credit to that strut in the definition of a National Minority, "a common psychological make-up manifested in a community of culture." It fitted us to a "T." To you, we Radical Faeries bring our insights. One of Marx's great formulations was his vision of the ultimate Communist relationship: "From each according to his abilities, to each according to his needs." As the Radical Faeries see it, this may well be one of the very first political appreciations of compassion, the human dimension totally missed—to their ultimate disaster and defeat—by the Hetero-male-dominated Second and Third Internationales.

With all this, we have to say that we Queers, having won our autonomy with no help from anybody, shall continue to maintain that autonomy. We shall be happy to walk with *any* group so long as we *and they* remain in a loving-sharing consensus. But the moment the consensus breaks, exercising our ancient prerogatives to totally self-reliant independence—we Faeries *vanish*! If you want us to re-appear, you shall have to make the first move to re-establish the loving-sharing consensus.

> Presented at "Queer Relations: The Lesbian/Gay Movement and the U.S. Left," sponsored by Modern Times Bookstore, *CrossRoads* magazine, Lesbians and Gays Against Intervention, the International Lesbian/Gay Human Rights Commission, and the San Francisco Women's Building. June 26, 1991, San Francisco.

Note

1. According to one of Hay's correspondents, Hausa homosexuals describe themselves by saying "I have two eyes and I can see." Rudolf Gaudio reports that the most common Hausa term for Gay men is *dan daudu* (pl.

'yan daudu); however, an "insider" term is *mai ido*, "one who has eyes."
These terms are not applied to Lesbians, who are usually called *'yar kifi*
(pl. *'yan kifi*) ("Male Lesbians and Other Queer Notions in Hausa," un-
pub. ms., 1995). In the past, the term *'yan daudu* referred specifically to
gender transformed male participants in the *bori* possession cult (Fre-
mont E. Besmer, *Horses, Musicians, and Gods: The Hausa Cult of
Possession-Trance* [South Hadley, Mass.: Bergin and Garvey, 1983], pp.
18–19).

"Our Third Gender responsibilities"

WHEREAS PREVIOUSLY Hay had employed the phrase "We are a separate people" to reinforce Lesbian/Gay identity, in these remarks he adopts a new formula for describing Gay difference. We are, he claims, a separate *gender*—a distinct *third* gender that is neither male nor female. Hay argues that such a conceptualization, based on the example of the Native American Two-Spirit, is a more affirmative and accurate description than that provided by the term homosexual, which narrows our difference to a single, sexual dimension. "Gender" evokes a constellation of social roles and traits, a psychological pattern and temperament, and a set of complex symbols and contested meanings. In Marxist terms, one might say that "sexual preference" and "sexual orientation" are inherently idealist concepts, while "gender" refers back to the material world, the world of productive roles, social functions, and identities.

Hay has often been misinterpreted as calling on Lesbians and Gay men to revive ancient "magical roles." As he recently wrote, those "laboring under prejudicial racist comparisons, not uncommon in contemporary Gay WASP Society, totally fail to appreciate that such 'magical roles' in co-conscious Tribal Societies translate, in our current perceptions, as *community services*. Community Services, inspired by our rather different Third Gender outlook on the World specific to our Gay Window's view, *are precisely what we Third Gender folk should be about*."[1]

Remarks on Third Gender

. . . It is time for us to reject the *lie* by which Organized Religions have attempted to obliterate us for two millennia. Sexual
Orientation isn't the *only* difference between Us and the Heteros.
As a result of the way we had been malignantly demeaned and di-
minished over the centuries, *it is the only difference* LEFT between
US and the Heteros. It's time we took a leaf from the lessons Third
Gender Brothers in other cultures have to teach us in how to re-
earn the respect and gratitude of our Hetero Communities for the
different people that we are—as well as for the talents and gifts we
bring to share. In other parts of Earth, in the Third and Fourth
Worlds, sedentary village cultures and quasi-civilized tribes—
some of which rose to City-State status and then subsided again,
some whose traditions still pertain today—noticed that though
most men seemed naturally inclined to be competitive, to be Warriors, Hunters, and Fathers, always there were those some who
seemed to be *men not for killing and men not for War*. These ones
were gentler types—they seemed to want to celebrate their Brothers rather than to compete with them. These ones seemed to have
particular powers of insight—they could distinguish between the
Seen and the Unseen; they could sense the anguish in someone's
heart and so act out stories or songs that magically dispelled the
torment. In later centuries this would be called Theatre. They
could mediate between the Known and the Unknown, and seemed
not always so awed or terrified of the dread Supernaturals that they
couldn't talk to them, or send messages to the shadowy Powers beyond the sky. In later centuries, this would be called prayer, and the
agency bringing not only rain but many other needed changes of
circumstances would be known as Temple.

Because these Brothers' contributions were essential to the cultural and spiritual well-being of the People, these different gentle ones were treasured—they would be seen as men of a different Gender. If Warriors and Husbandmen were men of a First Gender, then these Differents would be men of a Third Gender—and so they are still perceived, *and loved and treasured*, by the largest tribe of Native Americans in the American Southwest today, the Diné, whom the whitemen call Navajo. The Diné say, "When all the *nádleehé* [third-gender men and women] are gone, that will be the end of the Navaho."² And, equally, such different gentle men are seen among the largest Tribe in West Africa, the Hausa, as spirit mediators, while in Hawaii, contemporary inheritors of the traditional *mahu* role are playing a role in reviving the ancient art of hula dancing.³ In smaller, more compact Native American Communities such as Zuni, in western New Mexico, the supernatural counterpart of the *lhamana*, Kolhamana, traditionally represented the balancing of men and women.⁴

We Third Gender men of Indo-European stock equally have similar talents and treasures to share. Living in the cracks of Hetero Western World sidewalks for a millennium, we actually have learned a great deal, should we finally begin to put it to use. Because we Queers need nothing from either Hetero men or Hetero women, we have learned to see them as *they would like to be seen*—in make-up, in hairdress, in design, and in tailoring, for instance. Because we Queers need nothing from either Hetero men or Hetero women that we couldn't just as easily supply one another, we have learned over the centuries *to listen to them nonjudgmentally*. And this talent, now, can stand us in very good stead for its many modern uses and applications.

Over the centuries, listening to and observing Western World parliaments, we may have learned that for any self-loving, self-respecting Minority, the so-called Democratic process is never more than a Tyranny of the Majority. In the twenty-first-century world, when most urban areas in America will be aggregates of plural Societies, it would be unconscionable for Minorities to be always *competing with* one another and even more infuriating to have them always *voting against* one another. The only possible form of governance shall have to be an advance of political consciousness, in the electorate, to the recognition that, henceforth, they must learn to function and govern by means of the consensus process. The key to functioning by consensus is learning *to listen to one another non-judgmentally*! Radical Faeries have discovered that, by learning to slip the non-essential Hetero-male ego, we can really listen to one another with our inner ears. Listening with inner ears to discern principles held in common, community councils or coalitions might be enabled to collectively develop mutually respectful agreements on issues. To facilitate governing by the process of mutually respectful sharing consensus, Radical Faeries and, if they were of a mind, all Gay Brothers and Sisters, exercising their innate inclinations to process in subject-SUBJECT consciousness, might make a major contribution to Society by helping to create the most politically healthy of all possible communities. If Third Gender men and women could become Facilitator-Specialists in such governing processes, we might discover a loving appreciative need for us.

We need to make the leap in consciousness for a second reason, as well—to reclaim our own sense of an ancient and historical legitimacy, parallels to which are continually being held open for us to duplicate by our Brothers of the Third and Fourth Worlds. We made a wrong assessment of the strength we would garner as a result of claiming Minority status. When our Gay Liberationist Zappers hit the bricks in the 1970s shouting "We're a Minority—and we got rights just like every other Minority," we hadn't re-read our history books very carefully. When "the huddled masses yearning to be free" emigrated to the United States in the nineteenth century to earn a place for themselves in the bright and beckoning American Dream, they all, naturally, brought gifts to trade—gifts the United States was hungry for—huge quantities of raw labor power. What had *our* Gang brought?

Well, as a matter of fact they hadn't, consciously, brought anything—just their noisy deviant sexuality, which three-quarters of the country took one look at and said, "We don't like it, and it's *wrong* anyway." Of all the Minorities who came petitioning for the privileges of first-class citizenship, *we* alone hadn't thought to bring anything to share *or* trade. (As a matter of fact, we had, innately, brought tons of talent and treasures to share. But, liberated young Gays pouring out of our closets, we just hadn't thought about anything further than getting *out*. Truth to tell, in our Middle-class arrogance we just *hadn't thought*!)

But the notion of developing Third Gender is ready and willing to pay off. I spoke to a very politically involved Black Hetero friend in recent times and mentioned that I felt it might be time for us Gays to reclaim our Third Gender responsibilities, and he said, "Third Gender responsibilities? You've never said that before. That makes good political sense—that socially communicates something. Third Gender men are respected as valuable persons in a number of tribal societies."

At this point in time, I don't suppose we can expect the "bottom-line-driven" Western World Heteros, still mired in their almost obsolete and quite lethal subject-OBJECT consciousness, to be panting to discover how we Queers are necessary to *their* survival. But, to an ever-growing number of them, it is now becoming recognized that we who belong to the Third Gender carry a capacity for being able to leap to and develop a new and vitally needed social con-

sciousness—what Radical Faeries know as subject-SUBJECT consciousness—within which the collective functioning by sharing
consensus is *the natural way to go*. It could be that we are expect-
ing too much for the Heteros to comprehend how much they need
to learn to survive themselves!

So it is now that I am proposing that we take a hand-up example
from our potential allies in the Third and Fourth Worlds, whose
cultures may well be overtaking, and even out-numbering, our
Hetero Western so-called Free World sensibilities in the not-too-
far distant first decades of the twenty-first century. I propose that
we Gay Men *of all colors* prepare to present ourselves as the gentle
non-competitive Third Gender men *of the Western World* with
whole wardrobes and garages crammed with cultural and spiritual
contributions to share.

In the November 8, 1992, "Opinion" section of the *Los Angeles
Times*, columnist Richard Rodriguez said, "There is a great moan
in the American heart. Something is wrong with the way we live.
We have lost the knack, or the gift, of intimacy. We do not know
how to love one another." I would submit that the American Gay/
Lesbian Community, having shouldered almost entirely by itself
the mobilizing of American cities to confront and contain the pandemic of AIDS—*with little help from criminally insensitive Con-
gresses and three Administrations*—has rekindled vast surges of
community groups reaching out with love to one another on a scale
not seen in decades.

Equally would I submit that Third Gender Faerie men, in addition to forming superlative support groups for their own ailing
Brothers and lovers, are developing through their many Gatherings
across both the United States and Canada (not to slight "far Australia") whole new dimensions in the perceptions and sharings of
intimacy. It is time for us Third Gender folk, actually, *to rejoice in*

the gifts we bring! And, so saying, in such an endeavor—as my Hetero Black Friend and well-wisher suggested earlier—we even 300 might, in collective Gala, discover new Faerie ways to make such contributions both substantive and politically creative.

> Signed Harry Hay, March 2, 1994. Presented at the University of California, Los Angeles.

Notes

1. Letter to Richard Schneider, March 5, 1995.
2. Quoted in Willard W. Hill, "The Status of the Hermaphrodite and Transvestite in Navaho Culture," *American Anthropologist* 37 (1935): 274.
3. See Carol E. Robertson, "The Māhū of Hawai'i," *Feminist Studies* 15(2) (1989): 313–26.
4. See Will Roscoe, *The Zuni Man-Woman* (Albuquerque: University of New Mexico Press, 1991).

"The proud descendants of generations of gender outlaws"

I N 1994, when Senator Jesse Helms learned that the United
Nations had granted consultative status to the International
Lesbian and Gay Association (ILGA) and that one of the organizations affiliated with this body was NAMBLA, the North American Man/Boy Love Association, he introduced a resolution in the
Senate to cut off funding for the U.N. until it could be certified
that it did not recognize or grant official status to any organization that "promotes, condones, or seeks the legalization of pedo-
philia." The resolution passed 99 to 0.

Few issues divide the Lesbian/Gay community more than those
surrounding NAMBLA. Typically, the debate has centered on
whether NAMBLA should be allowed to participate in Lesbian/
Gay marches and other events, but at stake are fundamental issues
about the nature of human sexuality, that of children in particular, and the boundaries of today's Queer community.

Jesse Helms's attack in 1994 coincided with plans for a massive
Lesbian/Gay convergence on New York City in June to celebrate
the twenty-fifth anniversary of the Stonewall uprising. At meetings held in conjunction with this event, ILGA delegates voted to
expel NAMBLA. Hay was prominent in coordinating the opposition to this move, traveling to New York to participate in the
ILGA meetings and other events. Nor was this the first time he
spoke out on the issue. In 1986 he was almost arrested for carrying a sign that read "NAMBLA Walks with Me" in the Los Ange-

les Christopher Street West parade after that organization had been banned from the parade.

Hay has consistently argued the same points: First and foremost, that we should not allow our opponents to dictate to us who is and who is not a member of our community. Second, while Hay himself has never been a member of NAMBLA, he was once a young Gay man, well under the age of consent, who sought out sexual contact with an adult man and found it. To call this "child molestation" only stigmatizes homosexuality further and makes it more difficult for young Gay people to make contact with others like them. Indeed, Hay accuses Gay leaders of abandoning youth in their eagerness to cater to Right-wing homophobes.

The following article summarizes Hay's position and his analysis of the Helms-ILGA controversy. It includes some of the sharpest criticism he has written of the Lesbian/Gay assimilationist perspective.

Our Beloved Gay/Lesbian Movement at a Crossroads

During the same two weeks that we beheld the most comprehensive summitry the twentieth-century International Gay and Lesbian Movement has so far achieved—the all-inclusive Stonewall 25 celebrations—we also witnessed a fracturing of our movement's middle-class underpinnings, a rift which may unravel, if not tear apart, much of what we've gained in this century. The attempt by Gays and Lesbians to expel NAMBLA (the North Amer-

ican Man/Boy Love Association) from the Stonewall March and
from the International Lesbian and Gay Association (ILGA)
prompts my comments. My commitment to Gay and Lesbian self-
determination makes me ask, "Who is setting the agenda?"

During the days leading up to the march, a dissenting group
called the "Spirit of Stonewall" held a press conference at the
Stonewall Inn. We called upon the organizers of Stonewall 25 to
reexamine the liberating principles of the celebration's namesake,
the Rebellion of 1969, and reminded them that the original Stonewall uprising was a cry for full sexual freedom as a part of the
struggle for social justice. At that press conference, I made the following comments:

> I'm here today as a survivor as well as founder of the first on-
> going Gay liberation group in the United States, the Mat-
> tachine Society, formed in Los Angeles in 1950. I'm here be-
> cause things we discovered about ourselves, and the first
> principles we developed between 1950 and 1953, are now,
> forty years later, being trashed by Queers who don't know
> their own history. We decided from the beginning that hav-
> ing been almost obliterated for so many centuries, we
> wouldn't censor or exclude each other. If people self-identify
> themselves to me as Gay or Lesbian, I accept them as Broth-
> ers and Sisters with love. When we decided to rejoin the so-
> cial and political mainstream, we were determined to inte-
> grate on our own terms, as we saw ourselves and with our
> own set of values. Otherwise, we would not integrate at all.
> And finally, we no longer permitted any heteros—nationally
> or internationally, individually or collectively—to tell us
> who we were, or of whom our groups should or should not
> consist. If necessary, we would assert the prior rights of col-
> lective self-definition and self-determination. We Queers
> would decide such matters among ourselves! Those state-
> ments, developed forty-two years ago, still hold.

Jesse Helms, champion of Christian family values and our most intractable foe, is far shrewder than the self-appointed leaders of the Gay and Lesbian movement. Family Values hawks like Helms can easily exploit our movement's own Achilles' heel: two glaring contradictions we remain unwilling to face. First, we must acknowledge the vast differences in visions and values held by Gay men and Lesbians. Second, we must, as a movement, address the needs of our Gay/Lesbian youth whose experience of puberty, instead of providing a joyous self-realization and affirmational discovery, plunges them into a snake pit of self-loathing. And the adults of the Gay/Lesbian movement, lah-di-dah, resist doing anything about it.

Helms has fought for years to remove the U.S. from the United Nations by any means necessary; and he has fought to destroy the American Gay/Lesbian movement. In January of 1994, it looked like he'd be able to bean both birds with one shot by playing two, up to now, unrelated aims against one another.

In the summer of 1993, the International Gay/Lesbian Human Rights Commission (IGLHRC), headquartered in San Francisco, after years of lobbying, won a "non-governmental consultative status" for the International Lesbian/Gay Association (ILGA) at the U.N. Enter Jesse Helms! Helms managed to pass through the U.S. Senate (99–0) the following resolution:

> Contributions to International Organizations shall be reduced by the amount of $118,835,000 for each fiscal year, 1994 and 1995, and for each year thereafter, unless the President has certified . . . that no United Nations Agency or United Nations Affiliated Agency grant any official status, accreditation, or recognition to any organization which promotes, condones, or seeks the legalization of pedophilia, or which includes as a subsidiary or member any such organization.[1]

Helms didn't mention NAMBLA, but his meaning was quite clear. Likewise, he didn't name the European homosexual organizations, which have functioned as intergenerational groups since the turn of the century, that were also targeted. Of course, IGLHRC buckled at the first bark and demanded that Stonewall 25 expel NAMBLA from its ranks. The ensuing debate over this issue generated screaming and hollering all over the U.S., until June 30, 1994, when ILGA convened in New York City with an agenda to expel NAMBLA from its ranks.

That whole hearing had been rigged in advance. When some of us "anti-exclusionists" (a more accurate term than "pro-NAMBLA-ites") argued that Helms's remarks were aimed at European groups as well as American ones, ILGA responded by saying, "He has no jurisdiction over Europeans." In so saying, they exposed themselves as middle-class assimilationists with no knowledge of how ruling-class politics play out in "smoke-filled back rooms." They were ignoring the fact that the feckless, toothless caricature of a world parliament—the U.N.—needed American money in order to keep going *and would do anything to get it*!

Even though NAMBLA had been one of ILGA's longest-standing member organizations, ILGA voted NAMBLA's expulsion. When a NAMBLA youth delegate from Minnesota called for a Youth Caucus from the floor—a youth caucus includes ages 13 to 22—it turned out that the youngest ILGA youth delegate was twenty-four. Selling NAMBLA down the river was a short-sighted solution and it obscured the real issue of including and addressing the needs of our Gay and Lesbian youth. By appeasing Jesse Helms, the adults of ILGA said to the Gay/Lesbian youth of the world, "Fuck off! We've got more important things to do."

The Saturday before the Stonewall March, at the Irving Plaza Theater, young Gay and Lesbian folks, alternately furious or exuberant, in countless fascinating exchanges between audience and speaker, asked us elders what became of "sex" in the sexual liberation crusades being trumpeted for the last two and one-half decades. Forty- and fifty-year-olds squirmed. I stepped in to talk about the sexual climate of the Dark Ages. I told those too young to remember how, up to the 1960s, even what you said or mimed—even merely suggestive sexual language—could lead to time in state prison. Those who came of age in the more lenient 1970s need to know this history. I suggested that the newer generation of Queers would like to relate to our Radical Faerie perspective—that our beautiful and lovely sexuality is the Gateway to Spirit! The movement leaders of today don't understand that the continuing call for Gay liberation is not merely a call for our political liberation. It should remain a call for our liberation as sexual people.

On the following Wednesday and Thursday, during the ILGA Conference, it was horrible to have to watch the International Lesbian Delegates screaming "child molesters" and "monsters," joining their so-called feminist Gay Brothers in shoving and pummeling at those of us, not even necessarily NAMBLA members, who were against exclusion—particularly exclusion dictated by Hetero hate-mongering politicos. It was heartbreaking for me to watch my beloved Minority crumbling from within, all from lack of a developed Gay-conscious principle!

At the beginning of this last and fateful "closed" plenary, Lisa Power, a former ILGA Secretary-General, described the early ILGA as "a ghetto solidarity group." She then explained that ILGA is changing. "We are now becoming a human rights movement and we are now a more effective organization." In urging the members to support the expulsions, she said, "This is not a great day or a happy day for any of us, but we either go back into the ghetto or forward into the real world."

She does not say that "we will go forward as self-affirming, self-loving Queers into the real world." We are invited instead to assimilate into the dominant culture, reverting as usual to wearing the old hetero, escapist "human being" mask—a white, middle-class one, natch! Well, ILGA Sister, you don't speak for me or for millions of my Gay Brothers and Sisters worldwide! The Village in Manhattan (East or West), West Hollywood in L.A., or South of Market in San Francisco—ghettos? They are *neighborhoods*, certainly, in which some of us live and thrive, and into which all of us occasionally need to withdraw to lick our wounds, to comfort one another, to be comforted and to be spiritually restored. Then, refreshed and renewed in commitment, we are ready once again to take our places in the larger sphere. Our havens, ghettos? We are hardly so boxed in, either politically or socially, that we can't get out if we choose. That brave and pioneering "Camp Sister Spirit" in Mississippi, Sally Gearhart's "Wanderground" in northern California, and our several Radical Faerie sanctuaries in Tennessee, New York, Vermont, Wisconsin, Arkansas, Texas, Arizona, and Oregon are not ghettos. We'll thank you to be a little more respectful of other peoples' new horizons!

Forty-two years ago, my Mattachine Brothers and I saw, and my Radical Faerie Brothers still see, our work as taking place in the "real world," with our own people on our own Gay-conscious terms, and within our own Gay-conscious value-systems. We are the proud descendants of generations of gender outlaws, Brothers and Sisters who have successfully contributed to tribal societies for thousands of years. In each era, then and now, third-gender people, self-affirming, self-loving, proud and Queer, have served our many societies in life-enhancing, spirit-enhancing ways.

In the U.S. in the last decade, we have successfully applied our Queer perspectives to political innovations. With the help of almost no one in the Hetero establishment, and with little access to medical resources, we have taken care of our own in the AIDS holocaust. We have set an example, politically, for multi-cultural communities, helping them to side-step the cul-de-sacs obscured by obsolete democratic patterns. Groups of third-gender men and women have shown new political entities of multi-ethnic people non-judgmental ways of functioning, through the process of loving, sharing consensus.

NAMBLA was never the issue. The constitutional right of Gay and Lesbian groups to first-class citizenship, of Gay and Lesbian individuals to practice political and spiritual self-determination was. It still is!

In the face of his filthy-minded sneak attack, ILGA fell right into Senator Helms's lap. The resulting repercussions could unravel the movement. And appeasing the oppressor only teaches him a dangerous lesson: That he can win. Thirty days later, Helms let the other shoe drop. He amended an education bill on its way through the Senate by denying federal funds to any public school district that teaches homosexuality is a positive lifestyle alternative through class work, textbooks, or counseling. This language is so broad that even Project 10, a nationally known counseling program of Gay high school students, would be a key target of the ban. How misguided ILGA seems in retrospect. ILGA swore that with the corpse of NAMBLA in his lap, Helms would be satisfied and do nothing more. Yet now he blithely banishes a socially beneficial youth counseling program with a 63–36 vote of approval from his fellow senators. *C'est la vie!*

In a time like this the Gay and Lesbian movement should pull together and present an immovable phalanx to all attackers. Religious fundamentalism, based as it is upon the cleverly disguised sexual control of peoples' lives, is designed to spread hysteria. The

Radical Right's stampeding of state and federal political agencies during this time of confusion was fully predictable. During this period of economic uncertainty, when our standard of living—formerly based upon a larger share of global largesse than we're entitled to—has begun to fall, political and economic hysteria is on the rise. As members of the middle class try to hang on to the perks and privileges of their fading good life, they rush, as always before, to "cast their cares upon God." In so doing, they fall right into the traps set for them by Buchanan, Robertson and Limbaugh, those fundamentalist running dogs who present the new (and particularly American) face of neo-Fascism!

There is one way we can slap our Hetero-parent community to its senses and re-unite ourselves at the same time. At the Spirit of Stonewall press conference I said, "Insofar as child molestation is concerned, the most common, yet unrecognized, form is the *sexual coercion of Gay and Lesbian youth into heterosexual identities and behaviors.* This is practiced daily by the whole national and international Hetero community—parents, families, teachers, preachers, doctors, lawyers, and Indian Chiefs, not to overlook U.S. Senators and the pooh-bah news media. This outrageous coercion of Gay kids into heterosexual identities and behaviors is not only sexually abusive, *it is a spiritually devastating rape* because the child, unknowingly, is led into self-loathing at the same time!"

For this gigantic criminal trespass—against not only today's youth, but all of us since childhood, from the Queers my age, 82, down through all the generations of Queers now reading this page, to the Gay kids still being bedeviled by heterosexual coercion—we, the international Gay and Lesbian People, should unite *to sue the whole guilty hetero community for compensation*! And, while we're at it, we should request our first-class citizenship as well.

310

Now that the statute of limitations concerning child molestation has been nullified, this could be the class action suit of the century! Why not get cracking on this idea? Talk to your local ACLU. Think of the street theater we can devise—Glee into Rage into Laughter into Fury—at the snap of a limp wrist! And fun, too, as only we self-loving, self-affirming Queers know how to do it!

We can serve notice that once again in this dear land, we are here, as were the "strange" brotherhoods and sisterhoods of tribes past, before the pale-faced plunderers and marauders came. We are here, in our true dimension, with our Gay-conscious visions and values intact, with our split-level talents and four-dimensional insights at the ready, our eyes alight with laughter, prepared to resume our community places and our collective responsibilities.

Signed Harry Hay, August 31, 1994. A version appeared in *Gay Community News* (October 1994): 16, 18–19.

Note

1. Helms Amendment No. 1248 to the Foreign Relations Authorizations Act was adopted January 26, 1994.

Reflections

"One of the Great Earth
Mother's gifts to us all"

R UDI GERNREICH was born in Austria in 1922 and arrived in
the United States as a refugee in 1938. When he met Hay,
he had recently left the Lester Horton Dance Theatre to launch a
career in fashion design. Although he is remembered today as the
avant-garde designer who introduced the topless bathing suit and
geometric patterns in the 1960s, Gernreich played a critical
role in the early Mattachine movement when he became Hay's
first recruit. Gernreich's enthusiasm was the catalyst Hay needed
to translate his ideas into action.

After the resignation of the Mattachine founders in 1953,
Gernreich devoted himself to his career in fashion design. At the
time of his death in 1985, he enjoyed an international reputation.
Although he never came out publicly, he and his life partner
endowed a trust to support litigation of Lesbian/Gay cases
by the American Civil Liberties Union.

Remarks on Rudi's Passing

One of the truly great creators of modern design, one of
the very few artists to have received the COTY International Design Award several times in a row, Rudi Gernreich, died last Sunday, April 21. Practically every magazine and journal in the not-

314

unrelated worlds of Art and Fashion will be doing him honor—assembling and re-assessing the innumerable achievements, discoveries, insights, and innovations of his spatial and visual perceptions of our beloved human body in motion and in the many rhythms of the beloved body in repose. I say "beloved human body" because this is how Rudi would have always perceived it, and anyone closely studying his approach to design can only marvel at how rapturously he always reached to celebrate it.

For my part, I should like to do honor to three years of Rudi's life not heretofore mentioned in the public press—the time span from July 6, 1950, into May of 1953, encompassing that dream of Gay People awakening to their full historical potential, that vision of Gay Brothers and Sisters inventing and re-inventing new spatial perceptions of themselves through loving affirmations of each other, whose very first American consciousness-raising circles would come to be known as the Mattachine Society of 1950–1953.

Almost from the very first moment of our meeting, at a rehearsal of the Lester Horton Dance Theatre on a Saturday morning, July 6, 1950, we were in love with each other and with each other's ideas. Rudi was specifically taken with my vision of an American Gay Brotherhood, in terms of a Call I had developed and assembled some two years before and had gotten almost nowhere with since—until the moment of my meeting him. Rudi had immediately a whole program of enthusiastic renewals of activities we might undertake, similar to ones I had been involved with in the previous time but with more potentially viable people—even as he, simultaneously, urged the greatest of caution. "If we repeat the errors of Hirschfeld's German Movement," he'd say, thinking of how Senators Joe McCarthy and Richard Nixon were, even at that moment, kicking out of the Civil Service every Queer they could dream up a suspicion of, "we could set the potentials of an American Gay Movement back for decades to come."

The story has been told several times now how Rudi and I, now a Society of Two, set about discovering new adherents in the summer of 1950 (the Korean War having been started only weeks before) by collecting 500 signatures to the Stockholm Peace Petition[1] on the two slices of beach Gays had quietly made their own—the section below the Palisades just west of Marian Davies's huge waterfront estate now known as Will Rogers State Beach, and that slice of Malibu between the pier and the spit, which would be taken over by the Surfers in the 1960s. It is significant of the self-inflicting Homophobia of the times that 500 not-so-unobvious Gay Brothers and Sisters were willing enough to designate themselves Peaceniks by signing our petitions in the teeth of the Korean War and its accompanying patriot-mongering, even as they were *not* willing to commit themselves to participating in easily disguised semi-public forums oh-so diffidently fingering the newly published Kinsey Report.

"Do not despair," Rudi would say. "When we learn to translate our vision into words our Brothers and Sisters find relevant to their lives, they will join."

When it seemed we had exhausted all other avenues, Rudi said to me, "Didn't you tell me there were two guys in your music history class whom you suspected were Gay? Why don't you show them your Call and see what happens?"

"But Rudi," I protested, "these guys don't have two nickels to their names. They're as poor as we are."

"Well," said Rudi, "at least they will have integrity and self-respect. Try them out."

Rudi's instincts were sound. These other two, just like us, had gravitated to the Left because, as sexual outlaws, they found them-

selves in total empathy with the programs and goals of our Hetero
outlaw friends in labor and politics.

And Rudi was right about attracting members when we successfully translated our vision. In the spring of 1952, when we fought
an entrapment charge against the Los Angeles City Police Department and *won*, our Discussion Groups doubled overnight. When
these new members, in turn, began to experience the revelations of
sitting in groups talking about ourselves and each other in *positive*
values, and finding each other good, the collective jubilation was
so contagious that Discussion Groups proliferated all over the
place. By December 1952, we had fifteen Discussion Groups from
San Diego to San Francisco—ranging in membership from fifteen
to two hundred—and a sphere of influence of 5,000 people in California, who would serve as the beginning readership of *ONE*
magazine, whose first issue appeared in January 1953.

But, Radicals that we were, operating openly in our own names,
as members of the Board of Directors of a group brazenly question-
ing the Los Angeles City Council on the constitutionality of Entrapment—in the very teeth of the McCarthy witch-hunt—we
could not expect to escape being investigated by Congressional
witch-hunting Committees. What we had not allowed for were the
depredations of Gay Republicans within our own memberships. In
the Spring of 1953, the Mattachine Society was split open; the
strict unanimity process by which we had carried out all our func-
tionings and deliberations up until that point collapsed. And the
incandescent ambiance of the Mattachine Dream was suddenly
only a crumbling white ash.

For three years, without a murmur, Rudi Gernreich had given
the Mattachine Vision the highest intensity of his energy and love.
When it collapsed in the Spring of 1953, he knew it was time for
him to pursue other avenues of his personal visions of Freedom.

The terrible heartbreak many of us suffered from the collapse of the Mattachine Dream took longer to heal in Rudi than in the others. He never identified with the Gay Movement again.

Earlier this year, in an interview with the *Los Angeles Times*, Rudi Gernreich was quoted as saying, "The only relevant issue now is Freedom." But throughout all of his creative life, the only relevant issue to Rudi Gernreich was Freedom—freedom to create areas wherein he could mold into manageable dimensions those spatial relationships of color and rhythm and motion, those perceptions of our brain's right hemisphere that may lie forever beyond the powers of our two-dimensional binary language to express or to control. And within such passions to invent and always re-invent such Freedoms *to express*, Freedoms of personhood were never far off. And freedoms of personhood projected in turn against the backdrop of right-brain spatial projections can reveal the lovely body of a Faerie's vision as costume in itself. No wonder so many Hetero Men had trouble with the anti-Puritan aspects of Rudi's fashions. But not women. Women knew that Rudi Gernreich moved to free them forever from the costume restraints of Puritanism.

To those of us who knew Rudi Gernreich and loved him, in those first years of the American Gay Vision of Liberation through self-affirmation, he was always the personification of the Free Faerie Spirit. Dazzlingly beautiful and forever burgeoning with sparkles of devastating wit and laughter, he was one of the Great Earth Mother's gifts to us all. Enfolded in his love and laughter, we always felt blessed. . . .

And now . . . our memory of him re-invoked and rekindled . . . we still are!

Signed Harry Hay, April 24, 1985.

Note

318   1. The Stockholm Peace Pledge campaign was a major effort undertaken by the Communist Party of the United States of America in early 1950 (Joseph R. Starobin, *American Communism in Crisis, 1943–1957* [Cambridge, Mass.: Harvard University Press, 1972], p. 304).

"Views and vistas bubbled forth"

JOHN CAGE (1912–1992) once referred to the early years of his life in Los Angeles, before his marriage to Xenia Kashevaroff in 1935, as the period when he was "not yet 'Cage.' " These years remain hazy in Cage's biographies. The reason, no doubt, is that during this period he was avidly pursuing a Gay lifestyle, living with his lover, and hanging out with Gay bohemians like Harry Hay. While Cage enjoyed Gay relationships throughout his life, he never publicly came out.

As Hay wrote in a letter to one of Cage's biographers, "I was shocked when the young man doing my biography [Stuart Timmons] elicited from John that he had practically no recall of his 1930s years. Although my life, like John's, has been a pretty crowded one, I recall those lovely, tender years when we both were 20, 21, 22, fairly vividly, if admittedly, spottily. Certainly I was not about to forget the sparkly-eyed Avatar of the post-WWI break-out of all the Arts who came home—broke—from a two-year stint in Europe with a live-in lover in the fall of 1932 and emerged from the cocoon of a shy aloof young intellectual, whom I had known briefly in the spring of 1929 when I was a High School Senior preparing to win the same Southern California Oratorical Contest he had won the year before, and he was a Freshman at Pomona College (now the Claremont Colleges) who came back to coach me."[1]

Not long after this, Cage left for Europe, while Hay enrolled at Stanford. It was in the fall of 1932, after Hay had left Stanford, that his mother noticed an announcement in the local paper concerning the return of the son of John and Lucretia ("Crete") Cage, the well-known inventor and his socially ambitious wife. At his mother's encouragement, Hay contacted Cage—and discovered that he now had a lover, Don Sample. Over the next year and a half, the three young men became close friends. Hay sang some of Cage's early compositions before the Santa Monica Women's Club in November 1932, and still treasures a number of Cage manuscripts from that performance written on staves—despite the composer's claim in later years never to have made use of such "restraints."

John Cage and Don Sample

My relationship with John and Don changed, from three bright intellectual Faeries playing together, to one more dominated by Don—a fairly demanding taskmaster—that day at Maddie's house on Montana Street in Santa Monica, in maybe early October of 1932, when she said she had this new song she was interested to hear but she hadn't played it yet.[2] The song was "At Dawning" by that old Quean Charles Wakefield Cadman.[3] I said, "Oh, I know that. We sang it in the Glee Club at high school. And I've used it many times for encore." And Maddie said, "Oh please—would you sing it if I play the accompaniment?" Of course, these emotional-type hearth-and-home songs were exactly what John and Don detested. So Don quickly got up and started picking up our bags and beach umbrella, saying, "Well, Maddie, before you start that, we'd better be going. We just stopped by to see if you'd like to go to the beach and picnic with us." But Maddie pleaded with Don, "O please, can't your friend sing it for me—*just once*?" "Oh, why not, Don?" said John.

So Maddie started the introduction, and I sang it. Afterwards, when Maddie was thanking me, John interrupted. "You never told us you could sing *like that*." And Don said, "Migawd, Honey,

that's a first-class voice. Come on, guys, we've got to get home."
Maddie said, "But I thought you were inviting me to go picnicking
at the beach with you?" John said, "Yeah, and we've made all this   321
lovely food." "Yes," says Don, "but that was before Harry sang.
Now we have to recognize that you and he have a Concert in November. We'll tell Cornelia we're changing the program. After all,
she did say she thought we ought to lighten it a little. Harry can do
a couple of songs from the Poulenc collection we got in Paris and a
couple of songs from Hindemith, and your two Greek Odes—with
the Gertrude Stein for an encore—for half the program; and you'll
do your piano studies for the other half."

John's face fell. He obviously didn't enjoy having his day pulled
out from under him and being re-managed. But very shortly he,
too, was bubbling along again, elaborating on Don's new idea.
Their relationship had probably been like that since Don had spot-
ted John, subdued and shy, and emotionally all buttoned up two
years before in Paris. Certainly, according to John's stories of the
house they lived in for six months in Majorca, and as it still was in
the Cage mansion in Pacific Palisades, even without furniture or
hot water, John lived and breathed that love-bonding as passionate
and as totally inter-fulfilling as Mary Renault characterized He-
phaestion and the young Alexander in *Fire from Heaven*. Don
probably was the one originally in love with the Bauhaus School of
design. He was the one who found the new Aalto and Saarinen furniture catalogs that John and I fell in love with. It was Don who
located the Schindler houses in the area for us to go and see, and
who first made friends with Pauline Schindler.[4] (I imagine it was
Pauline who introduced Don to Richard Bühlig,[5] the great Vien-
nese pianist, but that was after Don came back from New York and
rented an apartment in Pauline's house on King's Road in the fall
of 1935.) It would have been Pauline who influenced them to go
visit Flora Weston in March of 1934.

Don obviously provided a disciplined Father figure–lover for John, which could very well have been exactly what John *didn't* need in that early formative time of his life. My guess is that Crete Cage, that formidable, managing, ambitious League-of-Women's Clubs pioneer (from her original home base in Eagle Rock) had totally managed her brilliant if somewhat erratic and dreamy Inventor-husband, and her equally brilliant Faerie-son John, almost to death. What John may not have needed, upon coming out into his very different Gay-consciousness, was a *first Lover who took her place*.

What I do know is that John and Don—exhilarated with their stay at Carmel with Flora Weston and her entourage, with poetry readings at Robinson Jeffers' when Lincoln Steffens was a guest for the evening—eagerly set off in mid-April of 1934 for new adventures in New York. Almost immediately, John met up with Edgard Varèse,[6] and within a month Don was back in Los Angeles—and with temporarily disastrous consequences (which is quite another story, my mother playing the Florence Nightingale role). Insofar as I remember, and I was fairly closely involved with Don for the next three or four years, he never so much as mentioned John to me again, although he seems to have interested Galka Scheyer, whom he met through Pauline Schindler and with whom he would go on to develop the discipline of Remedial Reading for the WPA, in bringing John Cage west again in the late 1930s to work with Oskar Fischinger.[7]

In the late 1970s, in New Mexico, my John and I one night were watching one of Merce Cunningham's choreographies for TV. Suddenly, I said to John, "You know, that last *pas de deux* would have been stunning, not to say breathtaking, if it had been danced between *two young men*." My Darling fervently agreed. Thinking about that now, I believe I could venture that, with Don, John Cage

might easily have persuaded Merce to so stage it, while on his
rather puritanical *own* he never would.[8] John *has* that Gay window, because, back in the magical relationship we all had in 1932–   323
1934, views and vistas bubbled forth from it, in response to challenges emanating from Don and me, from our versions of the same,
quite regularly—and there have been others who seem to have similarly motivated him since.

Signed Harry Hay, April 12, 1988.

Notes

1. Harry Hay to Franz van Rossum, March 22, 1989.

2. Hay is unable to recall "Maddie's" last name. She was a piano
teacher who lived in Santa Monica canyon.

3. Sentimental song writer, Charles Wakefield Cadman (1881–1946)
was one of the first American composers to become interested in the music
and folklore of Indians.

4. Pauline Schindler was the wife of modernist architect Rudolph M.
Schindler (1887–1953), an Austrian émigré who settled in Los Angeles
and designed a series of famous houses. Cage, for a while, pursued an affair with Pauline. According to one biographer, Cage could not remember
how he met her (Thomas S. Hines, "Then Not Yet 'Cage': The Los Angeles
Years, 1912–1938," in *John Cage: Composed in America*, ed. Marjorie
Perloff and Charles Junkerman [Chicago: University of Chicago Press,
1994], p. 85).

5. A different account of their meeting appears in David Revill, *The
Roaring Silence: John Cage, A Life* (New York: Arcade Publishing, 1992),
p. 40, and Hines, "Then Not Yet 'Cage,'" p. 91.

6. Edgard Varèse (1883–1965) was a French-American composer.

7. Cf. Hines, "Then Not Yet 'Cage,'" p. 90. Fischinger was a modernist painter and abstract filmmaker. The recognized expert on his life and
work is Hay's close friend William Moritz.

8. Cage and Cunningham had been creative partners since the 1940s.

"Nor all thy tears wash out
a word of it"

I N 1994, Hay received the Emil Freed Award from the Southern
California Library for Social Studies and Research in recognition of his lifetime of activism. Hay used the occasion to reflect
on three heroes in his own life—Joe Hill, Harry Bridges, and his
father. Although the similarities between "Big Harry," as he
was called in the family, and his son are apparent to anyone who
has heard Hay describe his father, it took many years of self-
examination before Hay himself could see and accept them. The
insights he relates here came after a series of dramatic personal
events in the early 1980s, culminating in a powerful dream of his
father, which occurred during a faerie gathering. Following this,
Hay began to speak of his father in entirely different terms, recalling memories about him that had been dormant for years.

What Hay shares in these reminiscences is key to understanding
his character and life's work. His father's uncompromising moral
certitude insured that his eldest son would rebel against him. Yet Hay
clearly manifests the same trait in his uncompromising stands on
social justice and his sense of personal responsibility. This is the
source of what many have praised as his courage. In fact, beneath
the expansive personality is the same vulnerability every Queer boy
feels. It is his moral certitude, acquired from his father, and an
uncompromising sense of duty, not fearlessness or bravado,
that has led Hay to take the risks that have made him famous.

Reminiscing about Heroes

You know, it's conceivable that life and living conditions in the farm areas of Southern California in the 1920s weren't necessarily all that different from the living conditions in similar areas of the 1880s, when my Dad was working one year and going to High School the next.

He and his Father and Mother, seven brothers younger than himself, and a sister older than himself, immigrated from South Island, New Zealand, to San Pedro in 1879, when he was 13. Before leaving New Zealand Grandpa had bought a cattle ranch sight unseen in California. It turned out that the differences and distances between *Baja* and *Alta* California were somewhat blurred. The piece he had bought by mail order was some thirty miles south of Ensenada, in a parched and rugged terrain that hadn't seen a drop of water in twenty-five years. It was worthless, and it left the family penniless and stranded on the dock at San Pedro.

The boys, scrounging around, heard about a run-down and abandoned Dairy near Dominguez which could be rented on shares. The family took it, and my Dad worked with his Dad and all the Brothers all through the rest of 1879 and all of 1880, fixing fences, repairing barns and sheds, and putting in a running water set-up. By 1881, the Dairy was supporting the family, and my Dad then could think about enrolling at Los Angeles High School, the same one I would start going to in January of 1925. My Dad, by studying one year and working two (so's he could start saving to go to the University of California at Berkeley), graduated from Los Angeles High School, I think, in the summer of 1889 and from Cal (the University of California) in 1896.

In the 1920s, it was commonplace for farmboys and working-class boys to go to school until they were fourteen. Then, often as not, they quit school and went to work as young men. So my Dad, who had gone to work as a man at thirteen, thought nothing of putting me to work as a man, also at thirteen, at least in the summertime—in 1925. I worked in hayfield mowing-and-stacking migratory teams that summer, side-by-side with I.W.W. members. When I worked for my Dad back home he always treated me like a chattel, and I hated him for it. These guys treated me like an equal and, work-wise, we *were* equals. I loved it, and so I was willing to do whatever they suggested. They told me all about the great working-class struggles of the nineteenth century, and about their great Hero, Joe Hill, who'd been executed for organizing by the bosses, nine years before. Because I had a good bass singing voice, they taught me some of Joe Hill's songs.

Joe Hill was their working-class Hero, so he was mine, too, from 1925 until 1934. I recall the thrill I had back in February of 1986 when I read that the Southern California Labor Library was giving a Lifetime Achievement Award to Harry Bridges. You see, Harry Bridges eventually took over first place in my pantheon of working-class Heroes. It's not quite true to say that Bridges replaced Joe Hill, because Joe Hill went on being important to me also, particularly after Earl Robinson's wonderful song of 1937, "I dreamed I saw Joe Hill last night . . ." I always think of my Working Buddies of the summers of 1925 to 1932, whenever we sing it, even now. It's just that Joe Hill was alive in *their* experience, and Harry Bridges was alive in *mine*.

Harry Bridges has been for sixty years my icon of what an American working-class Hero was *and should be*. I remember that day in July 1934, when he first leapt into my vision, speaking in honor of the two workers who had been shot down by the Governor's National Guard at the funeral which climaxed the great Pacific Coast–wide General Strike of that year. The shocking shudder of terror mixed with fury flooding me, as that hail of fatal bullets whistled past my ear on that bloody Thursday so long ago, changed my life. Will Geer, a Gay fellow actor and my lover at the time, and I had gone up to San Francisco that July to support the Strike by doing Street-Theatre, what at the time was called "Agit Prop," to help keep morale high and flying.

Already, I was dreaming that someday my "Strange Brothers" and I would develop a similar kind of powerful fraternal Brotherhood as the San Francisco Maritime Workers were building. (But I also knew that on this same issue my darling Will Geer thought I was dangerously out of my mind—and he wasn't the only one. "What in god's name would such a group even have in common to talk about?" he'd storm at me, cutting me short.) The icy shriek of bullets past my ear that bloody Thursday conjured up in me suddenly a chilling presentiment, somewhat accurately as it turned out, of what a long, lonely, and maybe unpopular political struggle against an insufferable oppression might be like.

Even so, from that long-ago day to this year, never in my life did it ever occur to me that I, also, might in turn be receiving one of the same splendid honors that my life-long Hero, Harry Bridges, received. Now this impossible event has happened—but he still goes on, *miles ahead*, being my Hero!

Of course, I'm talking (all round Robin Hood's barn, so to speak) about another Hero *I stubbornly refused to recognize in his lifetime*—my Dad! Because he worked me as a chattel without ever letting me feel that he respected either me or my opinions, I hated him. Gaelic Highlanders, all of them—the parents, the eldest daughter, and the seven sons. They none of them really knew how to show love. The sons, taught by example, or self-made—each one's word was his bond all his life long, as had been their Father's. Love was each one's warm silence; the cold icy glare, disapproval.

The one exception, because my stubbornness matched my Father's, he whipped me with his seven-leafed razor-strop. For this, I hated him so much that I would have died rather than give him so much as the satisfaction of a whimper.

Love is very assuredly its own encompassing reward. On that we are agreed—and John's and my experience these last thirty-one years verifies this.

But non-bottoming unyielding Hate harvests, in my experience, almost unbearable Grief. So unyielding was my hate for my Father's inability to bend when I needed him, as a boy, that I *missed* his splendid gift of love to me when I was man-grown. He stood, once, head thrown back, four-square against the character-plundering and pollution of a blackmail to slander his Queer Eldest Son as a seducer of Minors—in the bleak year of 1935, before so much as a single ray of knowledge that Queerness, as yet, in other cultures, was a blessing, was a vision of healing. My Dad stood up for me—and I couldn't unbend, in his lifetime, to thank him, let alone to love him back. How devastatingly well did old Khayyám fathom this bottomless grief: "Nor all thy tears wash out a word of it!"

Signed Harry Hay, March 15, 1994.

Afterword

by Will Roscoe

Harry Hay and
Gay Politics

MOST OBSERVERS TODAY agree that the Lesbian/Gay community is organized and functions like other American ethnic and racial minorities, and that most Lesbians and Gay men think of their sexual identity as equivalent to an ethnic identity. This is, of course, the very model adopted by the Mattachine organizers. "We said, 'Why can't we do the same sort of things the Jews do?'" Chuck Rowland recalled. "If you had five hundred thousand Jews in the community, they would have several temples. They would have a symphony orchestra. They would have ballet. They would have several theaters. They would have a hospital. Why can't we do all those kinds of things?"[1] And, indeed, we now have many of these resources in major cities throughout North America. So it would seem that Hay has lived to see the highest vindication one can receive for one's ideas—the verdict of history itself.

Yet, the grassroots popularity of the cultural minority model is neither welcomed nor advocated by most Lesbian and Gay theorists today. Far from it—the minority model and Gay identity itself have been subject to relentless criticism since the early 1980s. John D'Emilio, the historian who recovered the history of Mattachine, now believes that "a fatal weakness attends any Gay political movement which defines itself as a fixed minority in quest of equal protection based on its minority status."[2] Bruce Bawer considers all notions of Gay culture and commonalty the result of navel-gazing by "subculture-oriented" Gays.[3] Others have characterized the "ethnic/essentialist" model as conservative, elitist, even reactionary.

This rejection of the minority model is largely based on the school of thought known as social constructionism. In social constructionist theory, the introduction and deployment of labels is the central fact of Gay identity and history—specifically the label "homosexual" and its use by the dominant institutions of society, by medical doctors, psychiatrists, educators, social workers, police and so forth starting in the late nineteenth century. For constructionists, contemporary Gay identities are just that—modern inventions arising from social forces and labeling practices unique to Western societies.[4] More recently, a growing number of self-proclaimed Queer theorists have made even more radical extensions of these ideas.[5] Where constructionists were content to point out the historical contingency and variability of homosexual patterns and identities, Queer theorists (especially the followers of Michel Foucault) now argue that because identities are constructed by social power, to have an identity is to be subjugated. This has led many of these theorists to dismiss anything deemed to be "identity politics."

The criticisms of identity-based politics such as Hay advocates can be summed up as follows: (1) they are inherently apolitical and subjectivist, fostering narrow, single-issue politics and political fragmentation; (2) identities are too unstable to base a politics on; (3) identity politics promote the "fiction" that identities are fixed and "unitary," and for that reason are exclusionary and elitist; (4) and, in the final analysis, Lesbian and Gay identities can't be compared to those of "real" ethnic groups. Hay's writings in this collection offer answers to all these criticisms, making a strong case not only for the effectiveness of identity-based politics but their necessity, as well.

The first criticism is the source of most dismissals of identity politics. It is based on the misconception that they are necessarily narrow and reformist in scope. Clearly, a simplistic application of the slogan "the personal is the political" that makes individual experiences of oppression the central point of reference to the neglect of an analysis of exploitation is apolitical and subjectivist. (Although the outlaw status of homosexuality ensures that almost any assertion of a Queer identity will, as Hay likes to say, "scare the horses.") However, Hay shows how identity politics still can be linked to a comprehensive analysis of social inequality rooted in Marxist materialism. Hay pursues identity politics not as end in themselves but as a means for achieving the broader goal of social equality—through grassroots movements that provide their participants with a sense of belonging and alternative values. In this formula, the "personal" is not equated with the political but viewed as the chrysalis where political subjectivity and agency arise (much as the Lesbian/Gay community cannot be equated with the Lesbian/Gay political movement even though it provides that movement with the conditions of its possibility). The challenge is to balance affirmation of identity with analysis of the sources and nature of inequality in society, and of how all historically formed identities are linked through a relationship to the larger system of inequality. If the pitfall of identity politics is that cultural and social differences can be difficult to mediate, the alternative, minimizing or setting aside differences for the sake of unity, is a social contract women, minorities, Gays, and Lesbians are no longer willing to enter.[6]

Some critics even claim that identity politics are dangerous. Steven Epstein, one of the few Gay theorists to embrace the ethnic identity model, nonetheless warns, "If there is perceived to be such a thing as a 'homosexual person,' then it is only a small step

334   to the conclusion that there is such a thing as a 'homosexual disease,' itself the peculiar consequence of the 'homosexual lifestyle.' "[7] Similar concerns have been expressed in regards to Black
nationalism—that the emphasis on difference will only reinforce
the majority's worst fears about African Americans, which equate
difference with defect. But this is akin to blaming the victim. If our
enemies say that the state of being homosexual is synonymous
with being diseased this is because of their homophobia, not
because we dared assert Gay personhood.

The fact is, the answer to what causes homosexuality and
the question of how homosexuality should be evaluated are not
logically linked. Theories of biological origins and those of social
construction can be used both to defend Gay rights *or* to argue
against them. If, for example, Gayness is caused by genes, then
one could argue that it is natural and should be accepted—*or* that
it is a defect that should be corrected. If both homosexuality and
heterosexuality are socially constructed and Gay identity is a
choice, then neither heterosexuality nor homosexuality is more
natural than the other—*or* what has been constructed can and
should be un-constructed. As Eve Sedgwick points out, the danger
of any explanation of cause is that it can feed into the "overarch-
ing, hygienic Western fantasy of a world without any more homosexuals in it."[8] But homophobia does not arise from beliefs about
the cause of homosexuality, it comes out of irrational hatred and
fear of homosexuality. Where the difference between theories of
origins becomes salient, however, is in their application to the
political project of mobilizing sexual minorities, in which case
Hay and I argue that a theory that uncovers commonalties and
builds strong identities is more useful than one which decon-
structs them and offers nothing in their place.

The multidimensional definition of a minority that Hay
employs provides an answer to the second common criticism of

identity-based politics. Social constructionist and Queer theorists often speak of identities as if their assignment were completely arbitrary and all identities were equivalent—as if African-American, Lesbian and Gay, Chicano, or Jewish identity had the same status as that of "Californian" or "recovering co-dependent." Hay's model makes it possible to distinguish histori-cally formed collectives, the former, with a definable relationship to the system of production from identities, such as the latter, which lack the criteria of a cultural minority—language, psycho-logical make-up, shared culture, and so forth.

At the same time, acknowledging commonalties of social and psychological experience between Gay people is not the same as claiming that Gay identity is "unitary" or that identities are stable or fixed—the third criticism of identity politics. It is precisely the voluntary dimension of ethnic identities that makes their asser-tion the founding act of modern political subjectivity. This is something Hay and the other Mattachine founders recognized at the outset. As Chuck Rowland wrote in 1953, "A Mexican-American homosexual, for example, would participate in the homosexual culture, the dominant American culture, and the Mexican-American culture. He would also participate in the Mexican-American homosexual culture. He would use English at work and Spanish at home. He would make homosexual sexual contacts in both languages and in both cultural areas. He would swish (if he were so inclined) in both English and Spanish or be butch within the framework of all three cultures as he felt the situ-ation demanded."⁹

Obviously, our understanding of Lesbian and Gay identity can-not be based on a single example—that of white, middle-class Lesbians and Gay men. Social constructionists, however, are just as guilty of this error when they focus exclusively on historical developments in northwestern Europe and North America leading to the construction of "the modern homosexual." This marginalizes historical and non-Western Queer identities. Certainly, same-sex love and sexuality were part of the lives of Native American Two-Spirits, Classical Greek lovers, and eighteenth-century English Mollies, as they are a part of Gay life today. To say that one of these identities, that of contemporary, Western Lesbians and Gay men, is *the* "homosexual role" is ethnocentric. Gay Asians and contemporary Native Americans, to name two examples, can trace their homosexuality to non-Western traditions and practices—does this make them less "homosexual," less "Gay," or less "modern"?

To study and compare "Queer" identities from different times and places is not to say that they have the same social meaning. Most Gay African Americans do not have the same self-conceptions as white Gay men and Lesbians, but who would argue that they lack ways of distinguishing themselves from heterosexual African Americans? Hay's multidimensional model makes it possible to recognize that individual identities are constructed in different ways without relying on a single "essential" trait to define that identity. Just as each minority group emerges in history as the result of a distinct combination of factors and traits, none exactly like any others' except in their accumulative impact, "Gay" identity is a template or model that can be filled out with specific histories, specific social backgrounds, and culturally specific acts and practices, and still share important characteristics with other non-heterosexual identities in other times and places, and with other Queer identities, such as bisexual and transgender, in the present.

Today, and in any imaginable democratic culture in the future, every citizen has multiple identities, interests, and loyalties. Further, individuals vary in the way they identify with group symbols, labels, and histories, and the extent to which they participate in

their communities. Merely knowing an individual's identity does
not entitle one to assume their political beliefs (e.g., that all African Americans are liberal Democrats.) Nor does the existence   337
of African-American or Lesbian/Gay communities require one
hundred percent participation by all who identify as African
American or Gay. Identity and community are not coterminous.
However, these communities of culture do require (and deserve)
from African American, white, Gay, and non-Gay alike acknowl-
edgment of their historical and cultural contributions toward bet-
tering the lot of their own people and society at large. Whatever
potential exists for building movements that effectively challenge
racism and homophobia resides in these communities and the
channels of communication they provide to those who identify
with them.

The final common objection to the minority model of Gay politics is that even if homosexuals are different in meaningful ways it
does not mean that they can be compared to other minorities and
ethnic groups. Here we need to ask how ethnicity is being defined
(and to what extent a degraded or narrow view of Lesbian/Gay
cultural accomplishments might underlie this complaint). In fact,
scholars in ethnic studies recognize the fluidity and historical variability of ethnicities.[10] Ethnic identities may be assigned at birth,
but they are sometimes abandoned in adulthood. Even racial
identities and boundaries can be crossed. Children of one group
are sometimes raised by parents of another. In circumstances like
these and others, individuals can acquire an ethnic or racial identity later in life, not through their immediate family, much as Gay
men and Lesbians do. Indeed, I would venture to say that our
common experience of social isolation and gender role noncon-
formance gives us a more solid basis of commonalty, in terms of
formative emotional experiences, than that shared by second-
generation immigrants whose social life is thoroughly American

and whose cultural identity has been reduced to cuisine and a few holiday customs. As Epstein concludes, "Gays may now be more 'ethnic' than the original ethnic groups."[11]

Studies support this assertion. Lesbians and especially Gay men trace their sense of difference to their childhoods and to primarily non-sexual experiences. Bell, Weinberg, and Hammersmith, for example, found that homosexual males were almost twice as likely as heterosexual controls to report feeling "very much or somewhat" different from other boys during grade school (72 percent compared to 39 percent). Lesbians, too, were also more likely than heterosexual controls to have felt "somewhat or very much" different from other girls. Gay men were also more likely than heterosexual controls to report that they felt odd because they did not like sports (48 percent compared to 21 percent), or because they were not sexually interested in girls, or were sexually interested in boys. They were also much more likely to report having enjoyed solitary activities not associated with gender (like reading, drawing, or listening to music) than heterosexual males (68 percent compared to 34 percent).[12]

These findings suggest what is lost when Lesbians and Gay men are spoken of as if the word homosexual adequately described them—namely, the myriad often subtle ways in which they vary from the prevailing sex/gender system. The fact is, for most Lesbians and Gay men homosexuality is not a construction, not something acquired, not an accident of childrearing, but a profound, ongoing motivation. Perhaps they were born that way; in any case, it is not something that can be changed at will, as some constructionists and Queer theorists imply.

Without allowing for some element of essentialism—in terms of traits or talents that the individual brings to her social role—it is impossible to explain why a given individual is labeled "homosexual" and why anyone would accept such a stigmatizing label

and enter such a deviant role. Social constructionists have claimed
that introduction of the term "homosexual" facilitated the construction of Gay identity. In fact, as Hay's life and writings testify,   339
Gay identity was not the predictable by-product of social forces or
semiotic processes or epistemological ruptures in Western intellectual history. The only thing that the term "homosexual" made
possible was to see oneself as mentally ill and morally debauched.
Stigma may foster resistance, but it does not determine the content of that resistance nor provide it with a ready-made counter-
discourse. As this collection documents, *Lesbians and Gay men*
constructed the identities that made it possible for them to overcome self-hate and become political subjects.[13]

Harry Hay realized in 1948 that activating the political potential of homosexuals in the United States depends, in Marxist
terms, on their becoming a class "for itself," aware of their common interests, rather than merely a class "in itself." Recognizing
oneself in others is what psychologists generally mean by "identification." This is an active process of relating oneself to symbols
and histories, and not merely a matter of passively accepting a
label. To be aware of belonging to a group is to have an "identity."
Being a member of a group acting on its own behalf is a very different thing from merely having an intellectual commitment to
social change. Such a sentiment might be the basis for helping or
supporting a given struggle but not for devoting one's life to it
because it is the only hope of relief from the oppression one experiences. Without consciousness of themselves as a class—without
identity—mobilization of Gays and Lesbians *for* Gay issues is chi-
merical. Without a broad base of people representing themselves
in politics, the project of liberation devolves to political action
committees and single-issue lobbying.[14]

Any movement in any historical period needs powerful symbols
and ideas to inspire its participants. When its members have been

subjected to grueling assaults on their fundamental self-esteem, labeled deviant, twisted, perverse, ill, and criminal, the need for affirmation is acute. This is precisely what social constructionism cannot provide. It is not a stance that lends itself to unequivocal statements of the value and joy of Gay being. (Of course, it should be apparent by now that the Queer identity and culture Hay celebrates is not a sanitized or pastoral version by any means.) Epstein pinpointed the dilemma of modern Gay/Lesbian politics when he wrote, "So while constructionist theorists have been preaching the gospel that the hetero/homosexual distinction is a social fiction, Gays and Lesbians, in everyday life and in political action, have been busy hardening the categories. Theory, it seems, has not been informing practice. Perhaps the practitioners are misguided; or perhaps there is something about the strict constructionist perspective which neither adequately describes the experiences of Gays and Lesbians nor speaks to their need to understand and legitimate their places in the world."[15]

Identity-building politics have inspired and motivated Lesbians and Gay men. Gay assimilationism, from its garden-variety manifestation in the "We're-no-different-except-what-we-do-in-bed" position to its obtuse formulations by Queer theorists never has. This is just as true today as it was in 1950, when a nervous band of political and sexual outlaws launched Gay liberation. Identity politics involve tried and tested principles of organizing, mobilizing, and uniting that anyone who works in mass movements learns. It is helpful to have Hay, in this collection, remind us of them.

An additional contribution of this collection is the recovery of the radical origins of Gay liberation in the Mattachine movement of 1950–1953, along with new perspectives on the later homophile

movement and 1970s Gay liberation. These writings and documents are especially timely in light of recent interpretations of this
history by some theorists.

Steven Seidman, for example, in an essay entitled "Identity and
Politics in a 'Postmodern' Gay Culture," argues that social constructionism and postmodernism are the true inheritors of the
"core ideas" of radical Gay liberation, while the kind of cultural
minority model Hay advocates is accomodationist, even elitist.[16]
To reach this conclusion, however, he portrays the homophile
movement prior to Stonewall as uniformly conservative and
makes no mention of early Mattachine and its successes. Instead,
he speaks of the homophile movement as if it had a single orientation from 1950 to 1969, asserting that "many in the mainstream
homophile movement described homosexuals as a minority." In
other words, he attributes the minority model of early Mattachine
to the assimilationists who took over after 1953.[17] In fact, the
post-1953 leaders rejected *any* suggestion that homosexuals
constituted a minority. The very concept was anathema to them,
tainted with the radicalism of Hay and the other Mattachine
founders. "We know we are the same," chimed Marilyn Reiger,
a leader of the conservative faction at the climactic May 1953
convention, "no different than anyone else."[18]

Seidman goes on to characterize post-Stonewall Gay liberation
as "decidedly constructionist." Although he acknowledges that
Gay liberation theory was not unified, he cites only two texts from
this period and claims that one of them, Dennis Altman's 1971
Homosexual Oppression and Liberation, contains the "common
core of liberation theory." This "core" is apparently a Freudian-
inspired view of sexuality as "naturally" polymorphously perverse, neither heterosexual nor homosexual.[19] Combined with
a feminist critique of sex-roles, this led many to argue that the

goal of sexual liberation was to free everyone to be bisexual and androgynous. On this basis, Seidman claims that Gay liberation was a precursor to the anti-identity politics of poststructuralist Queer theory.[20]

Calls for universal androgyny and bisexuality were indeed common in the early 1970s, but Altman's version of these concepts proved to be a political dead-end. (There's little trace of them, for example, in the Los Angeles Gay Liberation Front Statement of Purpose included here on pp. 176–78). For Altman, the minority model of Gay identity and community "represents a new form of social control."[21] "It is in fact probably true," he argues, "that individuals are often forced into exclusive homosexuality because of both the way in which society brands those who deny its roles and the penalties meted out to those who are unwilling to accept them." The final chapter of his *Homosexual Oppression and Liberation*, "The End of the Homosexual," was not a prediction of a coming holocaust, but a description of the utopia to be ushered in by sexual liberation. The book ends with the sentence, "If man/womankind reaches the point where it is able to dispense with the categories of homo- and heterosexuality, the loss will be well worth the gain."[22] Although Seidman credits Gay liberation with rejecting assimilation, it's hard to see Altman's politics as representative of anything but the most absolute assimilation possible—the complete disappearance of homosexuality as a recognizable way of being.

The second text Seidman cites, by Allen Young, also endorses the idea that Gay liberation means a transcendence of social categories, but does so without negating Lesbian/Gay identity: "Homosexuals committed to struggling against sexism have a better chance than straights of building relationships based on equality because there is less enforcement of roles. We have already broken with gender programming."[23] Although Seidman dismisses Young's claim as "vanguardism," it is precisely this line of thought that led Hay, five years earlier, to coin the phrase "subject-to-SUBJECT" to describe the egalitarian quality of Gay relationships.

My own feeling as a participant in the 1970s movement is that Allen Young's vision, in which Lesbians and Gay men were seen as manifesting a liberated mode of life that could and should be fostered, represents the version of Gay liberation that had the greatest and widest appeal—not Altman's longing for self-abnegation. Even Carl Wittman's 1970 manifesto, which Seidman cites as representative of Gay liberation thinking because it critiques homosexual/heterosexual categories and idealizes bisexuality, includes an unequivocal rejection of Gay assimilation: "*Stop mimicking straights, stop censoring ourselves.*"[24] Indeed, if there is a "core idea" of Gay liberation it is de-assimilation, not deconstruction. "Don't blend in with Straight people—that's oppressing yourself," declared "Sister" Brian Chavez in *Gay Sunshine* in 1970; "BLATANT IS BEAUTIFUL."

Equally questionable is Seidman's account of Gay politics and culture in the late 1970s. These were the years in which the street tactics of the Gay Activists Alliance of New York were replaced by the coat-and-tie lobbying of the National Gay and Lesbian Task Force and when a millionaire named David Goodstein bought the only national Gay news magazine and used it to inveigh against Lesbian and Gay progressives and every manifestation of Queer culture that might offend middle-class sensibilities. Assimilationists, in the pursuit of reformist, single-issue politics, opposed every assertion of Lesbian/Gay identity in these years, whether in the form of Gay Pride marches and parades with their ostentatious displays of costume and mirth or ACT-UP's confrontational activism.²⁵ Meanwhile, Gay liberationists like Carl Wittman and Harry Hay found a home in the spirituality, eco-feminist, and progressive movements of the late 1970s, and continued to pursue identity- and community-building politics.²⁶ (At the time of his death from AIDS in 1985, Wittman was an active participant in radical faerie networks and a close friend of Hay's).

Seidman claims the opposite to have been the case: grassroots Gays and Lesbians *betrayed* Gay liberation ideals by embracing the minority model of identity and representing themselves "as an ethnic group oriented toward assimilation." "Although this model proved effective in socially mobilizing Lesbians and Gay men, its emphasis on a unitary identity and community marginalized individuals who deviated from its implicitly white, middle-class social norms."²⁷ On its face, the characterization "ethnic assimilationism" is oxymoronic. How does one assimilate by asserting cultural difference? In any case, the Lesbians and Gay men who contributed to the florescence of community-building and cultural expressions in the 1970s and 1980s can hardly be accused of assimilating. When asked what they were trying to achieve, they invariably stated their goals in terms of identity politics and the Gay ethnic model. Their efforts represent the true continuation of the anti-assimilationist spirit of Lesbian/Gay liberation. The marginalization of non-white and working-class Lesbians and Gays, on the other hand, is largely the consequence of the politics and policies of the middle-class assimilationists who now dominate the leadership of the movement and the same racism that pervades other sectors of American society, not identity politics.

Seidman would conflate Gay identity politics with Gay assimilationism and oppose both to his version of Queer postmodernism. I believe a truer representation of the political landscape would recognize the affinity between the assimilationism of moderates

344

like Bruce Bawer and the anti-identity politics of Seidman and oppose *both* to the cultural minority model that Hay advocates and to community-based, grassroots politics. Anti-assimilation and de-assimilation have been the consistent themes of progressive Lesbian/Gay politics, from early Mattachine, to Gay Liberation, to the brief but momentous appearance of Queer Nation.

Consider, for example, the constant devaluation and dismissal of Lesbian/Gay identities in the writings of social constructionists and Queer theorists. According to John D'Emilio, "The identity and the oppression are bound together. . . . So long as we accept these preset terms we have lost much of our freedom of choice. . . . It is time to carve out new personal and political paths, and to lay claim to the possibility of choice, to embark on new journeys of sexual definition." Jeffrey Weeks, too, would like to "celebrate the flux, to indulge in a glorification of the 'polysex-ualities' to which, on a radical reading of the Freudian tradition, we are all heir," but "the unfortunate problem with this is that most individuals do not feel 'polymorphously perverse.'" In the end, he resigns himself to Gay identity, even though it "may well be a historical fiction, a controlling myth, a limiting burden." Lesbian-feminist Monique Wittig considers "the most absurd of all things, the need and necessity . . . to support and advocate . . . a 'right to Difference,'" and she ridicules the idea that salvation "is in a tremendous exaltation of what they call alterity under all of its forms: Jewish, Black, Red, Yellow, Female, Homosexual, Crazy." For his part, Seidman would dissolve "any notion of a substantial unity in identity constructions leaving only rhetorics of identities, performances, and the free play of difference and possibility."[28]

The excitement of locating our presence in history, of lifting the veil on our past that launched Lesbian and Gay studies in the 1970s, has given way to boundless zeal for proving that there is no

Gay presence in history and for all purposes no Gay history. This preoccupation with the construction of homosexuality belies an assumption that its *absence* is the normal state of affairs, that only its presence needs to be explained. But such a premise is antithetical to Lesbian/Gay studies and politics alike. While recognizing the diversity of homosexual patterns and the possibility that one or more might be missing in some societies, the absence of homosexuality altogether can never be a normal condition. It can only be the product of concerted suppression.

At this point we might ask, how *does* the individual who considers her sexuality and identity to be products of social coercion proceed as a political subject? Avowedly "post-Marxian," Seidman advocates "multiple, local, intersecting struggles whose aim is less 'the end of domination' or 'human liberation' than the creation of social spaces that encourage the proliferation of pleasures, desires, voices, interests, modes of individuation and democratization." What this means becomes apparent when he contrasts Lesbian/Gay oppression, which is based on "cultural representations," to that of workers, which comes directly from economic and class relations.[29] Since this opposition fits perfectly with the traditional Marxist paradigm of class versus ideological struggles, base versus superstructure, I am at a loss as to how it is "post-Marxian." Rather, in capitulating to the placement of Gay issues outside of relations of production, the Gay politics Seidman advocates are simply non-Marxian—liberal and reformist, offering no alternative to capitalism and its forms of human exploitation.[30]

In the end, it is hard not to conclude that the radical posturing of Queer theorists serves to mask an assimilationist yearning to efface one's difference, to elude the debilitation of belonging to America's most hated minority. As Guy Hocquenghem, one of the first to articulate the anti-identity position, confessed, "People are always a little ashamed of being proud of being homosexual."[31]

346

This denial of identity seems to me a uniquely Gay form of self-hatred. I can think of no other contemporary minority whose intellectuals are so deeply invested in erasing their difference.

Hay's Gay politics represent an alternative to postmodernist Queer theory and dogmatic constructionism. Indeed, Hay is the only contemporary Gay thinker who could be said to offer a *unified* theory of Gayness—one that begins by defining its subject in multidimensional terms and then accounts for its individual and historical origins, its diverse forms and their history, the psycho-social development of Gay individuals, and the nature and sources of Gay oppression. Postmodernism offers at best a politics of resignation, one that rejects the possibility of an "outside" to power, of a subject-SUBJECT alternative to subject-OBJECT hegemony. For Hay, there is the possibility of a successor to subject-OBJECT social relations, and the means of getting there is through a politics that affirms Queer identities and cultures.

Hay is not bothered if his ideas are called essentialist or if his activism is deemed identity politics—he is happy to emphasize his differences with social constructionism and Queer theory—provided that the word *radical* precede these labels. The original meaning of this word, "to the root," serves well to convey the underlying theme of his philosophy and politics. The key principles of Hay's radical essentialism can be summed up as follows:

· It is, first and foremost, Gay-centered—a "situated knowledge" (to borrow Donna Haraway's terminology) reflecting the social standpoint of contemporary sexual minorities. It is not neutral on the question of Queer well-being; it seeks to create knowledge that contributes to that end.

· It posits Gay presence rather than absence as the usual state of human society.

348

- It conceives of its subject in multidimensional terms—not merely as a sexual preference but as a difference manifest in gender roles, social identity, economic roles, and sometimes religious roles, as well.
- It seeks to tell history from the bottom up, using those documents, records, and artifacts that reveal the common experience of the largest number of Queer folk and not only the discourse of elite heterosexuals and social institutions.
- It recognizes various levels of meaning—individual, social, transcultural, and spiritual. It does not assume that the way an individual describes herself will be identical to the institutional definition of labels that have been applied to her.
- It is multicultural and comparative. Rather than a unitary instance—"the modern homosexual"—it employs the notion of a family tree (like Wittgenstein's concept of "family resemblance") to conceptualize the relationship between the Queer identities and roles of different cultures and historical periods.
- It views history as a process of continuity-within-change rather than as a series of sharply defined periods or ruptures. Concept/labels like "Sodomite" and "Urning," "homosexual" and "Gay," have overlapped in their usage. Neither can be defined without reference to the other.
- It focuses on praxis. It seeks to analyze the interaction between individuals and their societies and cultures. It looks for instances of symbols and ideas in action as well as in discourse.

The mass coming-out that transformed the quiescent homophile movement of the 1960s into the dynamic Lesbian/Gay liberation and civil rights movements of the 1970s and 1980s was in large measure a function of the possibility of joining a community where a negative label could be replaced with an affirmative identity. Hay's writings show that this was no accident. The cultural minority model was a carefully thought out political analysis and strategy on the part of the Mattachine founders.

Over the years Hay's vision of Gay identity has had one overriding theme: Gay differences are the source of potential contributions to society at large. If he is right, then foregrounding one's Gayness is a way of manifesting commitment and giving service to one's community. In this and other ways, Hay shows how identity politics can be linked to a strong social analysis and the cause of freedom and equality for all. Today's theorists would do well to consider what identity politics has accomplished along with its risks. Every year in June the currency of the ethnic minority model is testified to by hundreds of thousands, if not millions, of women and men who fill the streets of cities throughout North America and the world for an event generally known as "Lesbian/Gay Pride Day." The popular appeal of identity politics should be reason enough to seek a way to preserve, indeed, embrace and foster them, while continuing to search for links between Queer politics and the transformation of systemic sources of inequality and oppression. Since 1948, Hay has been making the case for just such a version of progressive identity politics. It is now time for a new generation to re-articulate Lesbian/Gay liberation in its own language and dreams, and take the lead in exploring the uncharted realms of "this new planet of Fairy-vision," the freedom won for us by the generation of Harry Hay and the founders of Mattachine.

Notes

1. Quoted in Eric Marcus, *Making History: The Struggle for Gay and Lesbian Equal Rights, 1945–1990: An Oral History* (New York: HarperCollins, 1992), p. 34. Rowland (1917–1990) attempted to start a

Gay church himself through ONE, Inc. in 1956 (see Marvin Cutler, ed., *Homosexuals Today: A Handbook of Organizations and Publications, 1956* [Los Angeles: ONE, Inc., 1956]). In 1959, he returned to Minnesota and became a high school drama teacher. Following his retirement in the 1980s, he moved back to Los Angeles and founded that city's first Gay theater company, Celebration Theatre.

2. John D'Emilio, *Making Trouble: Essays on Gay History, Politics, and the University* (New York: Routledge, 1992), p. 187.

3. Bruce Bawer, *A Place at the Table: The Gay Individual in American Society* (New York: Poseidon Press, 1993).

4. Writings in the vein of social constructionism are legion. The canonical texts are collected in Edward Stein, *Forms of Desire* (New York: Routledge, 1992). David Halperin provides extensive citations (*One Hundred Years of Homosexuality and Other Essays on Greek Love* [New York: Routledge, 1990], pp. 154–68) as does Richard Mohr (*Gay Ideas: Outing and Other Controversies* [Boston: Beacon Press, 1992], pp. 285 ff.)

5. For collections of Queer theory, see the special issue of *differences* 3 (Summer 1991); Diana Fuss, ed., *Inside/Out: Lesbian Theories, Gay Theories* (New York: Routledge, 1991); Michael Warner, ed., *Fear of a Queer Planet: Queer Politics and Social Theory* (Minneapolis: University of Minnesota Press, 1993); Donald Morton, ed., *Queer Theory: A Lesbian and Gay Cultural Studies Reader* (Boulder, Col.: Westview Press, 1995). Important contributors to Queer theory include Judith Butler and Eve Sedgwick.

6. In this context, it might be helpful to recall Fanon's discussion of the role of national culture in liberation movements in former colonies: "The consciousness of self is not the closing of a door to communication. Philosophic thought teaches us, on the contrary, that it is its guarantee. . . . The building of a nation is of necessity accompanied by the discovery and encouragement of universalizing values. Far from keeping aloof from other nations, therefore, it is national liberation which leads the nation to play its part on the stage of history. It is at the heart of national consciousness that international consciousness lives and grows. And this two-fold emerging is ultimately the source of all culture" (Frantz Fanon, "On National Culture," in *Colonial Discourse and Post-Colonial Theory: A Reader*, ed. Patrick Williams and Laura Chrisman, pp. 36–52 [New York: Columbia University Press, 1994], pp. 51–52).

7. Steven Epstein, "Gay Politics, Ethnic Identity: The Limits of Social Constructionism," *Socialist Review* 93–94 (vol. 17, nos. 3/4) (1987): 9–54, p. 48.

8. Eve K. Sedgwick, *Epistemology of the Closet* (Berkeley: University of California Press, 1990), p. 42.

9. David L. Freeman [Chuck Rowland], "The Homosexual Culture," *ONE* 1(5) (May 1953): 10.

10. See, for example, Michael Omi and Howard Winant, *Racial Formation in the United States: From the 1960s to the 1990s*, 2d ed. (New York: Routledge, 1994).

11. Epstein, "Gay Politics, Ethnic Identity," p. 39. Stephen O. Murray reached this conclusion in 1979. He found that the Toronto Gay community was more institutionally complete than other ethnic groups and was de-assimilating rather than assimilating ("Institutional Elaboration of a Quasi-Ethnic Community," *International Review of Modern Sociology* 9 [1979]: 165–78).

12. Richard R. Troiden, *Gay and Lesbian Identity* (Dix Hills, N.Y.: General, 1988), pp. 82 f. As evidence that homosexuality is purely a matter of object choice, the "masculinity" of Gay male styles since the 1970s is often cited. In fact, the so-called "clone" image was a manifestation of an intense process of self-identification and bonding among Gay men. If Levi's were male clothes, we nonetheless wore them in a way that no heterosexual man had ever done—skintight with no underwear—which made us *more* visible in our own eyes and in the eyes of others than ever before. This was not a matter of traditional masculinity in any sense but of costuming and marking our bodies in the process of forging an erotic community.

13. Too often, rather than collect and analyze data that might indicate the actual ideas, beliefs, and identities current among homosexuals in the past century, social constructionists have assumed that whatever official organs have asserted has been what Lesbians and Gay men actually believed and did. George Chauncey Jr.'s recent study, *Gay New York*, is, in many respects, the first real social history of the modern Gay world because its conclusions are based on a broad sampling of the experiences and representations of Gay men themselves. Chauncey reveals that the medico-psychiatric category of the homosexual had little impact on how Queer men thought of and identified themselves until *after* World War II. In the period he documents, they most often called themselves "fairies"

and considered themselves not only homosexual but gender different (*Gay New York: Gender, Urban Culture, and the Making of the Gay Male World, 1890–1940* [New York: Basic, 1994]).

14. Mark Blasius is one of the few theorists to acknowledge the role of identity in making a Lesbian and Gay movement possible (see *Gay and Lesbian Politics: Sexuality and the Emergence of a New Ethic* [Philadelphia: Temple University Press, 1994]).

15. Epstein, "Gay Politics, Ethnic Identity," pp. 12–13. See also Donna Penn, "Queer: Theorizing Politics and History," *Radical History Review* 62 (1995): 24–42.

16. Steven Seidman, "Identity and Politics in a 'Postmodern' Gay Culture: Some Historical and Conceptual Notes," in Warner, ed., *Fear of a Queer Planet*, pp. 105–42. I have chosen to focus on this essay because it is exemplary of Queer theory methods and arguments. Questionable conclusions based on shaky historical generalizations are commonplace in this genre. See also Lisa Duggan, "Making It Perfectly Queer," *Socialist Review* (January–March 1992): 11–31.

17. Seidman, "Identity and Politics," p. 111.

18. Quoted in John D'Emilio, *Sexual Politics, Sexual Communities: The Making of a Homosexual Minority in the United States, 1940–1970* (Chicago, University of Chicago Press, 1983), p. 79.

19. Although it is often assumed that this means bisexuality, in fact, the polymorphous state lacks *any* specificity in object choice. Humans, without the Oedipus complex, would be as likely to mate with rocks and trees, as with other humans, male or female.

20. Seidman, "Identity and Politics," p. 116.

21. Dennis Altman, *The Homosexualization of America, the Americanization of the Homosexual* (New York: St. Martin's, 1982), p. 72.

22. Dennis Altman, *Homosexual Oppression and Liberation* (New York: Avon, 1971), pp. 81, 238. The most sophisticated statement of this position in these years was Guy Hocquenghem's 1972 *Homosexual Desire* (Durham, N.C.: Duke University Press, 1993).

23. Allen Young, "Out of the Closets, into the Streets," in Karla Jay and Allen Young, eds., *Out of the Closets: Voices of Gay Liberation* (New York: Douglas/Links, 1972), p. 29.

24. Carl Wittman, "Refugees from Amerika: A Gay Manifesto," in Karla Jay and Allen Young, eds., *Out of the Closets*, pp. 330–42; empha-

sis in original. Concerning bisexuality, Wittman also wrote, "We continue to call ourselves homosexual, not bisexual, even if we do make it with the opposite sex also, because saying, 'Oh, I'm Bi' is a copout for a gay" (p. 331).

353

25. In the 1970s, the National Lesbian and Gay Task Force declined to endorse marches or demonstrations of any sort. Interestingly, Seidman makes no mention of the real spokesmen of Gay assimilationism—writers like Bruce Bawer (*A Place at the Table*); Marshall Kirk and Hunter Madsen (*After the Ball: How America Will Conquer Its Fear and Hatred of Gays in the 90s* [New York: Doubleday, 1989]); and Gore Vidal—whose view of Gay identity as a kind of delusion based on an insignificant behavioral variation is equivalent to that of social constructionists.

26. Throughout the 1970s, Gay radicals continued to assert androgyny and the equality of Gay relationships as social ideals, and to affirm Lesbian and Gay culture as a site of political resistance. *No Turning Back*, a comprehensive position statement on Lesbian/Gay oppression and liberation prepared by the Movement for a New Society in the late 1970s, includes chapters on Lesbian and Gay culture, where one reads "The gay world is an oasis in the desert of mainstream society; many of us have reached it thirsty, and rejoiced when we found it. It has vitality and creativity" (Gerre Goodman et al., *No Turning Back: Lesbian and Gay Liberation for the '80s* [Philadelphia: New Society Publishers, 1983], p. 96). See also Terence Kissack, "Freaking Fag Revolutionaries: New York's Gay Liberation Front, 1969–1971," *Radical History Review* 62 (1995): 104–234.

27. Seidman, "Identity and Politics," p. 110.

28. John D'Emilio, *Making Trouble*, pp. 186–88; Jeffrey Weeks, "Questions of Identity," in *The Cultural Construction of Sexuality*, ed. Pat Cuplan (London and New York: Tavistock, 1987), pp. 31–51, esp. pp. 48, 49; Monique Wittig, *The Straight Mind and Other Essays* (Boston: Beacon, 1992), pp. 57, 56; Seidman, "Identity and Politics," p. 135.

29. Seidman, "Identity and Politics," pp. 106, 109.

30. Critiques of constructionism and Queer theory have been rare. Some, like Wayne Dynes and Richard Mohr, have criticized constructionism from the liberal to libertarian end of the Gay political spectrum (see Dynes in Stein, *Forms of Desire*). Others, like Stein, have offered criticisms on formal and logical grounds. To my mind, constructionism's most rig-

354

orous critic is Stephen O. Murray (see *Social Theory, Homosexual Realities* [New York: Gay Academic Union, 1984] and *American Gay* [Chicago: University of Chicago Press, 1996]). Recently, criticisms of Queer theory from a Left perspective have begun to appear (see Donald Morton, "The Politics of Queer Theory in the Postmodern Moment," *Genders* 17. [Fall 1993]: 121–50; and Rosemary Hennessy, "Queer Theory, Left Politics," *Rethinking Marxism* 7[3] [Fall 1994]: 85–111). There may even be some defection in the ranks. Leo Bersani, an influential postmodernist literary critic, writes, "By erasing our identity we do little more than reconfirm its inferior position within a homophobic system of differences" (*Homos* [Cambridge, Mass.: Harvard University Press, 1995], p. 42).

31. Guy Hocquenghem, *Homosexual Desire*, trans. Daniella Dangoor (Durham, N.C.: Duke University Press, 1993), p. 143. As bell hooks warns, "Should we not be suspicious of postmodern critiques of the 'subject' when they surface at a historical moment when many subjugated people feel themselves coming to voice for the first time." Criticism of reductionist, normative projections of identity "should not be made synonymous with a dismissal of the struggle of oppressed and exploited peoples to make ourselves subjects" ("Postmodern Blackness," in *Colonial Discourse and Post-Colonial Theory: A Reader*, ed. Patrick Williams and Laura Chrisman (New York: Columbia University Press, 1994), pp. 421–27, esp. p. 425).

Chronology

1912 Harry Hay born in Worthing, England, Easter Sunday, April 7.

1914 Family leaves England for Chuquicamata, Chile, where father manages an Anaconda Copper Company mine.

1916 After father is injured in a mining accident, the family relocates to Southern California.

1919 Family moves to Los Angeles.

1922 Harry joins Harry James's Western Rangers boys' organization. Spends summers of 1922, 1923, and 1924 at grandfather's ranch in Hernandez, learning to ride horseback and herd cattle.

1923 Sees the word "homosexual" in a locked-case copy of Edward Carpenter's *The Intermediate Sex*.

1925 Starts high school. In spring, observes Hopis perform ceremonies at a local beach and later dance for his Western Rangers group. Sent to work on relative's ranch in Smith Valley, Nevada, for the summer (returns seven times). Is taken to a gathering of local Indians and blessed by an elder known as Jack Wilson (i.e., Wovoka).

1926 Family moves to 940 S. Windsor Boulevard. After working during the summer in Nevada, returns to Los Angeles via coastal steamer and has his first adult sexual experience with a sailor named Matt.

1929 Graduates from Los Angeles High School, excelling in music, poetry, oratory, and scholastic studies, and as president of the Forum Society, ROTC captain, and graduation speaker. His father arranges a job at a downtown law firm. Discovers cruising in Pershing Square and meets Champ Simmons, who tells him about the abortive Society for Human Rights in Chicago.

1930 Enters Stanford University. On New Year's Eve, visits Los Angeles's first "Gay" speakeasy and makes contacts that lead to his introduction to San Francisco Gay networks.

1931 At Stanford, has affair with Smith Dawless and discovers acting talent. In the fall, begins telling Stanford classmates that he is "temperamental" (i.e., homosexual). Has affair with James Broughton.

1932 Leaves Stanford in February to recover from a serious sinus infection in Nevada. Is unable to re-enroll for financial reasons. Returns to Los Angeles in the fall and renews acquaintance with composer John Cage, singing three of his compositions for the Santa Monica Women's Club in November. Becomes the male understudy for eight actors in George K. Arthur's Hollywood Playhouse Repertory Theatre, and appears as a stunt rider in "B" films.

1933 Sings Cage's songs for California Composers' Circle. Becomes bass soloist in a Latvian choir. In October, attends first Communist Party meeting.

1934 In February is cast by the Tony Pastor Theatre as comedy lead and in character roles. Begins affair with leading man Will Geer. Participates in the Milk Strike demonstration and meets Clarabelle, queen of Los Angeles's Bunker Hill. In July, travels with Geer to perform agit-prop in San Francisco General Strike; witnesses police firing upon strikers.

1935 In spring, travels with Will Geer to organize migratory workers in the San Joaquin Valley. Forms the Hollywood Theatre Guild with Geer and others to produce Clifford Odets's *Waiting for Lefty* and *Till the Day I Die*. Becomes active in the Hollywood Film and Photo League. Father defends him against attempted blackmail. Performs percussion for the Lester Horton Dance Theatre. In November, appears in *Clean Beds* at the Holly Town Theater with Anthony Quinn.

1936 Has affair with Stanley Haggart. In January is introduced to writer Reginald LeBorg and collaborates on several projects, including *Heavenly Music*, which later receives an Oscar for best short subject. In March, father suffers a major stroke. With LeRoy Robbins and Roger Barlow writes, produces, and acts in *Even—As You and I*, a short surrealist film. Carries petitions on behalf of Hopis. Between 1936 and 1938, active in EPIC (Upton Sinclair's End Poverty in California campaign in 1936), the Hollywood Anti-Nazi League, the League Against War and Fascism, Mobilization for Democracy, Workers' Alliance of America, the Hollywood Writers' Mobilization, and Labor's Non-Partisan League.

1937 In February, helps Woody Guthrie sing on KEVD radio. In March, attends funeral of his uncle, which inspires story "Flight of Quail." Spends summer working at Hernandez ranch, where he survives a rattlesnake bite and helps organize a dance for locals. Father suffers a second stroke. In the fall, is invited to attend a Marxist-oriented discussion group of writers and artists.

1938 Referred to a Jungian therapist, who advises him to form a heterosexual relationship. Re-registers in Communist Party in May. Marries fellow party member Anita Platky on September 9; honeymoon is cut short by his father's death. Begins WPA job in November and becomes active in Workers' Alliance union.

1939 With Anita, documents poor housing conditions in Los Angeles slums for *People's World*. In November, moves to New York City and works at various short-term jobs. Active in Artists' and Writers' division of the New York Communist Party and the Theater Arts Committee for Peace and Democracy. Takes advanced courses in Marxist theory from Bernard Paul.

1940 In May, drives to Chicago to participate in America First Committee conference and meets Pete Seeger.

1941 Interviewed by Alfred Kinsey. Sees *Parsifal* at the Metropolitan Opera. Serves as interim head of the New Theater League. In May, begins seven-month clandestine affair with architect William Alexander. Works for Russian War Relief.

1942 Following Pearl Harbor, returns to Los Angeles, arriving in late February. Works briefly for Russian War Relief, then gets a job at a brass foundry. When foundry closes, is employed as a materials planner at Interstate Aircraft but then fired for union organizing. Reduces Party work due to long hours but remains active in Arts, Sciences and Professions Committee.

1943 Gets job at Avion Aircraft and discovers talent for what becomes the field of systems engineering. In September, adopts Hannah Margaret Hay. With other progressive couples, establishes nursery school facilities at Barnsdahl Park. Begins teaching political economy classes.

358

1944 Active in Echo Park Political Association (former Communist Party chapter) and teaches Marxist theory courses and current events classes. In April, collapses at work from exhaustion and hypoglycemia.

1945 In October, appointed temporary County Educational Director at Southern California Communist Party Congress. Serves on Communist Party's Women's Commission. In November, attends early "hootenanny" and hosts Pete Seeger. In December adopts second daughter, Kate Neall Hay.

1946 With Earl Robinson, Mario Cassetta, and others founds Los Angeles People's Songs. In spring, invited to teach Party's course on Lenin's theory of imperialism. In the fall, develops a class on folk music for the People's Educational Center. Works at Alfred Leonard's Gateway to Music.

1947 In the fall, following closure of People's Educational Center, offers ten-session course, "Music . . . Barometer of the Class Struggle," through the Southern California Labor School.

1948 Employed as production engineer at Leahy Manufacturing. In summer, learns about homosexual purges at the State Department. On August 10, after signing a petition to place Henry Wallace on the California presidential ballot, attends a Gay party and conceives idea of "Bachelors for Wallace." Begins seeking supporters to help launch a Gay organization. Redesigns course on imperialism into popular six-session format.

1949 In fall, offers expanded, twenty-session version of music course at Labor School.

1950 Meets Rudi Gernreich on July 8. From July to September, visits Gay beaches with Gernreich to circulate Stockholm Peace Pledge petitions and test interest in discussion groups on the Kinsey report. In fall, begins two twenty-week sessions of music course, continuing until spring 1952. In November, gives "Preliminary Concepts" to student Bob Hull, who shows it to Chuck Rowland and Dale Jennings. The five meet on November 11 and 13; the first semi-public discussion group is held on December 11.

1951 In April, Konrad Stevens and James Gruber join the steering committee. "Mattachine Society Missions and Purposes" statement adopted in July and first community dance held. Celebrates first anniversary of relationship with Gernreich. Divorce from Anita granted on September 23. Resigns from Communist Party. In October, all-day Mattachine conference is held at Rowland's home with nine steering committee members and delegates from five discussion groups.

1952 In February, five steering committee members attend Los Angeles City Council meeting to protest police brutality against Chicanos and other groups. In March, Mattachine decides to organize defense of Dale Jennings entrapment case. Gernreich initiates end of relationship. Jennings trial begins June 23. Hay teaches music history class in summer. Meets Jorn Kamgren. All-day, area-wide Mattachine conference held in October.

1953 *ONE* magazine begins publication in January. In February, in response to a newspaper reference to Hay as a Marxist teacher, Mattachine Foundation issues "Official Statement of Policy on Political Questions and Related Matters." On March 12, *Los Angeles Daily Mirror* columnist Paul Coates notes Mattachine's surveys of and letters to local political candidates; the steering committee reprints and distributes copies of the column to Mattachine members. In April, Mattachine convention held at Universalist Church. On the last day of the meetings, the founders decide to resign. On May 1, a second convention adopts a new structure and goals.

1954 Helps Jorn Kamgren open a hat business in West Hollywood.

1955 In May, summoned to appear before the House UnAmerican Activities Committee. Testifies on July 2. In fall, begins teaching music course at home of lawyer Frank Pestana.

1956 In January, presents talk at ONE Midwinter Institute. Travels with Jorn to Mexico on summer vacation, returning by way of New Mexico, where he meets Enki, traditional sacred clown of San Ildefonso Pueblo.

1957 In January, presents "The Homophile in Search of an Historical Context and Cultural Contiguity" at ONE Midwinter Institute. In August, spends two weeks in New Mexico, observing dances with Enki at Jemez and Picuris.

1960 During two week trip to New Mexico, Enki shows him site at Tsan-kawi ruins where "your" people lived. Exchanges letters with Robert Graves.

1962 In January, speaks at ONE Midwinter Institute. In June, Bob Hull commits suicide. Spends Christmas in New Mexico and observes dances in the church at Sandia and Mattachine dances at Santa Clara and San Juan Pueblos. Decides to end relationship with Jorn.

1963 Begins relationship with James Kepner and moves in with him in May. In September, meets John Burnside while attending a talk by Gerald Heard and again at ONE. They begin living together in December and vacation at year's end in Baja California.

1964 In July, leaves Leahy Manufacturing to work as office and production manager for Burnside's California Kaleidoscopes. Travels to New Mexico at Christmas and meets Antonio Garcia of San Juan.

1965 With Burnside helps form the Southern California Council on Religion and the Homophile. Margaret Hay honored at ONE.

1966 California Kaleidoscopes begins to employ members of the "counterculture." With Don Slater, organizes a fifteen-car Gay motorcade on May 21 to protest the military exclusion of homosexuals. Appears with Burnside on local television shows. In June, helps organize a Sexual Liberation Booth at the Renaissance Pleasure Faire in Southern California. In August, attends meetings in San Francisco to form the North American Conference of Homophile Organizations and participates in a three-day "theological conference" sponsored by Council on Religion and the Homosexual and the Glide Urban Center. Visits Harry James at Lake Fillmore for a reunion.

1967 In March, Hay and Burnside join Committee for Traditional Indian Land and Life. In May, CTILL begins to hold meetings at the kaleidoscope factory and mounts a national campaign against the Indian Omnibus Bill. In August, travels to first North American Traditional Indian Conference at Tonawonda, New York.

1968 Organizes logistical support for the Six Nations' White Roots of Peace caravan and coordinates lobbying against Indian Omnibus Bill, which is defeated in July. Helps organize aid for drought-stricken Papagos.

1969 In March, helps organize third colloquium of Native American Traditional Leaders. With Burnside participates in four-day workshop on Gay draft resisters with San Francisco religious leaders. In May, joins Don Slater, Troy Perry, Mike Steele, and Jim Kepner to protest appearance of a homophobic councilman running for reelection at ONE, Inc. In September, helps Morris Kight and Leo Lawrence organize meetings that lead to the formation of the Gay Liberation front (GLF) of Los Angeles in December and is elected first chair. GLF begins meeting at kaleidoscope factory.

1970 In February, helps organize pickets at Barney's Beanery and leads GLF delegation to Peace and Freedom Party state convention in Long Beach. Addresses Western Homophile Conference in mid-February. In May, moves to Kent Compound at San Juan Pueblo, New Mexico, and participates in managing the San Juan Mercantile. Works on *El Grito* newspaper, a Chicano paper backing Reies Tijerina. In the summer, meets anthropologist Sue-Ellen Jacobs.

1972 Attends Niman dance at Hopi with Sue-Ellen Jacobs and two Tewa friends; after coughing for an entire night, decides to quit smoking.

1973 Don Kilhefner visits in April. In July, fire destroys the Mercantile and kaleidoscope shop. Hay survives serious bout of pneumonia in September.

1974 Hosts weekend retreats for University of New Mexico Gay Student Union in spring and fall. Interviewed by Jonathan Ned Katz. Helps establish food co-op in Santa Fe. Joins weekly picket lines in support of United Farm Workers grape boycott. Networks with local Lesbian collectives and attempts to start a Gay discussion group in Santa Fe in October.

1975 Mother dies in May. Creates National Friends of the Rio Grande and successfully blocks plans for dam construction on the upper Rio Grande. In July, travels with Burnside to Seattle to do a ten-day workshop; returns through Oregon to meet Carl Wittman.

1976 Completes "Gay Liberation: Chapter Two" in April. Helps organize Lambdas de Santa Fe. In June and July, travels with Burnside to Wolf Creek, Oregon. Meets Mitch Walker in San Francisco and begins correspondence. Interviewed by John D'Emilio in October.

1977 Participates in march against Anita Bryant in Los Angeles on June 13; speaks at New Mexico's first Gay Pride march in Albuquerque. In September, travels to Los Angeles to appear at screening of *Even—As You and I* at the Los Angeles County Museum of Modern Art.

1978 Mitch Walker spends a month in New Mexico in February. In April, Hay flies with Burnside to Los Angeles for premiere of *Word Is Out*. Renews friendship with Kilhefner at Lama retreat. In June, speaks at Gay Pride march in Albuquerque. In November, participates in a workshop with Kilhefner at the Gay Academic Union in Los Angeles.

1979 Travels with Burnside to Los Angeles to participate in Kilhefner's "Gay Voices and Visions" course and search for a house. In June, Hay addresses Denver Gay Pride march. In July, moves from New Mexico to La Cresta Court and establishes collective with Kilhefner. With Kilhefner, Burnside, and Walker, organizes first Spiritual Conference for Radical Fairies held Labor Day weekend in Arizona.

1980 Becomes active in anti-draft activities. At second Radical Faerie gathering in Colorado in August, introduces "faerie sanctuary" project of the Gay Vision Circle. Begins corresponding with Will Roscoe and Bradley Rose, who visit in the fall. In December travels to Oregon to view possible sanctuary sites.

1981 Roscoe, Rose, and Mark Thompson join the Gay Vision Circle collective, which meets at Big Bear Lake, California, in April and in San Francisco in June, when Kilhefner and Walker withdraw from the project. In July, hikes with Roscoe and Rose into Desolation Wilderness Area.

1982 Roscoe and Rose live at La Cresta Court from April to September. Gay Vision Circle incorporation papers filed. Hay injures ankle at a Halloween party. In December undergoes exploratory surgery for prostate cancer—results are negative.

1983 In January, Anita Hay dies. In February, Hay travels with Burnside to New York City and Boston. In June, travels with Roscoe and Rose to Hoopa Valley in northern California to look for land. In late June, addresses Cincinnati Gay Pride event and then the San Francisco Lesbian and Gay Pride Parade. In August, travels with Roscoe, Rose, Pat Gourley, David Woodyard, and Joey Cain to New Mexico and stays in the Kent Compound for two weeks. Attends gathering in Napa, California, in October, where he has a dream about his father and, following a healing circle, his ankle finally begins to heal.

363

1984 In San Francisco, Roscoe, Rose, and others start holding meetings leading to the formation of Nomenus as the successor to the Gay Vision Circle. In June, Hay speaks at Boston Gay Pride Day and visits Walden Pond with Charlie Shively. Active in Lavender Caucus of the Rainbow Coalition. Attends second Napa gathering.

1985 In April, Rudi Gernreich dies. In May, Hay speaks during Gay Awareness Week at University of California at Santa Cruz. Suffers serious hearing loss and is no longer able to enjoy music.

1986 Visits San Francisco in February, May, and September on Nomenus business. In May, serves as grand marshal of Long Beach Lesbian and Gay Pride Parade. In June, causes controversy at Christopher Street West Gay Pride parade with sign supporting Valerie Terrigno and protesting the exclusion of NAMBLA. Marches in San Francisco Lesbian and Gay Pride Parade. Attends Napa gathering in October.

1987 Speaks at Georgia State University in Atlanta. In June, participates in question-and-answer session at San Francisco Lesbian and Gay Historical Society. Nomenus purchases Wolf Creek, Oregon site. Marches in San Francisco Lesbian and Gay Pride Parade. Participates in March on Washington.

1989 In March, speaks at University of Southern California. In April, West Hollywood city council issues a proclamation honoring his activism. Speaks at twentieth Stonewall anniversary in New York in June.

1990 Participates in Leadership Training Conference in San Francisco and marches in Lesbian and Gay Pride Parade. In July, holds first Sex Magic workshop at Wolf Creek. In September, addresses Colorado Gay and Lesbian Congress. In November, speaks at University of North Carolina and delivers keynote address at Celebrating Gay Spirit Visions Conference. Publication of biography, *The Trouble with Harry Hay*, by Stuart Timmons. Chuck Rowland dies in late December.

1991 In May, receives Black and White Men Together Achievement Award and speaks at ONE Institute. In June, participates in Crossroads forum in San Francisco. Travels to Soviet Union as a member of the International Gay and Lesbian Human Rights Commission delegation. Attends Malibu gathering in November.

1992 Organizes a panel on homophobia for Los Angeles Progressive Unity Council. In July, speaks at national conference of Committees of Correspondence in Berkeley. In November, presents third-gender workshop at Malibu gathering.

1993 In May, fire severely damages the "faerie sanctuary" at La Cresta Court and forces move to West Hollywood. In August, Hay delivers paper at Western Historians' Association. Presents workshop at Malibu gathering.

1994 In March, speaks at UCLA and receives lifetime achievement award from the Southern California Labor History Library. In June, participates in twenty-fifth anniversary of Stonewall in New York. Helps organize radical faerie retreat in November.

About the Editor

Will Roscoe has been active in the Gay movement since 1975, when he helped found Lambda, the first Gay/Lesbian organization in Montana. He served the following year as an intern at the National Gay Task Force; in 1977, as coordinator of the Gay People's Alliance at the University of Oregon, he spearheaded the formation of the Oregon Gay Alliance, a statewide coalition of Gay/Lesbian groups. In 1978, he completed an internship at the Pacific Center for Human Growth in Berkeley, where he organized a successful campaign to win membership in the local United Way, the first Lesbian/Gay social service agency in the country to do so. He also served as voter registration coordinator for the No on 6 campaign in San Francisco (the Briggs initiative). In 1979, he attended the first radical faerie gathering in Arizona, where he met Harry Hay, and became involved in efforts that led to the founding of Nomenus, which today operates a retreat in Southern Oregon. In 1980, with Tede Mathews and other local artists, he organized "Mainstream Exiles: A Lesbian and Gay Men's Cultural Festival" and between 1980 and 1982, he published and edited with Bradley Rose *Vortex: A Journal of New Vision*. In 1984, he became Project Coordinator for the Gay American Indians History Project and published *Living the Spirit: A Gay American Indian Anthology*. Roscoe's research on the Native American Berdache or Two-Spirit tradition has appeared in numerous journals and publications. His book *The Zuni Man-Woman* received the Margaret Mead Award of the American Anthropological Association and a Lambda Literary Award. In 1991, he completed a Ph.D. in History of Conscious-

366

ness at the University of California, Santa Cruz, and since then has taught anthropology and Native American studies at the University of California, Santa Cruz, San Francisco State University, and the University of California, Berkeley, while pursuing research as an affiliated scholar with the Institute for Research on Women and Gender at Stanford University. His most recent book is *Queer Spirits: A Gay Men's Myth Book*.